Deport Deprive Extradite

Deport Deprive Extradite

21st Century State Extremism

Nisha Kapoor

VERSO
London • New York

First published by Verso 2018
© Nisha Kapoor 2018

1 3 5 7 9 10 8 6 4 2

Verso
UK: 6 Meard Street, London W1F 0EG
US: 20 Jay Street, Suite 1010, Brooklyn, NY 11201
versobooks.com

Verso is the imprint of New Left Books

ISBN-13: 978-1-78663-347-7
ISBN-13: 978-1-78663-349-1 (UK EBK)
ISBN-13: 978-1-78663-350-7 (US EBK)

British Library Cataloguing in Publication Data
A catalogue record for this book is available from the British Library

Library of Congress Cataloging-in-Publication Data

Names: Kapoor, Nisha, 1980-, author.
Title: Deport, deprive, extradite : 21st century state extremism / Nisha
  Kapoor.
Description: New York : Verso, 2018.
Identifiers: LCCN 2017052579 | ISBN 9781786633477 (hardback)
Subjects: LCSH: Terrorists—Legal status, laws, etc. | Extradition—Cases. |
  Detention of persons—Cases. | Deportation—Cases. | Emigration and
  immigration—Government policy. | Political crimes and offenses. | BISAC:
  POLITICAL SCIENCE / Political Freedom & Security / Human Rights. |
  POLITICAL SCIENCE / Political Freedom & Security / General. | POLITICAL
  SCIENCE / Civics & Citizenship.
Classification: LCC K5445 .K37 2018 | DDC 342.08/2—dc23
LC record available at https://lccn.loc.gov/2017052579

Typeset in Sabon by MJ & N Gavan, Truro, Cornwall
Printed and bound bt CPI Group (UK) Ltd, Croydon, CR0 4YY

For Mama

Contents

Introduction

Creating Conditions

Life Sentence

> to kill
> is to erase an image
> off a mirror:
> swift glance &
> side-step,
> no body
> just a gaping hole
> upon an indifferent world
> *Syed Talha Ahsan, 2011*[1]

It was after 3 am when Lotfi Raissi woke to a bang on his front door. On opening it he was faced with armed policemen with a warrant. A piece of paper was flashed before him and a gun held to his head. He was being arrested, they told him, in relation to the 11 September 2001 attacks. He was forcibly stripped and held in a police van before being taken to a local police station. His wife and brother, also arrested, were taken elsewhere. Some days later his family members were released, and though on the seventh day the charges against Lotfi were dropped for lack of evidence, he was immediately re-arrested under a provisional extradition warrant issued by the United States. He would remain incarcerated in Belmarsh prison for four and a half months.[2]

An Algerian national living in London, Lotfi appeared in national press headlines as 'The Terror Instructor', a caption that referred to the basis of his arrest which concerned accusations by US authorities that he had taught four of the men involved in the 9/11 attacks at a flight school in Arizona.[3] He was alleged to have particularly close links to Hani Hanjour – the man who flew the plane into the Pentagon – with purported video footage of Lotfi and Hanjour together. Prosecutors argued that theirs was not just an association but a shared conspiracy, with active correspondence, video footage and telecommunications evidence to support the charge. Lotfi, they alleged, had access to forged documents and to large sums of money to finance flight simulator instruction. An FBI source had described Lotfi to the press as 'by far the biggest find we have had'.[4]

Lotfi was first alerted to his impending arrest when *Sunday Times* journalists arrived at his home the day before the police raid and told him he was on the FBI watch list. Twenty-four hours later he was headline news with some sections of the press reporting that anti-terror police had 'foiled a plot to hijack a passenger jet and crash it into the centre of London'. The story played a critical role in supporting the notion already floating that another terrorist attack was imminent in Britain and media stories which claimed that in Britain 'dozens of terrorists were on the run'.[5] On the same day as Lotfi's first court appearance, British ministers expressed fears to the press of further attacks in the UK by al-Qaeda.[6] Around the same time, the White House confirmed that special forces from Britain and the US were already active in Afghanistan. Media campaigns made it clear that fighting the terrorist threat meant tightening domestic security as much as it did escalating military intervention overseas, and Lotfi's case became emblematic in this emergent national imagination fixated on the imminent threat of terrorism.

Three years earlier there had been another dawn raid, this one at the home of Adel Abdul Bary, an Egyptian human rights lawyer who had fled the Mubarak regime in the 1980s and was granted political asylum in Britain. In the aftermath of the bombings of US embassies in Kenya and Tanzania in 1998, British police in white contamination suits broke down Adel's front door and separated him from his family while they ransacked their house. Adel was then taken into police custody and, after five days of questioning, released when authorities could find no terrorism case to charge him with. He was charged instead with possession of a gas canister, bailed and subsequently acquitted by a jury. Some six months later, however, he, too, was re-arrested on behalf of the US. While detained in Brixton prison in July 1999, he was incarcerated alongside Khalid al-Fawwaz who had also been indicted in relation to the embassy bombings. Their status as Category B prisoners was upgraded after the 9/11 attacks, when they were reclassified as Category A prisoners and moved to high-security facilities.[7] Both men would remain incarcerated for another ten years as they battled extradition before they were eventually transferred in 2011.

While their stories of criminalisation bear much resemblance, the final outcomes for Lotfi Raissi and Adel Abdul Bary were quite different. Though in both cases the evidentiary basis for the extradition requests was weak, their experiences of the justice system varied.

In Lotfi's case, the basis of the extradition request from the US concerned minor charges – namely that he had failed to disclose on a Federal Aviation Administration form a previous knee surgery, a visit to a healthcare professional and a previous minor conviction for theft in London. The prosecution argued that these, however, were interim 'holding charges', asserting that they had grounds to believe Lotfi was a terrorist involved in the 9/11 atrocities, and accordingly requested a sixty-day adjournment of the extradition case so that they could bring a further charge against him relating to a terrorist offence.[8] As the extradition case proceeded, it was revealed that even though Lotfi and Hani Hanjour had attended the same flight school there was no evidence that they had ever met and that the video image found on Lotfi's computer which the FBI believed to show Lotfi together with Hanjour was in fact Lotfi together with his cousin. There were also accusations that there were pages missing from his logbook that related to the time when he was training the dead pilots. Later, it was noted that the logbook had been taken apart for copying and reassembled in the wrong order. The allegation was withdrawn.[9]

While he was detained, the *Washington Post* published a report showing that the extradition request was largely for the purposes of intelligence gathering. An FBI official speaking to journalists about Lotfi's case pointed to their uncertainty about his connection with the 9/11 hijackers, stating, 'We put him in the category of maybe or maybe not, leaning towards probably not. Our goal is to get him back here and talk to him to find out more.'[10]

In Adel's case, the evidence gathered against him by British police, which was not deemed sufficient to charge him in the UK, was transferred to the US and formed the basis of the indictment against him. It included a fax obtained from his office reporting the embassy bombings, information which had been widely distributed at the time, and the testimony of an anonymous witness, 'Confidential Source Number 1'.[11] Later, it would be revealed that this source had never met Adel nor had mentioned him in the evidence he gave to the US authorities.[12]

Whereas in Lotfi's case the US extradition request was ultimately dismissed in 2002 when the prosecution failed to provide credible evidence and the judge ruled that 'such evidence did not exist', Adel's appeals were not successful and his extradition, along with that of Khalid al-Fawwaaz, was ultimately granted in 2001.[13] He remained incarcerated in prison without trial for thirteen years in Britain before his eventual extradition to the United States in 2011. After a further two-and-a-half years in solitary confinement in the US, he accepted a plea bargain and in 2015 was sentenced to twenty-five years for conspiracy-related charges and for acting as a 'communications facilitator'.[14]

What was common and therefore also analytically central to both cases was the racial representation that cut through how the initial charges were levied, how the media covered the stories, and how the cases were ultimately appraised. In an interview shortly after his release, Lotfi told the *Daily Telegraph* that he was a victim of his 'nationality' and 'religion', thus that racial profiling had played a key role in his wrongful arrest and detention.[15] He was vindicated in the newspaper by his family's respected name, as his uncle was a senior officer in Algeria's anti-terrorist branch, an association which qualified him to be a 'good Muslim' in the media. To the contrary, Adel's affiliation with Egyptian Islamic Jihad (EIJ), which had sought the overthrow of the Mubarak regime, in the 1980s and 90s, pre-dating the organisation's links with al-Qaeda, was drawn on to mark him as a 'bad Muslim'.

Simultaneously, the racism which dehumanised both subjects proceeded alongside a pervasive media and political discourse that insisted the disciplinary techniques available to the state were insufficient for dealing with the threat that terrorism posed. The bureaucratic wrangling which prevented the extradition of Lotfi Raissi spurred on the agenda of the then home secretary, David Blunkett, for improving the efficiency of extradition arrangements between Britain and the US by reducing levels of judicial scrutiny. Blunkett would tell the House of Commons in October 2001 that since Britain's 'love of freedom' did not 'extend to offering hospitality to terrorists ... the emergency terrorism Bill [which became the Anti-Terrorism Crime and Security Act 2001] and 'a separate extradition measure' would ensure Britain had 'robust and streamlined procedures' in place.[16] In practice this would mean that in the future the US would not be required to provide prima facie evidence to support its extradition requests. Executive power, police power, judicial protocols, and laws for dealing with counterterrorism both in the domestic context and at the level of international policing between states were argued to be inadequate, unnecessarily stifling and longwinded. Populist calls for greater efficiency, for more effective state power spurred on political agendas concerned with negotiating the problem of further enhancing law and order against constraints of the liberal rights framework.

The use of these two devices, race – a floating signifier that connects systems of bio-cultural classification based on assignments of racial or ethnic identity with the disposition of power, and bureaucracy – techniques of state administration which operate not independent of or outside the law, as Hannah Arendt suggested, but through it, to fortify executive power, are central themes that concern me here.[17] It is the enforcement of excess levels of state power as legitimate and necessary for policing the exceptional figure of the 'terrorism suspect', the continuous negotiation around how this can be legally sanctioned within the parameters of humanitarian frameworks, and what the resulting disciplinary action illuminates about the broader governing arrangements of society that is the focus of this book.

On Racism and the Security State

Between 2003 and 2015 there were nine individuals extradited from the UK to the US for terrorism-related offences, a small proportion of the total number of deportations over this period and a very small proportion of the number who have been caught up in the wider scope of securitised policing through immigration control, stop and search, community surveillance programmes and so on. The significance of these high-profile extreme cases – extreme not simply because they are few in number but because they involve some of the most extreme excesses of state power – is that they demonstrate the full extent of disciplinary power. In doing so, these cases are positioned at what Saskia Sassen refers to as the 'systemic edge', the point at which a condition is made so extreme that it is not easily captured by standard systems of analysis of, in the cases of interest to me here, citizenship, policing or human rights.[18] Their extreme nature, in its starkness, makes more visible what may be obscured in less extreme forms, and so brings to light broader trends of securitisation and dispossession. Through these stories of the extreme cases, we see there are connections to unravel between the expulsion of terrorism suspects and the broader manoeuvres of mass-scale deportation, preventive policing, programmes of 'earned' citizenship, and the repositioning of protective safeguards in the form of civil and human rights.

One of the signature traits of the War on Terror has been the creation of a suspect population that is globally dispersed. The effect of this has been to create, connect and condense a plethora of otherwise distinct political struggles across empire and at home. The War on Terror has also sanctioned the use of counterinsurgency policing, a mainstay of colonial governmentality, to be intensified through its day-to-day employment in the domestic spaces of the West. Militarisation and securitisation have been expanded and enhanced. In this shift, as the trope of the terrorist comes to increasingly define how the Muslim in the West is positioned and read, the connections between 'imperialism over there' and 'racism over here' are brought into clarity and made ever more proximate. The trope of the terrorist is mobilised as a supra-national threat, used to routinise emergency policing.

When we situate these cases in the context of the UK–US state, the policing of these men is one part of the more widescale state practice of detention and deportation, both key mechanisms of population management and control, and among the starkest expressions of state racism. Between 1990 and 2016 the prison population increased in England and Wales by 90 per cent, in Scotland by 62 per cent and in Northern Ireland by 49 per cent.[19] The demographics of these prison populations are disproportionately poor, black and Muslim, the population of the latter group in prison having doubled between 2002 and 2016.[20] Deportation figures, too, have risen sharply from the low thousands in the early 1990s. Between 2010 and 2015, approximately 40,000–45,000 people were deported annually.[21] Both detention and deportation securitisation regimes have been sustained through the pervading ideology of an enduring risk to national security in the form of the threat of terrorism. The idea of the presence of 'terrorism suspects' at home has helped to sustain calls for greater securitisation.

At the same time, the extradition of these terrorism suspects obtains a central importance in this broader project of imperialist policing. Much of the political negotiation over how these men should be treated is framed within and referenced against procedures used in Western military operations. Particularly evident is the entanglement of civilian and military techniques. The database of terrorism suspects managed by the Obama administration, which they referred to as the Disposition Matrix, included a range of options for dispensing with identified targets.[22] Among them were: capture and death by special forces, death by drone strikes, 'extraordinary rendition' – a technique involving kidnapping and extra-judicial transfer to a clandestine or military prison, 'rendition to justice', a variation of 'extraordinary rendition' which incorporates the civilian justice system and brings suspects to a civilian courtroom after the initial practice of extra-judicial rendition, and extradition, the transfer of suspects between countries that takes place under bilateral or unilateral agreements between states and with civilian judicial oversight. The novelty of the Disposition Matrix was that it illustrated the existence of two different sets of disciplinary techniques, some of which were recognised as within the framework of civilian or military law and others that went beyond the scope of such boundaries, that could be used simultaneously. As the different techniques of death-dealing reinforce and reimpose the dehumanised status of the 'terrorism suspect', those techniques that are considered more humanitarian help to legitimate and normalise the process. Executive decisions to 'modernise' extradition protocols that have eased the expulsion of undesired subjects, for example, have been legitimated through judicial support. Although international human rights organisations and bodies, such as the Council of Europe, have condemned and lobbied against illicit practices such as rendition, there has been relative silence on the juridified practice of extradition, which for all intents and purposes is used against some accused of terrorism to achieve the same means.[23] For the way in which it draws out the fine line between the ordinary and exceptional with the liberal disciplinary frame, extradition as

8

it is used for managing terrorism suspects is a key process that warrants attention.

In some senses, the figure of the terror suspect forms the testing ground upon which Western versions of 'democracy' and 'human rights' are deliberated. It is via the representation of these individuals that cases are made in support of summary killings, bigger bombs, drone strikes, ever more grotesque forms of torture, and clandestine and indefinite detention. It is also through the policing of such individuals that mechanisms have been put in place in Britain for the growing use of secret justice, the retraction of the provisions of citizenship and the move away from human rights protections. It is not that the democratic institutional principles associated with liberal states were ever previously universally imposed. Indeed, part of the aim of this book is to show the continuities between the contemporary counterterrorism policing and earlier colonial practices. But the terrorism cases I focus on here do help to indicate how such practices are being reformulated in the postcolonial present.

The historical employment of legal and cultural practices to construct, hierarchise and differentiate between categories of people tell us that enjoyment of full political, civil, social, cultural and legal rights was never universal but always conditional. Given that race has long operated as the dominant ontology for categorising, sorting and hierarchising populations on a global scale, we already understand legal processes that position some as 'less-than-citizen' and cultural discourses which work to legitimate and rationalise such practices as part of the work of racial and racist states.[24] The significance of the way in which exclusions are administered through the framework of the War on Terror is that while the *techniques* of vilification and disposal of subjects draw on the same kinds of cultural strategies and political-legal infrastructure, the cultural framing of racial threat posed by the Muslim subject is articulated in political-ideological terms.

Examining the stories of Muslim men suspected of terrorism-related offences provokes questions of how and where these subjects sit in connection to the modes of racial violence being mobilised and intensified by the state in the current conjuncture.[25] Is it appropriate to speak of racism, state violence and injustice in the name of individuals suspected or identified as themselves advocating or engaging in violence? Does the state violence conducted in the name of policing terrorism parallel other forms of state racial violence? The invocation of anti-imperialist arguments and even of human rights in the names of subjects whose political-ideological position is framed as being contradictory to principles of an inclusive, democratic, equal and just society, is questioned. Some political and academic commentators discussing human rights have argued that those who choose to engage in 'terrorism' have already denounced their allegiance to the liberal state, and so forfeit their right to protections. Christian Joppke, for example, suggests that denaturalisation is the appropriate response to terror because 'terror, particularly of the Islamist kind, is no ordinary crime but an attack on the fundaments of citizenship'.[26] Others argue that there exists an important distinction between human rights principles – against acts such as extra-judicial killings – and the politics of the subject for whom those human rights are being lobbied. Chetan Bhatt, for example, points to the contradiction in the Centre for Constitutional Rights advocating on behalf of Anwar al-Awlaki, because he himself had advocated for the death of civilians.[27] Bhatt's argument is that the legal framework for human rights cannot be divorced from the social and political context in which they are advocated and that these factors need to inform an analysis and application of human rights.

Yet within these variations on the liberal position which argues that there are logical grounds for withholding 'rights' from those who threaten security of the nation, there is limited recognition of the cultural frame in which the figure of the terrorism suspect is produced. As far as human rights are concerned with offering protections on an individual basis there is perhaps some scope to consider discretely the merits of a particular case. But since the process of criminalisation in the policing of terrorism operates through a racially charged lens, it functions to criminalise collectively and, indeed, preemptively. Terrorism suspects come to include a whole category of people – Muslims stopped and questioned at an airport before being incorporated into a database, those proselytising Islam, and those expressing dissent against Western foreign policy. The description of activity that now falls under the rubric of terrorism is expansive. In the case of Anwar al-Awlaki, the role that US imperialist politics played in politicising him lends strength to arguments that he was more of a propagandist than a 'terrorist'.[28] It is not so much that there would not be individuals incorporated into this category willing or culpable of engaging in futile violence, it is that collective criminalisation makes it somewhat unhelpful and near impossible to think in terms that assume we can clearly differentiate between the 'good' and the 'bad', the 'guilty' and the 'innocent'. The cultural framing that informs how particular subjects are criminalised, the processes via which this occurs and then the ways in which these cultural readings are upheld through the justice system plays a critical role in how we read and interpret the problem.

In reflecting on the designation of 'terrorist' in reference to non-state actors, moral and ethical questions relating to the political motivations of subjects factor into whether or not they are viewed as 'freedom fighters' or 'terrorists'. Whether– to play on Mahmood Mamdani's observation of the 'good Muslim'/ 'bad Muslim' binary – they constitute 'good terrorists' or 'bad terrorists'. The proliferation of work examining Islamophobia or anti-Muslim racism since the late twentieth century has largely – and importantly – focused on negative representations of Muslims within social and cultural spaces, particularly within the media and in state policies, policing practices and legislation that disproportionately target Muslims, as well as in the everyday populist racisms that have flourished in this context.[29] It is the representation of all Muslims as terrorists which in essence criminalises an entire population that is most often contested by these intellectual debates.

In a report for the Equality and Human Rights Commission assessing the impact of counterterrorism measures on Muslim communities, Tufyal Choudhury and Helen Fenwick outline the effects of legislation and policing practices that have accelerated since 2001, and the impact they have had on Muslims en masse as the 'suspect community'.[30] They accept the real and grave threat of domestic and international terrorism as exemplified by individuals convicted for terrorism-related offences, on control orders, under surveillance or referred to intervention programmes. However, they argue for a separation of this minority of individuals from the rest of the Muslim population who are also subject to a range of policing measures operating in the UK that rely on racial profiling such as Section 7 stops at ports and airports, stop and searches under S44 of the Terrorism Act, and the Prevent programme. These policing interventions have become the daily and routine experiences of Muslims across the country, practices which, they convincingly argue, stigmatise, alienate, discriminate and fail to protect human rights. This framing for presenting Muslim subjects as racially othered subjects, victims bearing the brunt of unjust state oppression nevertheless concedes the validity of the criminal justice system in the cases of Muslims who have been successfully convicted or identified as suspicious.

Much other literature on the politics of the War on Terror and Islamic insurgency movements engages the Muslim subject through a different lens, a lens that seeks to account for the politicisation of Muslims – that is, the Muslim subject keen to join radical Islamist organisations and engage in acts of terrorism. The burgeoning literature investigating the links between Muslims and radicalisation places emphasis on identity crises, disillusionment, feeling a sense of 'injustice', and a failure to integrate to explain the choices of some Muslims to engage with groups identified with 'radical Islam'.[31] Robert Leiken, for example, in a pathologising narrative of postcolonial migration to European centres, unpacking why second-generation Muslim youth turn to 'jihad', cites disaffection from a 'clash of cultures' as key. In Marc Sageman's work on leaderless jihad and 'Islamic terrorism', we are again introduced to the politicised Muslim subject in orientalised terms as a way of understanding political action. Such discussions tend towards individual psychology, cultural deficits and, at times, 'inter-group conflict', often reifying the same racist stereotypes that, in contrast, the discourse on the connections between race and criminalisation of the 'innocent' argues against.

In both the literature which underscores the Muslim as a racialized subject and the literature which presents the Muslim as a radical subject, it is the extent to which emphasis is placed on political subjectivity which determines whether talk of racism is presented as appropriate or misconstrued. Indeed, the analyses offered by those such as Leiken to explain political behaviour typically rely on reductive cultural stereotypes, attributing politics to culture. In consideration of how Muslims are the subjects of racism, this framework of analysis requires delimiting their embodiment as political subjects, perhaps to 'innocents' unjustly criminalised for holding critical views of Western state actions overseas, an analysis in line with a broader liberal critique of state violence. Once we consider Muslim subjects in political terms, as political agents, such a framing moves them beyond the realm within which we view them as located within racial structures. Particularly powerful about the extradition cases that are the focus of this book which range from Abu Hamza, a controversial Islamist cleric, to Talha Ahsan and Fahad Hashmi, whose convictions fell under the expansive scope of 'material support', which in their cases involved, respectively, typing up an unsolicited document for a website and hosting an individual allegedly linked to al-Qaeda, is that they indicate the power that representation has for obscuring the weight of the disciplinary techniques that operate alongside.

Accordingly, the danger of venturing into the merits and motivations of individual subjects is that this approach overlooks the more pertinent point of the way in which such criminalised subjects are dealt with and disposed of. Racism is not rooted in individual prejudice or the treatment of an individual case in isolation, but in the structures and systemic practices which expose certain segments of the population to, as Ruth Wilson Gilmore notes, 'premature death'.[32] The representations and governing techniques that are mobilised and enhanced for dealing with extreme cases – which necessarily draw upon the ordinary infra-structures of disciplinary governing techniques that are already part of the racial state – have significant consequences, because they illustrate what is possible in terms of state disciplinary practice and by doing so uphold rule by fear in those communities most marginalised.[33] As such, our ability to critically assess processes of dehumanisation and their consequences should not be contingent on the *suspected* or *apparent* political actions or behaviours of a subject. Firstly, because the representational frames through which such actions are read form part of the dehumanisation of the subject. But also because the disciplinary techniques used against such marked subjects, while being more intense, still constitute an important reflection of the broader social, cultural and political landscape. It is not that the disciplinary techniques that have come to be associated with the War on Terror are wholly new or disconnected from what has been before. We know this is not the case.[34] It is that the ideological and representational work that operates specifically through high-profile terrorism cases, such as the ones discussed in this book, is critical to a process of legitimation for the enhancement of exclusionary mechanisms, securitisation and the retraction of state accountability more broadly.

The extradition cases discussed in this book exemplify the possibilities for complete expulsion from social, political and economic orders – in the transfer of bodies from one state to another to face incarceration in lifetime solitary confinement in 'supermax' prisons. They also support the ideological work that helps provide the mechanisms and justifications for similar (if at times, though not always, less extreme) forms of dispossession and precarity that occur on a larger scale. What can the stories of those criminalised as terrorism suspects and expelled reveal about shifts in the state of security? How do these cases help to further the agendas of securitisation, marginalisation and racial exclusion? These are the key questions this book sets out to address.

The Starting Point

Deport, Deprive, Extradite draws on a series of high-profile cases of Muslim men accused of terrorism-related offences and, in most cases, extradited from Britain to the US. The book explores processes of dehumanisation, criminalisation, and expulsion (by which I mean banishment from and denial of recognition within social and political systems) as they are enacted through these cases. By doing so, I aim to reconnect the policing of terrorism with broader debates on the nature of contemporary racisms, re-centring the relationship between imperialism and racism. The central contention of this book is that as these marginalised subjects become the dehumanised focal points of moral panics around security, their cases are drawn upon to legitimate the diminution of more progressive democratic systems and processes, and the enhancement of authoritarian elements of the liberal state.[35] As a set of extreme cases, these stories illuminate and sometimes legitimate the routinisation of militarised policing practices, and the growing explicit conditionality of civil protections in the form of human rights and citizenship.

The focus here on the extradition of terrorism suspects as a point of departure is not intended as an investigation into the legal ethics and rationales for or against extradition per se – in order, for example, to consider issues of sovereignty or international protocols as they play out between nation-states. Rather, I pose the notion of extradition, specifically the extradition of those accused of terrorism, as a form of modern day expulsion that conjures multiple forms of banishment: deportation, incarceration and citizenship deprivation. The inconsistencies and capricious justifications for US jurisdiction in a portion of these cases, as was exposed in the Lotfi Raissi case and was further indicated in the jurisdictional rationales for subsequent extradition cases discussed later, reveal the political motivations and arrangements underlying this process. Rather than ask why such individuals are prosecuted in the US, or elsewhere, rather than in the UK, I aim to consider how governmentalities of imperialist and domestic racisms operate together; how well-established disciplinary governing techniques are intensified, normalised and legitimated; and the significance of the numerous forms of expulsion used interchangeably or concurrently in these cases. *Deport, Deprive, Extradite* also flips the frame fixated on so-called 'Islamic extremism' to, in contrast, reference the 'state extremism' committed in expelling marginal populations, a frame of analysis which allows us to see a broader spectrum of the state's securitising possibilities and realities.

In Chapter One, I draw on the stories of Fahad Hashmi, who was the first person extradited from Britain to the US under the US–UK Extradition Treaty of 2003, and Mahdi Hashi, a former British citizen who was stripped of his citizenship while detained in Djibouti before being rendered to the US. As their arrival to the same New York prison, albeit at different times, illustrates the enmeshing of civilian and military policing techniques, their stories also illuminate the power of the trope of the terrorism suspect for sustaining this process. I begin with their cases as starting points for unpacking the cultural constructions of terrorism, the racialised lens through which terrorism suspects are made and the legal legitimation this is granted.

In the stories of Babar Ahmad and Talha Ahsan, discussed in Chapter Two, we see the enmeshing of civilian and military policing systems further. Their cases illustrate how the sophistication of counterterrorism policing practices is produced out of combining the historical expertise of counterinsurgency policing developed in Northern Ireland (and other colonial outposts) with the infrastructures advanced for policing public disorder and criminality domestically, largely in disciplining black and other working-class communities. The turn towards policing terrorism suspects within the confines of British domestic-state institutions has brought with it the growing use of secret evidence and colonial-style court systems that rely on closed procedures, as were used in the case of Abid Naseer. Such procedures have been extended from initial enforcement in national security immigration cases to other civil tribunal hearings and the criminal justice system, broadening a culture of secret justice. Where

Abid Naseer's case illuminates the secrecy that encapsulates the low threshold for convicting terrorism suspects in the Special Immigration Appeal Commission in Britain, it also evidences the power of cultural representation which allows for his criminal conviction in the US for activity that could not be brought to open trial in a criminal court in Britain.

Minh Pham's extradition to the US, discussed in Chapter Three, paralleled the deprivation of his British citizenship, which meant his deportation to and incarceration in New York coincided with effective statelessness. His case offers a starting point for exposing the precariousness of citizenship and the process by which legislative provisions have been passed enabling its easier retraction. It was through the home secretary's commitment to deporting the cleric Abu Hamza that the British government passed legislation significantly expanding the terms upon which citizenship can be deprived, provisions which were then expanded again in the name of expelling others accused of terrorism, such as Hilal al-Jedda. The development of state powers to withdraw citizenship, as has been legitimated through terrorism cases, forms part of a broader conceptual shift that posits citizenship as something to be earned, proven and policed. While citizenship has always been a privilege, the growth of citizenship deprivation legislation reflects the extension of border control from policing immigrants to disciplining citizens, reifying and furthering systems of racial exclusion. It is a shift that has involved growing reliance on and subservience to executive power.

In the background against all of this, the European Court of Human Rights (ECHR), meanwhile, holds an ambivalent position: on the one hand, it is the institutional symbol of the human rights designed to be withheld from colonial subjects; on the other hand, it represents a point of hope for institutional appeal for the same subjects denied such rights. In the story of Haroon Aswat, discussed in Chapter Four, whose request for extradition was initially denied by the European Court of Human Rights due to the severity of his mental health condition but was subsequently supported by the Court following diplomatic assurances

from the US, we see how a collusion between human rights rhetoric, human rights institutions and political power plays out.
While the ECHR has been relatively consistent in deciding that
extreme disciplinary techniques, such as deportation to states
with poor human rights records and incarceration for prolonged
periods in solitary confinement, would *not* violate human rights
conventions in terrorism cases, the very availability of human
rights provisions to terrorism suspects has formed the basis of
government justifications for withdrawing from the European
Convention on Human Rights altogether. Here 'rights' become
more explicitly attached to 'responsibilities'.

In each story explored in the book, the disciplinary techniques used to exclude or expel those marked as non-belonging
or non-entitled not only enhance state powers to banish, they
work to reshape the parameters of justice, citizenship, human
rights and, by implication, systems of democracy more broadly.
As I discuss in Chapter Five, however, the enhancement of totalising state power illuminated through these cases is not without
possibilities for resistance, which has taken many forms and
brought together multiple political agendas. At its most progressive moments, when in recognition that extradition represents
the hollowing out of democratic systems and is a reflection of
'Empire come home', anti-racist organising is effectively anti-
imperialist.

In the pages that follow, the tales of these extraditees shed
some light on the intensification of state violence. Their stories
of oppression and the struggles for justice in their name also
reveal something about what it means for the right to be human.

Digging from the ruins

The intensification of securitisation impacts the excavating of
the very data that documents it: policing dissent occurs in a
variety of ways but perhaps one key indicator of the escalation
of law and order is the suppression of what can be known and
who can know it. Even as the stories of the terrorism suspects

that I engage with here allow us to see the gross capacities of the security state and the multiple dynamics of expulsion in operation, the accounts of their stories and the detailed context in which they are situated have not been easy to acquire. Restrictions come in multiple forms and are present on numerous levels, but in this setting it is generally the logic of national, and at times global, security that is invoked for securing, classifying and restricting information. Classifying documents and curtailing access to information are well-established strategies for protecting government interests in the name of public safety, but its expansion in application to encompass all kinds of domestic policing is a significant characteristic of twenty-first century state securitisation, its legal sanctioning maintained and extended through counterterrorism policy and legislation. In Europe and the United States, it is the potential risks to national security that have been cited to justify a whole raft of obstructions to the supply of information about mass detention, 'special interest' and mass deportations, or the numbers of people being deprived of citizenship, as well as obstructions to legal action against the government for their complicity in torture and extra-judicial incarceration.[36]

The rationale of national security also underlies the entire judicial process for terrorism suspects, including justification for the conditions of confinement of prisoners. Unlike the stories of those who are killed whose accounts die with them, extradition and incarceration leave a paper trail in the form of judicial documentation. What paper there is to be found has been critical for revealing the nature of accusation and of state arguments and the ultimate rationalities for judicial decisions. Though these documents are invariably state accounts, they nevertheless can provide snippets of detail, including witness statements, that shed some light. There remain restrictions, however. The use of closed-procedure trials through the Special Immigration Appeals Commission in the UK (a court set up in 1997 for immigration-related national security cases, where information available to the defendant and/or their lawyer is restricted), and subsequently expanded to other courts, as well as closed procedures used in the US, means that records of legal arguments, judgements and documentation are often only available in part.

Equally, while the richest details of an individual's story generally come from speaking to the subject themselves, incarceration makes this difficult if not impossible. Mass incarceration is not only an indicator of broader economic, political, social and cultural trends, it is a way of silencing and shutting out dissenting voices, those expressing counter-hegemonic positions. The higher the deemed security risk, generally the greater the restrictions on communication for the prisoner. Most of the individuals I discuss here have spent some time in solitary confinement, some with additional security restrictions placed on them making dialogue difficult. Incarceration in such conditions also impacts mental health, and thus one's ability to speak or to think clearly. This is compounded further by the surveillance of prison administrative systems, which mean that every form of dialogue or correspondence is open to inspection. If criminal trials, sentencing judgements or parole hearings are pending, the risks involved in speaking out are high.

The securitising of information is applied also to statistical data that can illuminate broader patterns and trends. Access to such statistics are increasingly prohibited, but in an ad hoc, haphazard fashion. In line with the general trend of the withholding of material, my attempts to obtain information via Freedom of Information Act requests were often unsuccessful, though not always or not completely, and some data have been obtained via this route. Simultaneously, the information age grants easier access to documentation that would otherwise be unreachable or unknowable. Whistle-blowers, investigative journalists and lobbies for public interest make available large reams of data and documentation that would otherwise be near impossible to reach. While Wikileaks may represent the most significant and iconic global exemplar of this, multiple other blog and small-scale campaign sites also publish snippets of information, obtained from court cases but otherwise not readily publicly available or from the sporadically successful Freedom of Information Act requests, which can offer important pieces of the bigger puzzle.

The empirical data that I draw upon here has been obtained in this paradoxical fashion, limited by the restrictions engendered by national security but aided by the data circuits made possible in a digitised information age.

Against the restrictions of incarceration, partially open legal judgements and securitised government data, my knowledge of these cases and the broader contextual information that I detail here also rely on a mixture of mail correspondence with prisoners and, in the rare occasions of those who have been released, interviews, as well as interviews and conversations with lawyers, human rights groups and activists familiar with these cases. Without them, this would barely constitute a book, if a book at all.

1

Making Non-Humans

We will not act for revenge ... We act for justice. We act with world opinion behind us. And we have an absolute determination to see justice done, and this evil of mass terrorism confronted and defeated.

Tony Blair, 2001[1]

You could hardly begin (in the public space provided by international discourse) to analyse political conflicts involving Sunnis and Shi'is, Kurds and Iraqis, or Tamils and Sinhalese, or Sikhs and Hindus ... without eventually having to resort to the categories and images of 'terrorism' and 'fundamentalism', which derived entirely from the concerns and intellectual factories in metropolitan centres like Washington and London. They are fearful images that lack discriminate contents or definition, but they signify moral power and approval for whoever uses them, moral defensiveness and criminalization for whomever they designate.

Edward Said, 1993[2]

As if to illustrate the totalitarian nature of colonial exploitation, the colonist turns the colonized into a kind of quintessence of evil.

Frantz Fanon, 1961[3]

Somalian-born Mahdi Hashi was five years old when he arrived with his family in London after fleeing civil war. After being granted asylum, he obtained British citizenship at the age of fourteen. When he finished his GCSE exams at sixteen, Mahdi travelled to Egypt to study Arabic. During this time, he, together with other friends a few years more senior, were among the thousands detained by Egyptian authorities for suspected political dissent. The accusation against him which concerned an 'association with extremists' saw him deported back to the UK. From that point on, he began to be harassed by the British intelligence services.

Mahdi was active in his community. At nineteen he worked as a care worker and volunteered as a youth leader at Kentish Town Community Organisation. When he planned to visit his sick grandmother in Djibouti in April 2009, as he checked-in at Gatwick airport he was stopped by two plainclothes police officers, one of whom called himself 'Richard' and told him that he worked for MI5. Mahdi reported the incident to journalists and complained to the Investigatory Powers Tribunal, relaying that the officers attempted to befriend him and warned him not to get on the flight, stating, 'Whatever happens to you outside the UK is not our responsibility.'[4] Richard handed Mahdi a piece of paper with his name and telephone number on it and asked him to call, advising him again not to board the plane. Refusing to be intimidated, Mahdi went on with his journey. On arrival at Djibouti airport, he was stopped at passport control, detained for sixteen hours, and deported back to the UK on the request of the British authorities. When he arrived, he was detained again at Heathrow Airport. Richard appeared with coffee and breakfast, informing him that it was they who had called for his return because he 'was a terror suspect' and made it clear to him that his 'suspect' status and travel restrictions would only be lifted if he agreed to cooperate with MI5. Mahdi told journalists:

> I myself am sick and tired of this cycle of savage harassment for the last three years to the point where they are making me a terror suspect ... What have I done to deserve this and to be

wanted and known as a dangerous terrorist. It looks like there is no way out.[5]

After returning to Somalia to care for his grandmother in 2011, Mahdi was detained by al-Shabaab, the Somali militant organisation, some months into his stay in 2012 who accused him of working as a spy for the US. At the same time that he was held by al-Shabaab, he was stripped of his British citizenship on claims by the home secretary that he was involved in Islamic extremism and a risk to national security. Since the letter alerting him to the fact was sent to his parents' address in London, it was not until some months later, after his release, that he became aware of this and tried to appeal. While on his way to the British embassy in Djibouti to appeal his denaturalisation, Mahdi and two others, both Swedish-Somali men, Ali Yasin Ahmed and Mohamed Yusuf, were detained by authorities there. Held in a secret prison for months, all three men were interrogated by Djiboutian, CIA and FBI officials before being rendered to the US to face material support for terrorism and conspiracy to provide material support charges in New York.

At a time when it was still proving troublesome for British authorities to successfully extradite individuals accused of terrorism offences to the US, and in the aftermath of the negative exposure and reprimand of European states from the European Court of Human Rights for their role in the US-led 'extraordinary rendition' programme, the tactic of 'rendition to justice' used for disappearing Mahdi Hashi indicated the possibility of alternative disciplinary techniques that could be used by US forces, with British complicity, for achieving the same end.[6] The ECHR's condemnation of the rendition programme, as resembling 'a "spider's web" spun across the globe', was vocalised in terms of the human rights violations that went against Europe's legal and moral commitment to 'rights, democracy and respect for the rule of law'.[7] But as Mahdi's father, Mr Farah, remarked in a radio interview, 'It's easier, I think, just to pass him to the Americans instead of extraditing him later on.'[8] His capture by Djiboutian officials operating on behalf of the US made his transfer less arduous and less scrutinised than it would be through a formal extradition process, while it also permitted his exposure to forms of violence that were not constrained by humanitarian safeguards.[9] For the British state, this form of expulsion operated through their denial of accountability. Mahdi's family experienced this first-hand when they contacted the Foreign Office after learning of his capture and detention and were told that since he was no longer a British national he had no right to receive consular assistance.

Mahdi, along with the two others, were imprisoned for three months by Djiboutian officials in a secret prison, in a cell roughly five metres long by five metres wide, which, with the exception of the interrogation sessions, he was never permitted to leave. He was forced to sleep on a marble floor in a cell that was poorly ventilated and reached scalding temperatures.[10] While detained, he witnessed his co-defendant Ali Yasin Ahmed and another man being tortured by Djiboutian officials, and heard the continuous torture of other inmates. He was also repeatedly threatened with physical torture and sexual abuse himself. The collaboration between Djiboutian and US officials became clear when, after enduring these conditions for three weeks, he was visited by American personnel, who he believed to be of The Joint Special Operations Command or the CIA, who subjected him to further interrogation over a period of eleven days.[11] At no point during this time was he advised of any constitutional rights or offered access to a lawyer. Mahdi stated that Djiboutian officers warned him that 'Americans tortured uncooperative prisoners who refused to answer questions and strongly encouraged that I cooperate'.[12] During the interrogation sessions by US officers, at least one of the local Djiboutian officials who had threatened him with torture, and who he had witnessed torturing others, was present. Some days after this period of interrogation ended, FBI agents arrived and began a further series of interrogation sessions (about seven sessions in total). To indicate the sleight in juridical distinction, prior to meetings with the FBI Mahdi was read his constitutional rights under US law. But like before, interrogation continued while

Djiboutian officials again stood watch.

Disappeared and without access to a legal representative or support from the British foreign office during this time, it was only after Mahdi was secretly rendered to the US and appeared in a New York court room in January 2013 that his family learned of his whereabouts. On arrival in New York with Ali Yasin Ahmed and Mohamed Yusuf, the men were detained in secrecy for a further five weeks under the false names 'John Doe A', 'John Doe B' and 'John Doe C' before they were charged with supporting al-Shabaab and appeared in court. Prosecutors argued that Mahdi travelled to Somalia to attend a training camp and fight with al-Shabaab in Somalia's civil war. When Mahdi's lawyers contested the submission of Mahdi's testimony in Djibouti as evidence for the prosecution as it had been obtained under conditions of torture, US government attorney Loretta Lynch argued that his statements to the FBI officials were made voluntarily after he had been informed of his rights, and were therefore admissible. The court agreed.[13] He was detained in Manhattan Correctional Center in solitary confinement for over two years without trial before he entered into a plea bargain in 2015.

Some years earlier, in 2007, Fahad Hashmi had, too, been deported to the same prison in New York. He was also held in solitary confinement for three years without trial and like Mahdi Hashi was subject to further restrictions, known as Special Administrative Measures, which were intended to impede his ability to communicate with the outside world.

Fahad had arrived to the US from Britain, however, via a different route than had Mahdi. It was in June 2006 when he was preparing to travel to Pakistan from London's Heathrow airport that he was stopped by a British police officer at passport control and escorted to a private room by a group of men whom he assumed to be law enforcement personnel. When he arrived in the room he was met with two men in suits who appeared to be waiting for him. Fahad asked why he was being stopped and was told 'he was being arrested for extradition to America'. His arm was grabbed and handcuffs were tightly applied to his wrist. He instinctively pulled his wrist back because of the painful manner in which the handcuffs were applied, so the officers pushed him to the floor, twisting his arm behind his back. He felt more than one knee pushed into him and yelled from the pain of the hand-cuffs. The police picked him up and took him out of the room. He reports that while in there he was never informed of his right to remain silent.[14] Fahad was detained in the general popula-tion of Belmarsh high-security prison for over eleven months, before he became the first person extradited from Britain to the US under the more relaxed arrangements agreed in the US–UK Extradition Treaty of 2003.

One day in May 2007 while still detained in Belmarsh, a prison official informed Fahad that he needed to be drug tested. After he left the cell a designated search team packed up all of his belongings including his personal legal papers. It soon became apparent to Fahad that there was no drugs test but that he was being escorted to a secure police van for transport to the United States. On the way to Heathrow Airport he recalled one of the British officers telling him 'We're going to send you to Cuba.'[15] When they arrived at the airport, the van drove directly onto the tarmac next to a small jet plane with 'United States of America' printed on the side. He was handed over to US officials who included three US marshals and two FBI agents. Prior to leaving for the airport Fahad asked a prison official at Belmarsh if he could call his lawyers to inform them of the extradition since neither he nor they were aware that he was being extradited. The official told him he could call at the airport. When he asked American officials for this right at the airport they declined his request. Once on the plane he was strip searched, chained and not permitted to use the bathroom for the duration of the flight. During transit Fahad was approached by the FBI officials who asked if he would waive his rights and speak to them. He declined. Upon arrival in New York, he was taken directly to the Southern District Court in downtown Manhattan, refused bail on the grounds of the terrorism charges he faced, which were providing and conspiring to provide material support to al-Qaeda as well as making and conspiring to make a contribution of goods and services to al-Qaeda, and incarcerated in solitary confinement in Manhattan Correctional Center.

A US citizen, Fahad had grown up in the Queens area of New York in a community that had been one of the areas of focus of the secret surveillance programme established by the NYPD in 2001. Stepping up the practice of surveillance that the police force had long been known for, the Demographics Unit (a secret section operating within the NYPD Intelligence Unit), working closely with CIA officers, began to map and spy on multiple facets of community life, targeting mosques, community centres, schools, businesses, and social and residential spaces. Documenting social behaviours, such as levels of religiosity, NYPD agents charted activities such as 'how many times a day Muslim students prayed during a university white-water rafting trip, which Egyptian businesses shut their doors for daily prayers, which restaurants played Al-Jazeera and which Newark businesses sold halal products and alcohol'.[16]

As part of the programme, undercover officers, learned in different languages of the communities in which they were embedded, inhabited target areas to record local news, identify stories of interest, and gain a general sense of the community, while local informants were employed to infiltrate mosques and religious events, reporting anything of note.[17] The surveillance of Muslim student societies formed a key part of this programme, encroaching on the political expression and activism of Muslim students keen to respond to wars across the Muslim world and to protest the role of the United States in them. Of the thirty-one Muslim student societies identified across New York, seven were listed as being 'of concern' including that of Brooklyn College – the society in which Fahad had been actively engaged. He was particularly outspoken in his political views, protesting against US imperialism and advocating Islamic alternatives, including a caliphate in Pakistan.[18] He became a member of the New York–based group al-Muhajiroun, a spin-off of the London-based group by the same name, and was known to be an avid debater in class and student meetings.[19] Fahad was involved in supporting Da'wah stalls, stalls distributing leaflets and literature promoting the teachings of Islam, in different parts of New York. As part of his activist work, he demonstrated outside various embassies, in protest of the treatment of Muslims in Kashmir, Chechnya and Palestine.[20]

The New York–based al-Muhajiroun that Fahad was affiliated with had frequently rallied against the colonisation of the Islamic world. The stated key objectives of the group aimed for a reversal of historical 'colonialist designs' that had divided parts of the Muslim world between Western powers, such as the Balfour Declaration (the letter from British Foreign Secretary Arthur Balfour announcing the establishment of a Jewish homeland in Palestine), the Sykes-Picot Agreement (a secret agreement signed in 1916 between Britain and France defining their spheres of influence and control in parts of the declining Ottoman Empire), and the decisions made at the San Remo Conference in 1920 (a meeting between Britain, France, Italy and Japan to determine who would administer the territories of Palestine, Syria and Mesopotamia [Iraq]). The protest activities of the group had included holding and participating in demonstrations against the Israeli occupation of Palestine, against the Danish cartoons affair, a series of cartoons published by the Danish newspaper Jyllands-Posten disparaging the Prophet Mohammed, and against US imperialism more broadly. They had been vocal about showing no allegiance to the US flag or its constitution. In terms of membership, most, like Fahad, had grown up in Queens and were second-generation US Muslim youth politicised both by the surveillance of their communities and by historical and contemporary military interventions by Western forces across the Muslim world. Their actions reflected political identities situated in local and global histories.[21]

After graduating from Brooklyn College, Fahad moved to London to study for a master's degree at London Metropolitan University. During this period, he was visited by an acquaintance, Junaid Babar, an association which would prove critical to Fahad's subsequent arrest. Among Junaid's luggage there had been ponchos and socks, which the authorities later classed as 'military training gear' which they argued Junaid went on to deliver to al-Qaeda members in Pakistan. During Junaid's stay, Fahad had also used Junaid's cell phone. Fahad's association with Junaid in these two ways – allowing Junaid to stay in his apartment with the ponchos and socks, and using Junaid's phone – formed the basis of his indictment for charges of material support for terrorism.[22] Following his extradition to New York in 2007, character 'flaws', invoked in relation to his alleged hostility on arrest, were used as additional cause to refuse bail and justify the extra restrictions of Special Administrative Measures.

In a press release following Fahad's extradition, the New York Police Commissioner Raymond Kelly stated: 'This arrest reinforces the fact that a terrorist may have roots in Queens and still betray us'.[23] Although these comments indicated that the guilt of Fahad had as good as already been decided, the statement made by the police commissioner sparked little controversy or protest. At the end of the press statement, the US Attorney's office retracted the claims: 'The charges contained in the indictment are merely accusations, and the defendant is presumed innocent unless and until proven guilty'. For the state, however, his very capture was indicative of the existence of 'domestic terrorists', and the act of apprehending him relayed to the general public the reassurance that measures were being taken to intervene in this regard.

There are numerous similarities between the two stories, as there are distinctions. As both cases expose the entwining of military and civilian systems of policing and jurisdiction, they also indicate something about the process via which terrorism suspects are made. The low threshold for criminalising individuals on suspicion of engagement in terrorism is upheld through a cultural discourse around who and what we consider a terrorism suspect to be. It is the racialised cultural representations through which the trope of the terrorist operates, and its legal legitimation, which were integral to the criminalisation of Fahad Hashmi and Mahdi Hashi that I want to explore in this chapter.

The Disposition Matrix

> *These men will be held in a high-security facility at Guantanamo*
> *... And they will continue to be treated with the humanity that*
> *they denied others.*
>
> George Bush, 2006[24]

> 'We can't possibly kill everyone who wants to harm us. It's a
> necessary part of what we do'
>
> Former counterterrorism official, 2012[25]

Mahdi Hashi's name was likely one of the many names entered into an intelligence database that the Obama administration had been secretly developing as a blueprint for pursuing terrorists. The Disposition Matrix, as the administration named it, referred to a database cataloguing the biographies of individuals deemed to pose a threat to the US, their suspected location, and a range of options for their disposal, from which target lists would be drawn.[26] The matrix, which reportedly included the names of suspects with little or no evidence against them, incorporated the kill lists of the CIA and the US military special forces, but by integrating multiple strategies of disposal, one or more of several strategies might be employed to capture and/or kill the target subject, depending on the location and circumstances.[27] While individuals located in countries experiencing direct US military intervention could be targeted by drone strike or killed by US special forces, others would be tortured and incarcerated in US 'black sites' still operating in East Africa or in US proxy-run prisons across Central Asia. In some cases, terrorism suspects would be brought to justice via the US domestic judicial system and be relocated to a prison in the United States, either through rendition, as was Mahdi Hashi, or through official extradition arrangements, as in Fahad Hashmi's case.

While the Disposition Matrix was an expression of the consolidation of multiple techniques of disposal into one database, the methods of capture, interrogation and detention themselves had been in use for some time. 'Extraordinary rendition', first employed as a technique of capture by the US Central Intelligence Agency in the War on Drugs, was mobilised as one of the initial key responses for detaining suspects outside the US in the days after 9/11, absent a more developed military strategy.[28] It entails the kidnapping and extra-judicial transfer of targets either to clandestine detention sites, known as 'black sites', proxy-run prisons operated by foreign states collaborating or working for the US, or directly to US military prisons.[29]

For those who for political reasons, often because they are European citizens or located in the West, could not be captured in this way, sometimes a secret grand jury investigation would be used to instigate an extradition request. A technique used more prolifically from the 1970s onwards for fighting wars on drugs, crime, and terrorism, the US–UK Extradition Treaty of 2003 was passed to increase the efficiency of this process.[30] Fast-tracked into UK legislation without formal consultative parliamentary process, scrutiny or debate, the treaty made provisions for a unilateral agreement between the US and the UK whereby the UK would be expected to extradite any individual to the US without the need for the US to provide prima facie evidence – only to invoke a standard of reasonable suspicion – and thus disallowing the individual from challenging any evidence provided by the US in a British Court of Law.

The different modes of death-dealing encapsulated in the matrix reflect the continuous negotiation between the unconstrained violence licenced in spaces of colonial and imperial occupation and the slightly moderated techniques approved of under humanitarian conventions.[31] As Obama approached the start of his first presidential term, he faced a number of criticisms of US military actions by human rights lobbyists stemming in part from the media exposure of the 'extraordinary rendition' programme first revealed by the *New Yorker* in 2006 and its links to the use of (recognised) torture techniques. Criticism also stemmed from the continued detention of Muslim men under the militarised conditions of confinement at Guantanamo Bay detention camp, which were lobbied against by human rights organisations as contrary to liberal norms and which Obama himself had, during his presidential campaign, sworn to close.[32] Part of the solution for skirting these human rights conflicts was to increase the targeted killings and drone strikes and eliminate the problem of warehousing people indefinitely. Two days after Obama took office he signed an executive order which revoked directives of the Bush administration authorising torture and re-emphasised the need to adhere to international conventions and federal laws. The following day he authorised two CIA drone strikes in northwest Pakistan; estimates suggest that twenty-five people were killed in that strike, most of whom were 'non-combatants', including four to five children.[33] This became the counterterrorism strategy associated with the Obama presidency, and its use drastically increased from 2009 on.[34]

At the same time, there was some attempt to spin capture, interrogation and detention practices as more humane and democratic. Revisions to rendition practices in the form of 'rendition to justice' directly connected military and civilian systems, even as the unreformed system continued – now more quietly – in the shadows.[35] Under the revised system a person would be kidnapped and interrogated before being flown to face trial in the US and there granted access to a public defender. As Madhi Hashi's case shows, this system allowed for a suspect to be interrogated and tortured under conditions that would officially contravene human rights protocols, only later being informed of their legal rights, offered access to a lawyer and questioned again. As a process, rendition to justice directly connects practices of torture with the human rights conventions of Western democracy through an arbitrary separation between the evidence obtained via torture in the initial period of detention and the evidence gathered immediately post this period once the suspect had been read their legal rights. It is useful to the purposes of intelligence gathering for both forms of interrogation to occur in succession. The US courtroom then has the power and authority to distinguish between them, seeing evidence gained during the first interrogation as inadmissible and the latter as admissible.

The continuities between these various systems is heightened through the interchange of personnel.[36] Prisons guards in both civilian and military systems are trained to reinforce dehumanisation of those in their custody. As former guard at Guantanamo Bay Terry Holdbrooks remarked, 'We were told not to talk to them, not to treat them as humans, to not engage in conversation with them whatsoever'.[37]

The liberal framework in which some disciplinary techniques or forms of violence are made more legitimate than others has informed the response of authorities on human rights, illustrated by the contrasting ways in which the European Council and European Court of Human Rights have responded to them. After their involvement was revealed in 2006, the European Council's Committee on Legal Affairs and Human Rights condemned the complicity of European states in the practice of extraordinary rendition. Subsequently, Poland was found to have violated its obligation under the European Convention on Human Rights by the ECHR for supporting a CIA black site on Polish territory.[38] In contrast, extradition, as it proceeds through the civilian justice system, is presented as a more democratic process: to transfer and incarcerate. Whereas the European Council condemned Europe's complicity in the extraordinary rendition programme, the European Court of Human Rights, as I discuss in Chapter Four, did not view extradition to long-term solitary confinement as a violation of the human rights of terrorism suspects.

Yet for those who are subject to these techniques of violence, the practices are bluntly similar, particularly when comparing rendition and extradition for capturing terrorism suspects. A general account of the process involved in the capture of suspects through the extraordinary rendition programme is offered by Ruth Blakeley and Sam Raphael:

Prior to the transfer, detainees would be subjected to a 'preparation phase', or 'security check'. This was described to the Marty investigation by a CIA officer as a 'twenty-minute takeout', designed to reduce the detainee to 'a state of almost total immobility and sensory deprivation'. Detainees would be stripped, often by having their clothes cut from their body. They would be gripped from all sides throughout the process, and often punched, kicked or shoved. When naked, they were photographed, and be subjected to a full cavity examination. Suppositories were often administered anally, before being dressed in a diaper and a tracksuit or boiler-suit (jump-suit). Detainees were then blindfolded, sometimes after having cotton wool taped to their eyes. Headphones or ear defenders were placed on their ears, sometimes with loud music played through them. Loose hoods were then placed over the head, which reached down over the shoulders. Hands and feet were shackled, and may then have been connected to other detainees.[39]

Torture and indefinite detention usually follow transfer to a black site or space of military detention.

In reporting their experiences of transfer, Babar Ahmad's and Talha Ahsan's accounts of extradition to the US, which I discuss in the next chapter, are reminiscent of the general description given by Blakeley and Raphael. Both extradited at the same time, Babar reports being driven in a police convoy to RAF Mildenhall, Suffolk, where two private jets awaited him on the tarmac. Before he disembarked from the van, Metropolitan Police Extradition Squad police officers placed a blacked-out ski mask and ear muffs on him upon the request of US authorities. He describes walking inside a permanent US Air Force facility within the RAF grounds, which had 'boxes of American food lying around' and 'American toiletries in the bathrooms', and where he was handed over to officers who appeared to be US military personnel. They photographed and filmed him, placed leg shackles, handcuffs (and a locked belt linking the handcuffs to the leg shackles), blindfolds and ear muffs on him, then photographed and filmed him again before leading him onto one of the private jets. He was blindfolded and ear muffed once again an hour before the plane landed at a private airfield in New Haven, Connecticut.[40] Talha's account is similar, but noting additionally that while he waited for the officers to process other detainees, he was made to sit facing a corner with a Homeland Security handler standing watch. He notes that their 'bodies were examined, including below the waist undressed, and photographs were taken'. He was only permitted to use the toilet with the door open in full view of the handler, and was forbidden from communicating with his co-defendant sitting beside him. As he was boarded onto the private jet 'in handcuffs and leg shackles deprived of sight and hearing', he was flanked by two handlers who took him on a zig-zag route to the aircraft.[41] On arrival both Talha and Babar were taken to New Haven Federal Courthouse.

The multiple similarities in both extradition and extraordinary rendition as techniques of transfer are distinguished by a thin line of judicial oversight. The condemnation of the practice of 'extraordinary rendition' by the ECHR was conceived of in terms of its barbaric nature operating beyond routine protocols of civilian or martial laws of war. In contrast, extradition was sanctioned precisely because it proceeded within these bounds of recognised legal arrangements. In exposing the fluidity of transfer between systems, the processing of terrorism suspects through the Disposition Matrix shows the continuities between civilian and military policing systems and how seemingly discrete systems of governance were intimately tied together. Doing so also exposes the double-edged sword of liberalism by explicitly demonstrating how the framing of democratic processes are manipulated and exploited in the name of subjects made non-human. At the same time, the fixation with achieving a threshold of violence acceptable by humanitarian standards overlooks the rationale in the decision-making process by which an individual is incorporated into a matrix that catalogues people marked for disposal. Thus, to fully grapple with the operations of the matrix, it is necessary to also consider the racial ideologies which informed the processes of representation and identification of subjects marked as terrorism suspects, ideologies which work sufficiently to dehumanise and permit their treatment with impunity. That is, fixed cultural readings of these marked individuals which placed them as only recognisable in uncivilised, 'non-human' terms, I suggest, are a necessary prerequisite for inclusion into a catalogue deciphering how they ought to be captured and/or killed.

Orienting Terror

Images of zombified beings, goggled, hooded, chained and incarcerated in dog cages in Camp Delta during the early days of the War on Terror, came to represent one of the many iconic imaginings of the terrorist in recent times. Beyond this initial onslaught of barbarism, the most grotesque images, such as those from Abu Ghraib, have been supplemented by impressions that appear more ordinary and unremarkable, and are visible everyday. Turbaned, bearded men and burqa-covered women have, through political and media discourse, come to signify and represent the terrorism suspect. As these images circulate ever more intensely, an acute visual and affective sense of Muslim non-humanity has become concretised, signalling in turn an important expression of race-thinking. Framed in this way, the trope of the terrorism suspect, a schema through which Muslims are made less-than-human, must be understood as a racialised trope, a trope against which self-aggrandising standards of Western civilisation can be affirmed.[42] The 'terrorism suspect', like the figure of the criminal, is readily incorporated into an ideological base where racialised associations become central to its definition.[43]

In 1999, research was carried out by staff of the Federal Research Division of the US Library of Congress, subtitled *Who Becomes a Terrorist and Why?*, which aimed to depict the social and psychological profile of the terrorist. Distinguishing between the 'old' terrorism of the 1970s and 'new' terrorism of the 1990s, it pointed to the urgency of promoting a change in depictions of terrorism, lately altered by shifting recruitment patterns, including the recruitment of female and child terrorists, access to 'weapons of mass destruction' and growth in the use of suicide bombers. It was the advance of so-called 'religious terrorism' that was positioned as that which presented the most potential harm and as that which had the capability of causing the most destruction. Specifically, here, of the 'new breeds of increasingly dangerous religious terrorists [that had] emerged', it was declared that 'the most dangerous type [was] the Islamic fundamentalist'.[44]

Terrorism, framed as religious fanaticism rather than as an act erupting from particular political conditions, re-packages it as a religious-cultural trope and so depoliticises it as an act. One of the significant points of the Library of Congress report is that it characterises all those groups mobilising under Islam as performing 'religious terrorism'. From al-Qaeda to Hezbollah to Hamas, the context, motivation and instigation of violence is explained as culturally rooted, where the techniques of violence employed and the rationalisation for them arise out of an Islamic 'cultural and religious context'.[45] The choice to draw upon a religious instead of a political cause allowed for the possibility of fixing to those marked as Muslim a bio-cultural pathology, placing the origins of terrorism within the ideology of an alien culture.[46] The premise is that acts of terrorist violence are rooted not in political circumstances but in Islamic civilisation, read thus as a pre-modern or anti-modern entity that is the antithesis of the West. Jerrold M. Post, a political psychologist and the founder and former director of the Central Intelligence Agency's Center for the Analysis of Personality and Political Behavior, corroborates this idea, noting that 'unlike the average political or social terrorist, who has a defined mission that is somewhat measurable in terms of media attention or government reaction, the religious terrorist can justify the most heinous acts "in the name of Allah"'.[47]

As the principal ideological target of Western imperialism moved from communism to terrorism, institutionalised through the War on Terror, the discourse of the Islamic extremist has developed and been refined. Different political factions, from the centre-left to the centre and far right have invoked the connection between Islam and terrorism in varied ways. At times the entire religion of Islam is demonised while on other occasions there is an attempt to distinguish between Islam as a whole and certain readings of it which are said to be misplaced and 'extreme'.[48] The longevity of the generic cultural reading of terrorism is pronounced through publications such as the Global Terrorism Index which, in 2016, continued to cite the significance of religious ideology in underpinning political Islamic movements.[49] Within this reading, the fixation with (artificially) separating the 'moderate' Muslim from the 'extreme' has endured. Theresa May, for example, attempted to maintain such a distinction in her remarks following the spate of terrorist attacks in Manchester and London in 2017, making quite explicit claims to the superiority of Western civilisation as she did so. She noted that the attacks were 'bound together by the single evil ideology of Islamist extremism that preaches hatred, sows division and promotes sectarianism. It is an ideology that claims our Western values of freedom, democracy and human rights are incompatible with the religion of Islam'.[50]

This oft-cited distinction, a mainstay of liberal rhetoric regarding the War on Terror, warrants more critical attention. Contrary to its seeming attempt at ideological 'moderation', such a separation works to further entrench racialised representations, as the canonical work of Mahmood Mamdani has shown. In preference for a cultural reading, which Mamdani has referred to as 'culture talk', motivations for terrorist violence are attributed to essentialised and orientalist notions that equate Islam or some factions of it with barbarism, irrationality and, in general terms, pre-modernity.[51] The trope of the terrorist in this framework is constructed from a set of narratives rooted in European colonialism that reduce the complexity of vastly different civilisations of the East to pathological tendencies towards savagery, misogyny and despotism.[52] This reliance on orientalism is depicted in the shorthand or abbreviation of such 'culture talk' by simply referring to those identified as terrorism suspects as 'evildoers'.

The nuanced distinction made by some liberal quarters between 'good' Muslim and 'bad' Muslim attempts to mediate this to offer salvage for some. Yet the attempt to separate the 'moderate' Muslim from the 'extreme', to make a distinction between 'good' and 'bad', maintains the reliance on culture as cause, while at the same time the targeted political response of Western governments bares the falsity and superficial nature of such a separation. As Theresa May indicated in some initial proposals for how the government would step up its counterterrorism response, pre-emptive intervention and punishment were as necessary for those at risk of radicalisation as military intervention was in the aftermath of an attack.[53] The pre-emptive profiling upon which counterinsurgent strategies are based by their very definition stipulate policing the 'moderate'.

As this orientalist lens has framed the discourse of terrorism invoked to support and sustain military intervention and occupation in Afghanistan, Iraq, Pakistan, Somalia, Libya, Yemen and Syria, it has simultaneously fed into the political narratives of race in Britain, layering onto the pathological cultural discourses already in circulation in reference to Britain's black and Asian post/colonial communities. Cultural explanations are periodically reasserted by political officials and commentators to explain structural injustices created and maintained through a politics of racism – whether in the political response to the eruption of riots, through the mundane everyday vilification of multiculturalism or through the rationalisations given for longstanding inequalities in health, education and employment. Within this broader evocation of culture/cultural pathology, the repertoires of what we understand as orientalism has often played a central role and the enduring presence of imperial subjects within mainland Britain means that such narratives are well established within British race and immigration discourse.

Orientalist notions attributing to post/colonial migrants from the South Asian sub-continent an excess of (backwards) culture that inhibited their integration, and which ranged from ideas of weak proficiency in English to misogynistic cultural practices, were reconstructed with a particular Muslim lens from the late 1980s onwards with the Salman Rushdie affair.[54] Local and national government responses to the 2001 riots in Oldham,

Bradford and Burnley, as one example, explained the grievances of those experiencing social, political and economic deprivation, under-employment and over-policing as not the products of structural racism but of Muslim communities living 'parallel lives'.[55] It was the lack of integration and specifically Muslim 'self-segregation' that official inquiries held responsible. Against this backdrop of racial pathologisation, the trope of the terrorist allows for a re-articulation of cultural essentialism now linked more explicitly to a propensity for 'Islamic fundamentalism'.

The distinction made between foreign national terrorism suspects and British Muslim communities in the early years of the War on Terror, which still managed to align both in terms of discourses of non-belonging and calls for more controlled citizenship, soon collapsed. Where the arrest of Babar Ahmad in 2003 brought home to many in South London's Muslim communities the continuities between the military intervention in Iraq justified through the rhetoric of terrorism and the policing of British Muslims, the convergence of the 'foreign' and 'home-grown' terrorism suspect was cemented after the 7/7 bombings in London and Tony Blair's declaration that the 'rules of the game had changed'.[56]

The dissolution of the distinction between the 'foreign' and the 'home-grown' has become ever more pronounced as the War on Terror has progressed and numbers of disaffected Muslim youth have responded to economic and political disenfranchisement at home and to Western imperialism abroad. Terrorism and its euphemisms – fundamentalism and Islamic extremism – are embedded as catch-all explanations for wide-ranging social, political and economic problems, obscuring more than they illuminate. Uncivilised cultural tendencies are now not only linked to a lack of integration but to a risk of radicalisation and engagement in terrorism. Self-segregation now does not simply lead to domestic tension; it breeds radical extremism.[57] The 'gang culture' attributed to black communities in areas such as Moss Side, is now compounded by the presence of Muslim 'Jihadis', so that the representation of African Caribbean, Somalian and Libyan youth are reconstructed in line with the discourses underpinning contemporary politics.[58]

Contextualising Terrorism

Where orientalist 'culture talk' has been pivotal to the hegem-onic accounts of political Islam and the political-economic positioning of Muslims more generally, the appropriation of the notion of terrorism to account for dissent against state power also sits within the broader colonial and imperial imaginary. In the context of the British Empire, where in the aftermath of the French Revolution the state appropriated the term 'terrorism' in reference to Irish anti-colonial resistance, the conceptualisation of 'terror' moved distinctly away from a notion of institution-alised violence. Instead, terror was typified in more abstracted terms. Terrorism, referencing the coercion, terrorisation and destruction of a target was related specifically to anti-colonial insurgency.[59] As Fenians came to be synonymised as terror-ists and political actions associated with Fenianism referred to as 'terrorism', the violence of British occupation, with all the resource extraction that this entailed, was framed as part of the rightful order of empire and civilisation.[60] In this way, the ter-rorist trope offered a useful way for disavowing certain forms of political dissent at a time when liberal sentiment was commit-ted to the belief that freedom to resist those in power should be protected as a fundamental part of democracy in practice. John Stuart Mill, for example, could lobby for the rights protections of dissenting liberal revolutionaries as a fundamental aspect of liberty while simultaneously disavowing the actions of Fenian agitators as illegitimate for their use 'foul' weapons.[61]

The trope of the terrorist as it comes to reference Fenian anti-colonial resistance operates at the interface between national considerations of citizenship and colonial concerns for manag-ing and containing the Empire. Its invocation through the Irish question meant it was given a double function, subsuming both a domestic threat endangering the Union and an imperial threat for British Empire. As a concept, the racialised axis of the terrorism suspect is signified through its infiltration into debates demarcat-ing the borders and boundaries of citizenship under empire. At the moment when franchise was extended to working-class men in the 1860s, and citizenship became more explicitly invoked in biopolitical terms, moving away from property requirements and towards the 'character' of a subject (through race-classed and gendered taxonomies), the Irish question was situated as somewhere between the savagery of Jamaicans and the purity of the Anglo-Saxon race. The ambivalent inclusion of some Irish people as citizens of the nation enabled through reforms, justified in racial terms because they as a group were considered more proximate to the English than other imperial subjects, was offset by those identified with the growing Fenian movement, who were excluded from the same privileges. With the whitening of some segments of the Irish population, the discourse of terrorism worked to blacken the unruly and dissenting segments of the same population and so provided the reasoning through which their exclusion could be maintained.[62] It is at this moment in history when the hegemonic idea of citizenship develops that, as Amy Martin insightfully observes, 'the idea of "terrorism" in its modern incarnation appears' and becomes a way of disavowing and disenfranchising those who cannot be made docile while securing the subservience and consent of the wider populous.[63]

The cultural signifiers and racial traits used to depict Irish terrorism were adapted to revolutionary fighters in India at the turn of the twentieth century. Stephen Morton notes, for example, that a cartoon in the British *Punch* magazine in 1870 entitled 'Hercules and the Hydra' depicted Gladstone as Hercules, preparing to fight 'Fenianism', a multi-headed serpent, was recreated in a strikingly similar fashion in the Hindi *Punch* magazine in 1908, as a cartoon entitled 'Down with the Monster' which portrays the Indian viceroy Lord Minto as Hercules, killing the twin-headed hydra of Indian anarchism and revolution.[64] These representations re-morphed again to depict the Mau Mau and resistance fighters in Malaya in the 1950s, where cinematic representations correlated with British government propaganda on terrorism.[65]

As anti-colonial resistance developed more fervently across the Empire, the trope of the terrorist was frequently the representation featured in government justifications for the implementation of martial law and states of emergency.

The longevity of wars against 'terror' has prompted comparisons with earlier histories and moments of resistance. In responding to the question, 'Was It Like This for the Irish?', Gareth Peirce, deeply familiar with Britain's long history of domestic counterterrorism, notes the continuities between the state violence perpetrated against those suspected of IRA involvement and the current brutalities faced by Muslim communities, acknowledging that while the strong Irish-American political influence offset the precarious position of the Irish in the UK, there appeared to be no political equivalent that might do the same for Muslims in the foreseeable future.[66] The pertinent distinction is that the cultural pathologies of the Irish that were developed to portray them as an inferior race operated in tandem with discourses that recognised their potential to belong as citizens, not to mention the very material legislative act that encompassed Ireland within the Union. The trope of the Irish terrorist worked very much along a biopolitical paradigm to differentiate between Irish subjects worthy of life and those who could be treated with impunity. The logic of Islamic terrorism, on the other hand, is framed by a more overreaching colonial discourse where there has been no such counter play between demonisation and political incorporation. There is no political or rhetorical drive to operate the project of exclusion in tandem with any counter political move that pushes for greater political recognition or incorporation.

There are, still, a number of assumptions implied in the one-sided framing of terrorism that I am alluding to here that warrant further reflection. On the one hand, colonial histories reveal that violence which is conventionally rooted in anti-occupation, anti-imperialist struggle has been recurrently delegitimised through the spectre of terrorism. Violence enacted by colonised subjects was represented as a form of 'anarchy', as 'semi/uncivilised and savage', and as 'irrational' since it did not conform to recognised protocols.[67] As the definition of terrorism has become more formalised it is conceived of as 'premeditated' and 'politically motivated', 'perpetrated against non-combatant targets' and 'usually intended to influence an audience'.[68] At the same time that this definition is broadly accepted in Western policy, the violence of the state, which could also be characterised in these terms, is itself not designated as terrorism.

This is not to suggest that the wide-ranging scope of violence that is characterised as terrorism is necessarily expressed or presented by those engaged in it as anti-imperialist in form. Indeed, we know that such acts can be imperialising. While some violence that is narrated in terms of terrorism can be more readily understood as a struggle against occupation, as for example Hamas in Palestine, other movements that come under the rubric of terrorism, such as ISIS, can be recognised as a reactionary struggle for Islam. Yet, as has been well documented, the generation of this kind of violence is intrinsically linked to the interventions, aid and support of Western governments, security services and military operations.[69] But since this latter element, which can be conceived of as racialised military action, is not named as illegitimate violence, it further signals the paucity and ideological loading of terrorism as a concept.

As a form of representation, the discourse of terrorism, like fundamentalism, is thus not impartial but an expression of the relations of power underpinning asymmetrical warfare. It is a concept that, as Edward Said indicates in his discussion of culture and imperialism from which I quote at the start of this chapter, is rooted in a historical process justifying the morality of imperialist violence while simultaneously disavowing struggles for liberation and simplifying insurgent movements produced out of the violence of occupation and war.[70] The pronouncement of terrorism is used to 'criminalise struggles for liberation', but not to describe 'US history and the racism of the pre-civil rights era', as Angela Y. Davis notes, or the violence of colonial occupation. Thus the rhetoric of terrorism which is presented as the reason for Western imperialist intervention conceals the fact that the 'threat of terrorism is an instance of metalepsis: an effect of colonial discourse that is presented as a cause'.[71]

The Terror of Law

The representational framework through which the discourse of terrorism is articulated is sustained through the liberal discourse of violence in relation to the rule of law, advancing the premise of a polar distinction between liberalism and terrorism. Debates concerned with issues of state securitisation (mostly in the West) posit terrorism as the antithesis of liberal democracy. 'While liberalism is about toleration, civility and progress', writes Tim Dunne, 'terrorism takes us down an altogether different path – one of violent intolerance where human life is lived in fear and dies in anger'.[72] The position is not so much that violence is never legitimate, but that only certain forms of violence, usually those forms which are condoned through the law, are justifiable though there are exceptional moments when violence even beyond the scope of everyday norms can be justified. Through an engagement with the work of Michael Walzer, Talal Asad notes this very contradiction in the liberal framework which establishes when violence is legitimate.[73] In *Arguing about War*, Walzer's mission is to debate the terms of when war is acceptable, and advocates a place for war when it complies with international rules and regulations, although there are instances when rules 'can be and perhaps have to be overridden' that are open for debate. In contrast, there are certain forms of violence, namely terrorism, that are automatically disqualified from this discussion and which are never legitimate to debate because they are simply 'evil'. The general consensus for defining terrorism in this way is that as it is 'premeditated and designed to create a climate of extreme fear', that it creates insecurity of public spaces, that 'it inherently involves attacks on random or symbolic targets, including civilians', and that 'it is considered by the society in which it occurs as "*extra-normal*" violating 'the norms regulating disputes, protest and dissent' (emphasis added).[74]

The central distinction for Walzer between the two forms of violence is their relationship to the rule of law. Since the conduct of state-sanctioned or military led action is framed by legal procedure, it can be recognised as legitimate violence and the

individuals who conduct such forms of violence are acknowledged as subjects of conscience capable of ethical and moral
reflection. In contrast, terrorism is always illegitimate and to
be regarded as 'pure evil' because it occurs outside of legal
apparatus, thus operating against the protocols of international
law, and because of the fear it then instils. Asad points out that
such a distinction is misguided, since the law is not made up by
an objective set of given rules but are a set of arguments that
are never applied independently, and are intimately linked to
political objectives and global hierarchies of power (a point that
others have taken up and argued more extensively, noting the
role of law as a force of violence and a legitimating technique
for state-sanctioned violence).[75] Legal and military strategy can
always be rendered amenable to political objectives.[76]

Accordingly, if terrorism is defined by its ability to bring fear
into everyday life, to effect the violent destruction of symbolic
targets and make insecure public places, then it is a definition
that might also apply to state-sponsored wars. Yet the liberal
framing of 'just war' tends to disassociate such manifestations
of violence from its narrative. This allows for the justification
of different disciplinary responses towards those characterised
as engaging in terrorism or identified as terrorism suspects,
responses which need not comply with the humanitarian standards set by international law. The behaviour or mode of violence
to which they are connected – terrorism in general and, for Asad,
suicide bombing in particular – is drawn upon to produce the
marked subject in non-human terms as evil. This can be reified
or reproduced via the state-sanctioned disciplinary practice to
which they, as non-humans, may be subject to.

Taking up this debate, Judith Butler observes that what is
clear from this contradiction is that the framework of legitimate
violence is limited to state violence in defence of the 'community' when the community in question is recognisable according
to established and familiar norms of recognition, that is state
violence in defence of communities that are seen to matter.[77]
Justified violence is the privilege of certain kinds of states,
'usually those regarded as embodying the principles of Liberal

Democracy, or certain kinds of communities (generally those whose cultural or material life is already valued)'.[78]

In this sense, the issue is not so much the form that violence takes or what modes and mechanisms are used to commit it, but who it is committed by and who it is legitimate to commit it upon. Under interrogation, this liberal framework is clearly premised on an ability to recognise political complexity around violence performed by or on behalf of state actors, in defence of communities deemed to be of value. At the same time, it refuses to recognise any political complexity that might underlie the violence carried out by subjects operating outside of this framework. To this end, the point of contention is not the technique or strategies of violence per se but the process of rationalisation which informs when such techniques are warranted. Such a line of reasoning assumes unquestioningly and takes for granted that some bodies are worth defending and others less so. When one is recognised as a fully human subject, violence in defence is always permissible and justifiable, but violence is read as an expression of barbarism and irrationality when enacted by those read as beneath the standards of civilisation. These distinctions only make sense through a racialised logic which determines, as Butler notes, 'certain pre-conceptions about what culture ought to be, about how community is to be understood, about how the state is formed, and about who might count as a recognizable subject'.[79]

And So Non-Humans Are Made …

After over three years in solitary confinement, both Mahdi and Fahad agreed, as do most who are accused in the US criminal justice system, to plea bargains days before their trials were due to begin. While they were detained, the Special Administration Measures imposed on them meant they were only allowed limited contact with lawyers and immediate family. The conditions of confinement also meant they could not send or receive mail except with immediate family, they could not interact with other prisoners and they were only allowed minimal exercise, one hour a day in a caged space internal to the prison. As Jeanne

Theoharis notes, in Fahad's case, 'These conditions degraded his health — in pre-trial hearings, he appears increasingly withdrawn and less focused — and interfered with his ability to participate in his own defense'.[80]

Both men pleaded guilty to material support, a charge that is seen as a 'black box' for prosecutors since it allows all manner of deeds to be criminalised.[81]

In a post-conviction statement, the FBI reported that 'between approximately December 2008 and August 2012, the defendants [Mahdi and two other Swedish co-defendants] served as members of al-Shabaab in Somalia, where they agreed with others to support al-Shabaab and its extremist agenda'.[82] The complaints Mahdi had made to the *Independent* and to the Investigatory Powers Tribunal in May 2009 while living in London that he was being harassed by MI5, who made it very difficult for him to visit family in Somalia, were not mentioned in the FBI's report. He was sentenced to nine years in prison.[83] Before Fahad's sentencing, he was allowed to speak for the first time publicly since being arrested four years earlier. He expressed his 'gratitude to all his supporters, Muslim and non-Muslim, for their work on his behalf and commitment to seeking justice, took responsibility for his actions, and questioned the government's treatment of him and Muslims more broadly'.[84] He was sentenced to a maximum term of fifteen years. Outside the court room, Preet Bharara, the United States attorney in Manhattan, 'praised the investigative work of the Joint Terrorism Task Force'.[85]

2

Blind Justice and Blinding Crime

> The people know how real life works. Sometimes the script is written in advance.
>
> Arundhati Roy, 2017[1]

In the early hours of a day in December 2003, Babar Ahmad woke to a deafening bang outside his home. A car had crashed into the front of the house. When he rose from his bed to peer outside the bedroom window, what his ears had told him was a serious car accident his eyes registered as a column of riot police lined up in the front garden, perhaps about fifteen in total. With a second bang they burst through his front door; stomping boots traipsed up the stairs. Babar stood with his hands raised hoping his non-confrontational response would appease the officers and make them realise they had come to the wrong house. It did not, and after they landed a few punches, the police locked his hands behind his back and rammed him head first into a window. He soon learned that it was he who was their intended target.

The officers, who had been led to believe he was the leader of an al-Qaeda –linked cell, were told to prepare to confront a highly proficient terrorist, and accordingly to 'deck and dominate' the suspect in counterinsurgent fashion. Having removed his wife from the bedroom, they beat him with their fists and knees, verbally abusing him as they did so, stamped on his bare feet with boots, rubbed the metal handcuffs against the bones of his forearms, and applied life-threatening neck holds to him until he felt he was about to die. They took him downstairs to his prayer room, sexually assaulted him by fondling and cupping his genitals, and forced him into a prayer position. One of the officers taunted, 'You are in prayer now,' while others laughed. Another asked, rhetorically, 'Where is your God now?' and shouted, 'Pray to him'. Later, Babar would tell the criminal court during the trial of these officers, 'I had just been beaten and I was on the floor and they were laughing and there were jibes.'[2]

By the time he reached the police station he had sustained at least seventy-three forensically recorded injuries, including bleeding in his ears and urine. Six days later he was released without charge. During this time, his house was thoroughly searched, his possessions removed for examination, and his biometric data was sent to US intelligence authorities.[3] Two days after his release, an FBI agent faxed a forty-nine-page list of exhibits that the Metropolitan Police had seized in the operation to at least nineteen FBI offices and agents in the US. The UK police then began the process of formally handing over evidence seized by the Metropolitan Police from Babar's home and office to the FBI through the process of nine formal Mutual Legal Assistance Treaty (MLAT) requests.

Eight months later, in July 2004, following a thorough investigation of the evidence seized from his home, Babar was informed by the Crown Prosecution Service that there was insufficient evidence to charge him with any criminal or terrorist offence. But in August 2004, three weeks later, while on his way home from work, Babar was re-arrested pursuant to an extradition request from the US in which they alleged that in the 1990s he had been a supporter of terrorism, committing terrorism offences in the USA from 1996 to 2003. The accusations inferred he had tried to solicit support for terrorism in Chechnya and Afghanistan using websites that supported Chechen and Taliban rebel fighters during that time. Babar was, however, a resident in the UK during this entire period. Detained in prison, this time Babar would remain incarcerated without trial in Britain for eight years before being deported to the US in October 2012, where he faced the prospect of a lifetime in solitary confinement.

At the time of his arrest, Babar was an engineering postgraduate working in the IT Department at Imperial College London. Born and raised in the capital city, he had lived his teenage years in the Tooting neighbourhood of South London. He excelled in high school, a model student. He spent his teenage years as a member of the Royal Air Force section of the Royal Cadet Force and had been interested in joining the RAF, though this was an interest that he soon grew out of. When war broke out in Bosnia in 1992, Babar was revising for his A-level exams. An ITN news report on the Omarska concentration camp sparked his interest and he began to follow events more closely. Some months after he started university as an engineering undergraduate, he decided to travel to Bosnia. There he volunteered with local aid organisations, and visited different parts of the country, witnessing first-hand the weight of the war. He notes how the 'experience had a lasting impact' on him. During conversations with people living in refugee camps, he heard stories of the rape and slaughter of Bosnian Muslims by Serbian forces. He recalls how 'one evening he heard an account at a refugee centre in Travnik, central Bosnia, of a three-year-old girl that was gang-raped, slaughtered, then had her body flesh turned into mince which was cooked and force-fed to her mother'. He could not sleep that night. The next day he volunteered to fight with the Bosnian Army to help defend the Bosnian people.

Over the course of his undergraduate university life Babar spent much of his spare time raising awareness about the war, fundraising and organising aid convoys to support Bosnian refugees and made several return trips to Bosnia, to both deliver aid and fight when the opportunity arose. During this time Babar was also active in organising a local Friday circle, which came to be known as the Tooting Circle, a weekly gathering of local young Muslims who, as one of the attendees explains, 'had grown up with Muslim Brotherhood/Ikhwan educational initiatives and now took their own direction'. They spoke of political events impacting the Muslim world and organised in response. The group was active in organising Da'wah stalls. Soon after Babar graduated he travelled to Chechnya with the aim of supporting local forces against the Russian invasion. By the time he arrived the war had ended, but he worked in an orphanage for a while and travelled the country. On his return to the UK he set up a media outlet, Azzam Publications, which produced and sold accounts of the Bosnian war. This for him offered not only a forum for raising awareness about the full scope of the atrocities of war but was a way to preserve the 'legacies of friends' that he had lost along the way. With help from other friends he set up the website Azzam.com to market the books and audio tapes he produced. When Russia invaded Chechnya a second time, Azzam Publications began to translate and post daily news of the war, which were also available on their website. Most of their online content was second-hand material that had been copied or translated from other sources. Towards the end of the website's existence, two articles were posted advocating support for the Taliban. Though Babar did not post either of these articles he would later take responsibility for their presence on the website. The posting of these two documents would eventually form the basis of the charges against him and his prosecution for engaging in terrorism-related offences.[4]

While incarcerated in Britain, Babar's legal battle was fought on two fronts: the first against his impending extradition to the US and the second against the abuse he had suffered by the arresting police officers. The legal battle around his extradition was less a contestation of whether the allegations against him were substantiated or constituted terrorist activity, since the terms of the US–UK Extradition Treaty of 2003, which was ratified in the UK in 2004, meant the US did not have to provide evidence to support its allegations. Instead, it was much more a negotiation over the extent to which a person identified as an 'enemy combatant' and thus eligible to be subjected to the full excesses

of sovereign violence could be protected by European protocols and conventions on human rights. In the early stages of his
appeal against extradition, one of the key points of contestation
was his categorisation as an 'enemy combatant'. Being labelled
as such would open up his possible subjection to the Military
Order 'Detention, Treatment, and Trial of Certain Non-Citizens
in the War Against Terrorism', an order issued by US President
George W Bush in November 2001, which held that all those
identified as 'enemy combatants' would be tried for violations
of the law of war, and subject to military commission and the
death penalty. In response to contestations by defence lawyers
arguing that doing so would violate European human rights
conventions, US officials agreed that upon extradition Babar,
and others also facing extradition under similar circumstances,
would not be treated as 'enemy combatants', but tried in civilian
court to face life, and death, in prison.

At the same time, Babar sought an admission of wrongdo-
ing by the Metropolitan Police. In 2003, following his initial
arrest, Babar had filed a complaint with the Independent Police
Complaints Commission against the key arresting officers from
the Met's Territorial Support Group, Roderick James-Bowen,
Mark Jones, Nigel Cowley and John Donoghue. Photographs of
his injuries, medical reports and expert opinions documenting
the assault provided evidence to support his case. A report by
an accident and emergency consultant physician, Mr Manolis
Gavalas, noted that there was 'clearly unequivocal evidence
that he was subjected to harrowing physical and psychological assault'. His assessment of the injuries was that the aim of
the police officers 'whilst waving the flag of "fighting terrorism"
was to inflict pain, humiliation and intimidation'.[5]

The struggle for accountability of the officers that had
attacked Babar was fraught with the same kinds of issues that
had been highlighted by the Stephen Lawrence campaign and
subsequent inquiry years before.[6] In the police misconduct trial
that followed Babar's complaint, PC Roderick James-Bowen,
one of the officers involved, was cleared of any wrongdo-
ing and it was noted he ought to be 'commended and not

castigated'. When civil proceedings were later launched against the officers, the Met police offered Babar settlements, first for £20,000 then for £60,000, to prevent the case going to court. He refused. In an unprecedented victory, the civil proceedings led to the Metropolitan Police finally admitting full liability for subjecting Babar to grave abuse tantamount to torture and offered again to pay him £60,000 in damages.[7] As a result of the exposure this case gained, the then mayor of London, Boris Johnson, announced an inquiry into the police abuse and the Crown Prosecution Service subsequently charged the officers with actual body harm. However, when the case finally reached trial, the jury took only forty-five minutes to decide their verdict of not guilty and some jurors requested to meet the officers to shake their hands.[8] None of the officers faced a disciplinary hearing and all were returned to full duties.[9]

The arrest, detention and extradition of Babar Ahmad and the other Muslim men was made possible through the intersection of these two different repertoires of policing and criminalisation. The first incorporates counterterrorism policing techniques and infrastructures established in the British state system in response to Northern Ireland as well as to anti-colonial resistance in other parts of the Empire. This history set a precedent for the institutionalisation of counterinsurgent forms of policing. The second are the racialised policing practices of the civilian criminal justice system which disproportionately target black and working-class communities, and which operate in tandem with emergency measures to normalise and rationalise forms of state violence that could be otherwise presented as excessive or exceptional. There are many ways in which the police assault, arrest and incarceration of Babar Ahmad sits within the broader spectrum of routine racialised policing practices, but his story of extradition to incarceration in solitary confinement is fundamentally part of the imperialist policing of the War on Terror. Such extraditions of terrorism suspects illustrate the ease with which the two systems, colonial counterinsurgency and domestic racialised policing, ordinarily conceived of as distinct, operate together in tandem. On the one hand, the policing of terrorism suspects in this way reveals there is little extraordinary about the disciplinary measures imposed against them – they simply display the most extreme punitive techniques routinely available to the state. On the other, the calls for the extension of state powers in such cases means they serve to legitimate the enhancement of securitisation. The use and expansion of closed trials and secret evidence that develops out of the policing of foreign nationals suspected of engaging in terrorism, is one such example.

Policing Here, Policing There

Where orientalism provides the representational framework in which Muslim subjects are produced and policed as terrorism suspects, contemporary counterterrorism policing practices draw their technical expertise from the history of British counterinsurgency practices across Empire and the civilian policing methods that have developed in relation to moral panics around rising crime. Thus, the development of the counterterrorism policing system post 9/11 builds on a structure already established within the policing strategies and legal infrastructure of the British system such that there has been an almost seamless flow between the policing of one suspect community and the policing of another.

The situation in Ireland, Britain's domestic colony, occupied a pivotal role in bringing the Empire home, acting as both a testing ground for policing methods later transferred to other British and European colonies and as a receptor for such techniques developed and enhanced in counterinsurgent operations elsewhere, particularly in British Palestine, Malaya and Kenya.[10] Following from the long line of Coercion Acts, acts of parliament legislating for response by force to popular discontent and disorder, operating in Ireland since 1800, post partition, between 1921 and 1973, there were always special powers of some form operating in Northern Ireland.[11] The circularities of resistance, which brought Irish independence fighters in contact with subversive postcolonials from Asia, Africa, the Americas and the Caribbean who had moved between the colony and the metropole, forms the backdrop to the re-importation of counterinsurgent techniques to the metropolitan centre.

The ambivalent position of Ireland as both colonial outpost and imperialist agent, internal to the nation while simultaneously outside of it, and ostensibly to be governed with greater 'democracy' than other non-European colonies, means that the form of counterinsurgency historically employed there is one that had to be attendant to democratic norms of policing. One way this was done was by integrating counterinsurgency practice into civil institutions and public services. Another was to incorporate militarised policing practices usually restricted to the army within the civilian police force and to amend the law accordingly.[12] This was the creation of a model that has since then been exported to other liberal-democratic states looking to implement their own forms of counterterrorism policing systems as part of the global War on Terror, and has remained critical to the design of high-security policing in contemporary Britain.[13]

The rising presence of black and Asian communities in Britain's metropolitan centres following the Second World War and the attendant moral panic around crime, particularly in relation to black bodies, marked the establishment of another lineage of racialised policing practice that has manifested itself in community surveillance, pre-emptive stops and interrogation, and through public order containment.[14] While these communities, too, were also signifiers of 'the Empire come home', the racial representation of threat then was configured less in militarised than in civilian terms. It was a moral panic conceived of not so much as a political threat but a criminal one. Accordingly, the technical apparatus designed for policing black communities has largely developed from within the confines of the civilian criminal justice system, even as the expertise for designing models of public order policing have been drawn from other parts of the Empire.[15] This more routine form of public disorder policing has been especially visible during acute moments of social dissent or disruption, such as during the mining strikes and the Hillsborough disaster. Both policing systems have borrowed from and interchanged with each other, periodically being enhanced through expertise imported back from the United States.[16]

In Britain, the legacy of both historical elements has been to provide a robust system for administering a spectrum of 'hard' and 'soft' policing measures and which can manoeuvre between techniques that gain legitimacy via emergency powers and those which are validated via calls for day-to-day crime prevention. The negotiation between emergency powers passed in the name of fighting terrorism and the more routine governance of criminal justice legislation often finds solution in the implementation of ordinary counterterrorism provisions, passed not as emergency legislation but through routine parliamentary process, which expand the scope of criminalised activity through legislative means and present the policing of it as judicially sanctioned. The emergency nature of the Anti-Terrorism Crime and Security Act 2001, for example, which allowed for the indefinite detention of eleven nationals held without trial shortly after it was passed, was heavily critiqued for its disregard of due process. When this power was eventually overturned by the House of Lords who ruled that it was a violation of human rights, it was replaced with control orders which effectively substituted indefinite detention in prison with indefinite detention at home. Simultaneously the political criticisms of excessive use of executive orders were responded to by expanding the scope of what constituted terrorist activity and sanctioning it through law. In the Terrorism Act 2006, actions deemed to be 'preparatory to terrorism', 'encouragement of terrorism' and dissemination of 'terrorist publications' were all outlawed, which, as the Independent Reviewer of Terrorism Legislation noted, meant that at least sanctions would 'follow the conviction of crime, rather than being the result of administrative decisions'.[17] In 2015, the most common charge remained the preparation of terrorist acts and is reported to be the most used provision of terrorism legislation since 9/11.[18]

The product of this enmeshing of civilian and military policing systems is a sophisticated continuum of tactics which range from pre-emptive interventions that target – and indeed create – suspect communities, the institutionalisation of guilt by association and the expansion of general activities criminalised under the law, the move away from open courts and trial by jury to secret and closed courts of various kinds, and the use of deportation or exile of some form as an additional or alternative measure where prosecution through judicial avenues falls short.[19]

The legal framework which has sanctioned the perpetual enhancement to criminal and counterterrorism provisions has largely been centred around managing and disciplining 'dangerous' bodies in the name of public protection. The focus of both criminal justice and counterterrorism legislation has increasingly been fixated on preventing and impeding 'dangerous offenders', a sufficiently broad and vaguely defined category that works to collapse differently marked racialised bodies into a spectre of public threat.[20] Broadly encompassing categories of the 'terrorist', the 'criminal', the 'immigrant' and the 'foreign offender', the policing of 'dangerous offenders' has offered one conduit through which criminal and counterterrorism provisions have interchanged. Legislatively, this means that some of the provisions for dealing with terrorism suspects are accommodated under criminal justice legislation. One of the earliest extensions to pre-charge detention time, the length of time a person could be detained for questioning without charge, of terrorism suspects, for example, was passed through the Criminal Justice Act 2003. Similarly, provisions allowing for indeterminate life sentences implemented in 2003 for dealing with 'violent criminals' were extended to convictions for 'training for terrorism' under the Criminal Justice and Courts Act passed in 2015. At the same time, some of the powers passed through terrorism legislation have come to have wider traction, the extension of internet policing and cyber surveillance being notable examples.

At the operational level, the interconnections between counterterrorism and public disorder policing, which illuminate the increased counterterrorism capacity within the police force, are evident in multifarious ways. Under the Counter-Terrorism Act

2008, police constables were awarded additional powers, such as permission to take fingerprints and DNA samples and to search premises of suspects on control orders. Perhaps the greatest convergence is evident in the practice of stop and search, which in practice has relied upon the provision of enhanced powers under successive counterterrorism laws as well as the less extraordinary powers available under Section 60 of the 1994 Criminal Justice and Public Order Act. In 2004, Statewatch reported that the number of stop and searches occurring for counterterrorism purposes were more than double the official figures reported since 'a large number of police forces [we]re recording anti-terrorist stop and searches under Section 60' rather than under counterterrorism provisions.[21] When these powers to stop and search without suspicion under counterterrorism legislation were ruled unlawful by the European Court of Human Rights in 2010, modified powers were introduced which require there to be reasonable basis for stop and search, but have rarely been used since 2011, while provisions for stop and search without suspicion still remain under criminal justice provisions.[22]

The cross pollination between counterinsurgent and public order policing techniques have in some senses come full circle, with specialist units charged with the remit of managing public order being given additional responsibilities for counterterrorism. This came to the fore in Babar Ahmad's arrest.[23] As members of the Territorial Support Group (TSG), a specialist policing unit of London's Metropolitan Police Service, the officers who carried out Babar's first arrest were part of a division charged with providing anti-terrorism and domestic extremism capability in support of counterterrorist units alongside their principle duties dealing with incidents of public disorder and assisting other units dealing with knife and gun crime. The same unit of officers who provide additional counterterrorism capability also police mass public protests and riots, and deal with drug crimes. The Territorial Support Group is the successor to the Special Patrol Group, which was established by the Metropolitan Police in 1965 in response to the moral panic of 'outbreaks of housebreaking and hooliganism', and was modelled on the Tactical

Patrol Force operating in New York at the time.[24] The Special Patrol Group was subsequently transported to Northern Ireland and militarised further, the experience of which would show influences later in the Tactical Support Group's additional counterterrorism functions.

The re-orientation of police units and personnel in this regard has carried with it continuities in racist policing cultures. The Tactical Support Group is a unit that receives disproportionately high numbers of complaints for aggressive policing tactics. When Babar's case against the officers was brought to trial, it came to light that the arresting officers had collectively amassed over seventy complaints against them, the majority concerning assault, with the bulk of complainants black or Asian men. One of the officers, PC Mark Jones, who was a former Royal Marine, had personally received over thirty complaints, had been previously suspended from duty in relation to another charge of racially aggravated assault, and was suspended again at the time of the trial for the same reasons.[25] Between August 2005 and November 2009, over 5,000 complaints were made against the Tactical Support Group, over half of which were in response to 'oppressive behaviour'.[26] The large number of complaints directed at the unit as a whole prompted the Independent Police Complaints Commission (IPCC) to review the unit's conduct between 2008 and 2012. The review noted specifically the substantial number of complaints coming from black men. Of the twenty-eight sample cases that were voluntarily referred to the IPCC, twenty-two complainants were of an ethnic minority background, of which young black males formed the largest group.[27] The unit's predecessor, the Special Patrol Group, was notorious for enforcing SUS Laws and the excessive policing of black men in the 1970s, and infamously associated with the killing of Blair Peach, an anti-racist campaigner and activist who was knocked unconscious by SPG officers during an anti-Nazi league demonstration against the National Front in 1979.[28]

This racist violence of the police has manifested itself, too, through the technical processes relied on for administering

counterterrorism policing, which have drawn together administrative processes used in earlier counterinsurgent and anti-crime
policing strategies. The racial profiling and associated violence
that underpin intelligence gathering and surveillance in counterterrorism policing have been refined through the additional,
and growing, use of DNA databases. The key provision used for
intelligence gathering in the name of fighting terrorism remains
Schedule 7 of the Terrorism Act 2000, which permits the police
to stop and question people at ports. It has been used more than
half a million times since its implementation, making it the focus
of numerous human rights campaigns.[29] The powers granted
to the police under this provision drew from the Prevention of
Terrorism (Temporary Provisions) Act 1974, passed as emergency legislation, before the legislation in 2000 made permanent
provisions that were otherwise renewed every six months.[30] Just
as surveillance of the Irish population under the 1970s legislation saw a large discrepancy between the number of people
stopped and the numbers charged with an offence, so have very
few of those stopped under Schedule 7 provisions been detained
or charged.[31] While many of the provisions of the Terrorism
Act 2000 were similar to those before, it included the particular
advancement of the addition of DNA collection and the subsequent creation of a DNA database.

The recording and retention of DNA for policing crime has
been a growing trend since the mid 1990s. The same legislation
which institutionalised stop and search without suspicion for
day-to-day crime prevention also permitted the establishment
of the UK's National DNA Database. The Criminal Justice and
Public Order Act 1994 expanded the terms upon which DNA
could be collected and set in motion a process of formally building a repository linking genetics and criminality. By 2009, it was
reported that the DNA database for England and Wales was the
largest in the world, at 5 million profiles and growing.[32] The
expansion of powers since this time under successive criminal
justice legislation meant DNA samples could be taken by the
police without consent from anyone arrested on suspicion of
any recordable offence and could be retained indefinitely, until

the Protections of Freedom Act 2012 limited the duration to six months. That it is a system that depends on racial profiling was made starkly apparent when in 2007 it was confirmed that three-quarters of the young black male population of the UK were on the national DNA database.[33] It was estimated that by April 2007 a total of 135,000 black males aged fifteen to thirty-four had been added to the database – equivalent to 77 per cent of the population.[34]

Pressures to expand the recording and retention of the DNA of terrorism suspects led to the creation of an adjunct Counter-Terrorism DNA Database in July 2006, also administered by London's Metropolitan Police Service on behalf of the Counter-Terrorism Unit.[35] By building on these established infrastructures for fighting crime more broadly, Britain's counterterrorism database has operated under similar powers, recording the DNA of mass numbers of individuals whose genetic traces happen to be found in spaces – homes, places of work, public venues – that are targeted in counterterrorism operations. The framing of counterterrorism in terms of national and global security, however, has raised the stakes, extending the scope of the practice beyond that which has been more formally legislated. Now, DNA obtained for counterterrorism purposes, such as Babar Ahmad's, can be shared internationally with partner states with which the British government is working in cooperation. DNA collected for such purposes is also much more likely to be collected covertly, without the suspect's knowledge, and DNA records have been obtained from discarded cigarettes or drink containers, during surveillance operations or when a suspect visits the home of an informant.[36] In 2016, it was reported that 53 per cent of the 9,600 individuals on the counterterrorism DNA database had never been convicted of a crime.[37]

As the surveillance techniques used to create terrorism suspects signify the Empire come home, the globalised element of policing that these techniques illuminate is further compounded by the collaboration between the US and the UK that frequently underpins domestic counterterrorism policing.

That Special Relationship

'For instance, now,' she went on, sticking a large piece of plaster on her finger as she spoke, 'there's the King's Messenger. He's in prison now, being punished: and the trial doesn't even begin till next Wednesday: and of course, the crime comes last of all.'

'Suppose he never commits the crime?' said Alice.

'That would be all the better, wouldn't it?' the Queen said, as she bound the plaster round her finger with a bit of ribbon.

Alice felt there was no denying THAT. 'Of course, it would be all the better,' she said: 'but it wouldn't be all the better his being punished.'

'You're wrong THERE, at any rate,' said the Queen: 'were YOU ever punished?'

'Only for faults,' said Alice.

'And you were all the better for it, I know!' the Queen said triumphantly.

'Yes, but then I HAD done the things I was punished for,' said Alice: 'that makes all the difference.'

'But if you HADN'T done them,' the Queen said, 'that would have been better still; better, and better, and better!' Her voice went higher with each 'better,' till it got quite to a squeak at last.

Alice was just beginning to say, 'There's a mistake some-where—,' when the Queen began screaming so loud that she had to leave the sentence unfinished. 'Oh, oh, oh!' shouted the Queen, shaking her hand about as if she wanted to shake it off. 'My fin-ger's bleeding! Oh, oh, oh, oh!'

Lewis Carroll, 1865[38]

Interviewer: Can you tell me a little about your experience of the plea bargaining process and how you went about preparing, with your lawyers, for the sentencing?

Ahsan: First they picked a number – fifteen years, then we negotiated the charges to suit the number, then we argued facts to suit the charges.

Talha Ahsan, 2015[39]

At fourteen Talha Ahsan began attending his local Friday circle in Tooting, London, which was headed by Babar Ahmad and his brother. There, Talha and other local Muslim men held regular discussions concerning Islam and politics, informed by events such as the Bosnian genocide and the lack of global concern for the atrocities experienced by Bosnian Muslims. With regular attendance, Talha was invited to participate in further activities such as running the Da'wah stall.[40] Pursuing his interest in Islamic politics further, at nineteen he went on to study at the School of Oriental and African Studies, learning Arabic during this period. After graduating with first class honours in 2004, he worked in his father's business while he looked for work that would allow him to continue developing his intellectual interests, exploring possibilities of becoming a librarian or a teacher.

For six months, between March and August 2001, Talha assisted Babar in the running of his website, Azzam.com, processing orders received via their post office box in London and mailing products to customers in the UK and abroad. As part of his duties, he made electronic copies of the correspondence they received.[41] On one occasion he typed up an unsolicited document containing classified information on the movements of a US navy battle group. He was never involved in the website's administration, simply in filling the orders.

Five years later, and some eighteen months after Babar Ahmad's second arrest, in February 2006 the Metropolitan Police arrived at Talha's home. They searched his family's house, confiscated his passport, left with some of his belongings, but made no arrest. Nothing appeared to come of it and Talha settled back into his life. A few months went by before the police called again in July 2006 to say they would be returning his passport. The next day, four officers arrived at his home. One of the officers slid a plastic pouch towards Talha which contained his passport and a form to be signed, then indicated that another officer, standing outside, wanted to speak to him first. The second officer informed Talha that the US had made serious allegations against him and that he was to be arrested. He recalled, 'I was requested to place my hands in front to be cuffed. In agitation, my frantic hands searched around my belt for my phone to call a solicitor. The movements in turn palpably frightened the officer and he urged my hands being placed in front of him'. Talha remained detained for six years without trial in Britain before being extradited, where after two years in pre-trial solitary confinement he entered a plea bargain. There was never any trial.

The charges against Talha centred around his helping Babar Ahmad with the postal orders during those six months in 2001, specifically for typing up the document of navy movements, which was neither uploaded or disseminated, nor seen as grounds for prosecution by the British authorities.[42] Talha was never questioned by British authorities and was not made aware of the details of the allegations against him until he entered plea bargain negotiations in the US six years after his arrest, where he faced material support charges.[43] He explains:

> As my involvement in Azzam Publications was so tangential, most of the allegations in the indictment and accompanying affidavit were unknown to me. I suspected I had been indicted due to the ship document I had typed though that was not seen as grounds for prosecution by the CPS. As time went along, the magnitude of the case only seemed to expand and as if with rubbing palms and salivating mouths the prosecutors were presenting me as part of an enormous global al-Qaeda conspiracy.[44]

The spectacle of Talha's extradition was in part realised by a decision to remove him collectively along with Babar and three other Muslim men, all facing terrorism charges in the US. On an evening in early October 2012, two armoured police vans enclosed within police convoys transported Talha, Babar, Adel Abdul Bary and Khalid al-Fawwaz, both facing charges relating to the 1998 US embassy bombings, and Abu Hamza, facing charges relating to hostage taking in Yemen and conspiracy to establish a jihad training camp in Oregon, from Long Lartin Prison to RAF Mildenhall Airfield, where they were awaited by US Department of Justice aircraft and federal marshals.

Collectively referred to as 'Abu Hamza and others' in the media, the spectacle of their deportation in Britain overshadowed the questions that had been repeatedly raised regarding the appropriate jurisdiction over these cases.[45]

One of the recurring themes that presents itself in the extradition cases of those facing terrorism charges is the tenuous link between the nature and specificity of the crimes alleged and the claims of US jurisdiction over them. In Fahad Hashmi's case, discussed in the previous chapter, a US citizen studying in Britain and extradited to the US on material support charges in 2007, the entire case against him concerned events that had taken place in Britain.[46] Similarly, Abid Naseer, whose case is discussed later in this chapter, was accused of plotting a terrorist attack in Manchester, UK, and by extrapolating this into a planned international attack, linking these charges to alleged plots in Norway and New York, the US was able to make jurisdictional claims.

In the case of Abu Hamza, while some of the charges against him had clear links to the US – namely his alleged involvement in setting up a 'terrorist training camp' in Bly, Oregon – the sovereignty over other charges, those relating to taking hostages in Yemen and engaging in jihad in Afghanistan between 2000 and 2001, was contested.[47] For Babar Ahmad and Talha Ahsan, the only connection to the US was that one of the website servers of Azzam.com had ostensibly been for a short period hosted in the state of Connecticut.[48] Over the course of his detention in the UK, Babar Ahmad's legal team argued that the allegations against him would, under the expanded counterterrorism legislation, also constitute offences in the UK and contended that he thus ought to stand trial in Britain. As the details of Babar Ahmad's case emerged, it became clear that the police had never given the bulk of evidence recovered from his home to the Crown Prosecution Service for him to be prosecuted in the UK, but had passed it straight over to the US, prompting his indictment and the request for his extradition.[49] Days before being removed to the US, Babar reported that it had been the one of the officers under investigation for assaulting him who had transferred the documents to the US authorities.[50]

While much of the human rights resistance to the use of extradition has been an objection to the US–UK extradition arrangements as a reflection of the weakening of British sovereignty through continual acquiescence to the US, this assessment is not an entirely sufficient explanation of Britain's role in the extradition process. As human rights lawyers have indicated, the broad basis for criminalisation under the US material support statute and the intensity of the US plea bargaining system notwithstanding, there was plenty of scope within the British judicial system for these subjects to be dealt with by UK authorities.[51] At the operational level, extradition forms part of political negotiations in which deportation is sometimes in the interests of the sending state as much as apprehension is in the interests of the receiving state. So, in the case of Babar Ahmad, for example, the pursuance of his arrest and transfer to the US appeared to be as much a priority for the FBI officer leading the US the request as it was supported by the British police officers involved in his arrest.

At other times, political negotiations appear more one-sided. In Abu Hamza's case, there was much pressure from the public on the British government to deport him, and as the government of Egypt, his country of birth was refusing his return, there was some indication that the role the US played was to assist Britain with its predicament. The significant British state investment in Abu Hamza's deportation was divulged in the litigation papers, where it was revealed that the attorney general of the United States had written to the British secretary of state complaining about the delay caused by Abu Hamza's appeal of his extradition to the European Court of Human Rights as well as his intermediate incarceration in the UK following conviction of numerous offences in 2006 including soliciting murder and intent to stir racial hatred.[52] If extradition was further delayed until the end of the sentence that Hamza was serving, the attorney general pointed out, 'in the worst case, it might mean we [the US] would eventually have to abandon our extradition request.'[53] Conceding that this process was as much in the interests of the British government, reassurances were offered by the British state authorities that Abu Hamza's current sentence would not be a deterrence to extradition but that proceedings would continue regardless. These various negotiations indicate that the process of extradition was very much a collaborative one.[54]

The media spectacle that was made of the extradition served a broader political purpose, too. A few days after their extradition, Theresa May opened her speech to the Conservative Party Conference with, 'Wasn't it great to say goodbye to Abu Hamza and others?'[55] She went on to draw upon their deportation to reaffirm the strength of the security services while demonstrating the need for its continued support and enhancement. Their extradition also offered a way of quashing what had become a high-profile resistance movement that had lobbied against the deportation of Babar and Talha in particular, a struggle which threatened to expose the arbitrary nature of state power and the retraction of civil liberties that underpinned growing securitisation. The successful extradition of Talha and Babar effectively dispersed the crowd.

But beyond the momentary spectacle of justice that surrounds high-profile terrorism cases such as these, on arrival to the US there is an ease with which these men are processed and managed within the structures of the US civilian penal system. Though the designation of 'terrorism suspect' is drawn upon to sanction some of the most intense conditions of incarceration available within the civilian system, these well-established high-security prison facilities have been frequently compared to military penitentiary arrangements.[56] These ordinary conditions of confinement lay in wait so that techniques which are used customarily in federal criminal cases, particularly when the accused is regarded as a political threat, could be adapted, applied, and sometimes extended, to terrorism cases.[57] Talha and Babar were housed in pre-trial solitary confinement for over two years alongside death row inmates in Connecticut and the men extradited to New York and incarcerated in Manhattan Correctional Center were placed in pre-trial solitary confinement alongside other high-security prisoners. As do most others processed through the federal criminal justice system, Babar and Talha entered into a plea bargain where, as Talha's testimony indicates, conviction is secured more through political negotiation than through an independent or impartial judicial process. The enmeshing of different kinds of criminalised subjects was thus upheld by the continuities in the techniques used for disciplining them. In this sense, the exceptional treatment of terrorism suspects is exposed as only an illusion.

This entanglement is further illustrated in the imprisonment of Muslims convicted as 'international' terrorists within an already highly militarised system of incarceration. The federal supermax prison ADX Florence is the prison of choice for those deemed to be the most dangerous offenders, and houses a number of people convicted of international and domestic terrorism offences. In its treatment of those convicted of terrorism it is the successor to an earlier federal supermax prison, USP Marion, which operated a system of twenty-three-hour lockdowns to manage and contain the 'ordinary criminals' housed there. When ADX Florence was established in 1994 it was built on the 'lessons learned' from USP Marion.[58] The Muslim men now incarcerated in solitary confinement in ADX Florence can be subjected to the use of four-point spread-eagle restraints, forced feedings, cell extractions, mind-control medications and chemical weapons used to incapacitate prisoners, all reported to be in use at the prison. It was domestic 'state of the art' and supermax prisons such as this which later provided the blueprints for US military equivalents, and the same disciplinary techniques have all been reported to be in use at Guantanamo.[59] Communication Management Units (CMUs), which developed from special units to discipline political prisoners, have similarly been used to house those convicted of terrorism offences. Referred to as 'Little Guantanamos' by prisoners and guards, they are meant as less restrictive versions of ADX Florence, and imprisonment there means severely reduced access to phone calls, letters and visits – which are, anyway, non-contact visits.[60] The majority of the prisoners in CMUs are Muslim.[61]

Yet, at the same time that there has been an easy folding of terrorism cases into the normalised security apparatus of the criminal justice system, there has been a growth in the use of national security-style policing and judicial systems, notably in the form of closed courts and secret evidence. Namely, there has been an expansion of secret justice.

Secret Justice

Three months after Abu Hamza, Babar Ahmad, Talha Ahsan, Khalid al-Fawwaz and Adel Abdul Bary were extradited to the US, Abid Naseer, a Pakistani student who had been studying at a college in Manchester, UK, had his appeal against extradition to the United States thrown out by the European Court of Human Rights. He faced similar terrorism charges of providing material support to a terrorist organisation, of conspiracy to provide material support and of conspiracy to use a destructive device.[62] He had been one of twelve people arrested in 2009 by the North-West Counter-Terrorism Unit on suspicion of planning a terrorist attack at the Trafford Centre, a large shopping mall on the outskirts of the city of Manchester. Their arrests were a high-profile affair, designed to show that Gordon Brown's government was tough on terrorism and supported in this by media reporting that an 'Easter bomb plot' had been thwarted.[63]

Most of the men arrested were Pakistani students based at various universities across the North West of England, identified by the authorities as a 'Manchester group' and a 'Liverpool group'.[64] Charges against all the men were dropped within thirteen days of their arrest after no significant evidence against them was found. But on the same day that the students were 'released' without charge, they were handed over to the Border Agency for deportation on the grounds that their presence in the UK was not conducive to the public good or that they were in breach of their student visa status. The failure to bring a prosecution against these men was superseded by deportation powers. The conditions of incarceration meant that most of the students returned back to Pakistan 'voluntarily' and the home secretary signed exclusion orders banning them from returning to the UK.

Two of the students, Abid Naseer and Faraz Khan, did pursue

an appeal against deportation, arguing that if they returned to Pakistan their safety could not be guaranteed. Their appeal was heard by the Special Immigration Appeal Commission (SIAC), a court set up to deal with immigration cases where national security concerns are raised. Modelled on a colonial administrative system, decisions are made by three selected judges and no jury. The court hears evidence in a mixture of open and closed sessions, and decisions can largely be set out in closed judgements. In the closed sessions, appellants and their lawyers are not allowed to see the evidence against them but instead they are assigned a (security-cleared) special advocate to represent them, and with whom they are not permitted to communicate once the advocate has been privy to the evidence against them. The appeals of Abid and Faraz was paradoxically successful: while it was agreed they would be at risk of torture if they returned to Pakistan, their 'successful' appeals meant they could not contest their designation as terrorism suspects. The SIAC court endorsed the assessment from the Security Service that these men presented a threat to British national security, while still noting the absence of any evidence of the students' handling or preparation of explosives or their involvement in any plot.

In the deportation proceedings against Abid Naseer, the state argued that email exchanges between him and a friend in Pakistan, who the authorities declared to be an al-Qaeda associate, in which they discussed marriage arrangements, were encoded to disguise the plotting of 'a mass-casualty attack'.[65] The justification for such an assessment was never openly discussed in court but were the result of closed evidence, despite the open admittance by authorities that 'although meetings of the suspects were observed, there was little intelligence or information as to what was discussed at those meetings'.[66] The court ruled in favour of the government, asserting:

> For the reasons which are wholly set out in the closed judgement, we are satisfied, on balance of probabilities, that that assessment is right. We have reached that conclusion *despite the complete absence of any evidence of the handling or preparation*

of explosives by Naseer and his alleged associates. It is a fact that, despite extensive searches of buildings associated with them, nothing has been found, apart from an irrelevant trace of RDX in one of the properties. Mr Bennathan QC submits that this sets it apart from all previous Islamist terrorist plots to cause explosions in the United Kingdom.[67]

At the time of the arrests, the police and the Security Service believed that Abid Naseer was the central figure in the plot, arguing they were in possession of intelligence that indicated Abid was the common link between the Manchester group and the Liverpool group and the key link back to operatives in Pakistan.[68] After their release following their successful appeals, the authorities continued surveillance of the Pakistani email account with which Abid Naseer had been in contact, for the purposes of further intelligence gathering. British intelligence services suspected another attack was being planned, this time targeting the New York subway. Framed now as part of an international terror plot, the Manchester case was viewed as part of a much larger affair in which Abid was the UK ringleader and point of contact. With this elaboration, US interests in his case increased and the US instigated an extradition request for Abid Naseer to be tried for terrorism-related offences in New York. Though the request was largely based on the same evidence the British state deemed insufficient to charge him, the request was granted and he was extradited in January 2013. His appeal to the ECHR was dismissed following the ruling on Babar Ahmad's case, since he was appealing on the same grounds. In 2015, after two years in pre-trial solitary confinement in the US, Abid's case went to trial where he was found guilty and sentenced to forty years in a US supermax prison.

Notably, in the UK judgements made in Abid Naseer's case, even as much of the basis of the court's decision was premised upon evidence they had heard in secret, there was sufficient information disclosed in the open judgement to indicate the skewed rationalisations and arbitrary nature of decision-making at play. In SIAC, which administers most of the cases involving individuals suspected of terrorism offences (very few are dealt with through the criminal justice system), suspicion alone is sufficient basis for disciplinary action, usually to sanction deportation. The quiet use of secret evidence to scrutinise such suspicion has meant these kinds of procedures have raised little protest. But as the logic of this system for dealing with terrorism cases has been entrenched and normalised, it has promoted the growing use of closed court procedures and secret evidence in other courts too.

The initial implementation of SIAC came in response to a decision by the European Court of Human Rights in the case of Karamjit Singh Chahal. Having migrated to Britain from India in 1971 just as Britain was increasing immigration restrictions to curb postcolonial migration from the sub-continent, Karamjit gained indefinite leave to remain following the amnesty offered by the British government in 1974. Some ten years later, on a visit to Punjab at a time when tensions there were escalating – and shortly before the Indian army stormed the Golden Temple killing over 1,000 Sikhs in Operation Blue Star – Karamjit was detained, interrogated by the Indian police force, beaten unconscious, tortured with electrodes and subjected to a mock execution. On his return to Britain, Karamjit mobilised popular support and organised protests against the Indian government's actions, which lead to his detention under British Prevention of Terrorism legislation.[69] In 1990, the then home secretary Douglas Hurd, ordered Karamjit's deportation on the grounds that his presence was not conducive to the public good; he was not charged with any offence nor informed of the details of any criminal activity he was being accused of, merely told that there were serious allegations against him concerning unspecified terrorist offences. As counterterrorism legislation in India allowed separatists to be detained under special legislation which suspended legal safeguards, in Britain the same threat of terrorism was used to invoke national security concerns which allowed for deportation orders to be passed without right to appeal. When there was an appeal in such cases, defendants were not allowed legal representation.

Karamjit did, however, turn to the European Court of Human Rights, and remained incarcerated in Britain for six years while appealing the deportation decision on the grounds that if deported he would be subjected to torture. In a landmark ruling in 1996, the court agreed and ordered his release. This decision, which ruled that the lack of ability to appeal against deportation in national security cases was discriminatory, led to the ultimate creation of SIAC in 1997.[70] While there were only three appeals against deportation orders heard before SIAC between 1997 and September 2001, the use of the court grew significantly after 9/11.[71]

Heralded as a procedure that would enhance 'human rights' since it would allow for opportunities to appeal against deportation, the superficial nature of those rights is made quite evident in the operation of SIAC's judicial process which is designed to preserve the sanctity of executive power. It is effectively a colonial administrative judicial system in which state-appointed, security-cleared judges justify the routine use of closed evidence, providing the arrangement with legitimacy. Decisions on the portions of evidence are to be disclosed in open court and which sections are to remain closed are made by the secretary of state, and though this is subject to review by SIAC, the secretary of state cannot be forced to disclose material. Furthermore, even if the appellant successfully contests the accusations against them, the court can uphold the deportation order if the secretary of state points to intelligence material that asserts the appellant is a threat to national security.

Since the purpose of the court is to determine suspicion rather than the actual transgression of a person, a distinction legitimated by the court's key remit as deciding on issues of national security, SIAC is given licence to meet lower evidentiary standards than those that apply in criminal court settings. Accordingly, SIAC is granted great flexibility in the rationalisations and decision-making process that inform its judgements. The framing of these cases within a national security context means the evidentiary basis upon which the court decides is derived to a significant extent from intelligence assessments, which are not prepared with a view to prosecuting suspects in open court and do not need to be subject to the same evidentiary standards that apply in criminal court. Legal professionals who have worked within this SIAC system note that such intelligence reports are generally 'summaries of information, which may come from many different sources, including direct testimony of covert agents, hearsay from informants, various kinds of surveillance including interception, [and] information gained third-hand from foreign intelligence liaisons'.[72] In the post-9/11 context, it has become apparent that some of the government's secret evidence against those accused was likely sourced from interrogations in other countries that involved the use of torture. This may be information received by the intelligence services through its liaisons with countries such as Algeria or Pakistan, or information obtained from the interrogation of detainees in Guantanamo Bay and other clandestine military prison sites. In *Ajouaou v Secretary of State*, a case concerning an appeal by a Morrocan man, Jamil Ajouaou, against his pending deportation from Britain, SIAC rejected appeals that it should not consider such evidence, maintaining that the object of the court was not to consider 'proof' but 'reasonable grounds for suspicion'.[73] The heavy reliance on secret evidence, and the low threshold for what constitutes evidence means that, as the law reform organisation *Justice* notes, 'in every case between 2001 and 2004 save one, SIAC consistently upheld the Secretary of State's certification that the detainee was a suspected international terrorist'.[74] Between 2007 and 2017, when use of the court grew substantially, SIAC has been consistent in dismissing most appeals.

The use of closed court procedures within SIAC to protect state interests has been made more apparent under policies that further lower the thresholds for deportation. There are two main decisions that the court has to make: the first concerns whether the individual accused can be regarded as a legitimate threat to national security, a definitive terrorism suspect; the second concerns whether such a person would be at risk of torture or ill-treatment should they be deported. In the early years of SIAC's operation, it was generally the former issue that was considered in closed procedures while the latter point tended to be considered in open court. Following the government decision to enforce measures which would ease the deportation of terrorism suspects through a programme of 'deportation with assurances', SIAC began to hear more of the latter elements of the deportation appeal in closed court, too.[75] The government has justified this by arguing the arrangements for ensuring the safety of those to be returned are too sensitive to be discussed openly.

But perhaps the biggest impact of SIAC is that it has established a cultural precedent and fine-tuned operational capacity for the use of closed courts and secret evidence. As closed courts and secret evidence are reckoned to be perfectly legitimate for dealing with people criminalised as terrorism suspects, so have variations of such measures been applied in other jurisdictional courts tasked with deciding on terrorism cases in other contexts. So in 2005 when control orders were enforced as a substitute for indefinite detention of foreign nationals, the appeals against such orders were dealt with by the High Court. Such appeals occurred under the same conditions as in SIAC, enabling special SIAC procedures to move wholesale to the High Court. Similarly, such processes were used again in the High Court for dealing with offences related to the financing of terrorism legislated in the Counter-Terrorism Act 2008. As these exceptional procedures become normalised, they have been used in employment tribunals, in mental health review tribunals, and in immigration cases that are not marked as national security–related cases, but where individuals have been refused naturalised citizenship on grounds of 'bad character' because of suspected association with others deemed to be suspicious.[76] With challenges brought by former Guantanamo Bay detainees against the British government's complicity in torture, the Justice and Security Act 2013 was passed which permitted closed proceedings in civil courts for any case in which the government decides that the disclosure of sensitive material would be 'harmful to the public interest'.

Any initial reluctance to bring such measures into the ordinary criminal justice system has not prevented their routine use in tribunals operating under civil law. After the precedent of the SIAC was established, closed procedures were used in a parole board hearing in 2002 for a prisoner serving a life sentence. While in the same year, anonymous hearsay evidence was deemed sufficient basis for granting Anti-Social Behaviour Orders by the House of Lords.[77] It was not long after the Justice and Security Act 2013 was passed that the first attempt at a secret criminal trial in Britain was made when Erol Incedal (initially known as AB) and Mounir Rarmoul-Bouhadjar (initially known as CD) were brought to trial for terrorism-related charges in 2014. Public identification of the defendants was banned as was press coverage of the trial until an appeal by the *Guardian* saw this partially overturned, such that the earlier decision allowing the trial to take place entirely in secret now enabled some elements of the proceedings to be reported, but the 'core of the trial' remained secret.[78] There have also been reports of secret evidence used in criminal cases and hearings on police shootings, usually in gang and drug-related operations.[79]

The theatre of secrecy in these UK courts is in contrast to the theatre of open trials in the US. Though most terrorism cases, as most federal criminal cases in the US, are resolved through plea bargains, there is a slightly higher rate of terrorism cases being brought to trial in comparison.[80] When Abid Naseer was extradited to the US in January 2013, after being held in pre-trial solitary confinement in New York for two years, he maintained a 'not guilty' plea and his case was brought to trial – this time in open court, where he chose to represent himself. Before Abid's arrival in court prior to the first session, security was enhanced around the Brooklyn Federal Court, with a team of eight heavily armed Department of Homeland Security cops stationed around the building. The trial experimented with the use of 'light disguise', as the judge permitted British MI5 agents to appear in masks and wigs for their own safety. The evidence that formed part of the decision to convict Abid included statements by MI5 agents that he had appeared 'tense' while talking on the phone; it also included material collected from the Osama bin Laden compound, in which Abid was not named, and which did not indicate any direct links to the accusations against him.[81] The judge overruled Abid's assertion that the 'inflammatory' documents were not relevant because he was not named in them, replying, 'The more I read the documents the less significant I find them, but it seems to me on the face of it, it becomes relevant because of *who* it was said by and the allusions to the scope and activities of various cells'.[82] Additional evidence against Abid came from Najibullah Zazi, a man who entered into a cooperation agreement with the US government, who acted as a key witness for the prosecution. Najibullah Zazi pleaded guilty in 2010 to plotting to bomb the New York City subway and agreed to testify against others in exchange for a reduced sentence. When cross-examined by Abid, who asked him if they knew each other, Najibullah Zazi responded, 'I don't know. I don't happen to remember your face'.[83] Najibullah Zazi admitted to the court he had not heard Abid Naseer's name mentioned in any conversation while in New York and Pakistan.

While to some extent these trials maintain the illusion of democratic judicial systems, symbolising to the rest of the world the merits of US justice and perhaps reinforcing ideas of American exceptionalism, they fundamentally operate in conjunction with the routine use of secrecy. In a number of terrorism cases, including in Fahad's, Adel Abdul Bary's and Khalid al-Fawwaz's cases, Special Administrative Measures (SAMs) are imposed to restrict communication of the prisoner both with their lawyers and with the outside world. Operating in a similar way to the procedures followed in SIAC, lawyers are required to be security cleared before they can review secret evidence against their clients but are forbidden from discussing much of it with either the person they are defending or outside experts not security cleared.[84] As this significantly impedes the ability to mount a defence, it critically inhibits scrutiny of the nature of the criminal charges or the evidence basis to support them.

On Return

Both Babar Ahmad and Talha Ahsan entered into plea bargains after spending over two years in pre-trial solitary confinement in the US. Both pleaded guilty to charges of providing and conspiring to provide material support. In a rare twist to usual terrorism proceedings, during their sentencing the judge, Janet Hall, gave a positive character assessment of them both. She remarked that Ahmad seemed to be 'a generous, thoughtful person who is funny and honest', that he was 'well liked', 'humane' and 'empathetic', 'soft-hearted' and 'selfless', and that Ahsan had similar qualities. She concluded that neither of the two men 'were interested in what is commonly known as terrorism' and offered a more complex definition of jihad, noting that in reality jihad is not necessarily reflective of the way it is invoked by counterinsurgent intelligence forces.[85] Talha was sentenced to time served and deported shortly after and Babar to an additional year in US prison before being deported back to the UK. Their families and campaign supporters celebrated the outcome as significant for the way in which it disrupted the official terrorism narrative.[86] Yet even as this decision was as close to a declaration of 'innocence' possible under such prosecution in the legal system and despite the humanising remarks made by the judge, the disciplinary framework ensured the conviction of the accused. Even as the judicial decision laid out a narrative which produced these men as multifaceted political subjects and offered complexity to the meaning of religio-cultural concepts such as 'jihad', the outcome, which still held these men as convicted terrorists, did not negate the process via which they had been dehumanised so as to achieve this conviction nor undo its material realities.[87] Talha returned to Britain in 2014 and Babar in 2015. Both retain the legal status of convicted terrorists and all the restrictions on citizenship – access to employment, higher education, freedom of movement – that this entails.

3

Depriving and Deforming Citizenship

Citizenship is a privilege, not a right, and the Home Secretary will remove British citizenship from individuals where she feels it is conducive to the public good to do so.

Home Office, 2013[1]

Immigrants from the Commonwealth countries, though remaining British subjects under British nationality law, would be debarred from entering (and settling in) Britain except as and when required by the British economy ... In terms of British nationality law, this would mean that a British citizen was not completely a British citizen when he was a black British citizen.

A. Sivanandan, 1982[2]

In the basement of Field House, a building dedicated to hearing immigration and asylum appeals, Minh Pham appeared before the Special Immigrations Appeals Commission in the summer of 2012. In this court that consists of no jury and a panel of three judges, Minh, a British citizen, was not appealing against deportation, the concern that occupies most cases before the court, but against the deprivation of his citizenship, an order that had been made some six months earlier. His representatives were arguing that to deprive him of his citizenship would make him stateless, and thus that the order should be repealed.[3]

Minh had converted to Islam when he was twenty-one. It offered him a way out of his depression. He grew up in South East London after his parents fled Vietnam in 1983 and brought him by sea to Hong Kong when he was one month old. They moved to the UK when he was six. His family claimed asylum and were granted permanent residency by the time he was twelve.[4] Minh was the first-born son and the oldest of four siblings, his parents had little money and spoke little English, and he recounts that his early years in London were hard. Bullies at school targeted him with his small and skinny physique, a refugee with broken English. He was punched on several occasions, one time so hard that he was hospitalised. His parents' inability to navigate the administration of the local school system meant he did not initially get a place at the local high school; for his first high school placement, he travelled an hour and a half by bus each way, but was eventually transferred. He struggled at school in core subjects but found an outlet in art, at which he excelled. As his English improved, he could help his parents and other Vietnamese families in the area with interpreting. He would help local mums with doctors and hospital appointments, with shopping, and with translating official letters and documents. He started smoking cigarettes when he was eleven and by fourteen was smoking cannabis. He drank and partied hard. He worked at McDonald's, first in the kitchens before progressing to the role of cashier. He passed A-levels in Graphic Design and Art and went on to enrol in a local design college. It was here that he borrowed some books on Islam from a classmate and saw an alternative. He gave up smoking and drinking and started afresh: it was a chance for a new life.

Minh began attending the mosque on Old Kent Road soon after his conversion and met other youth who were active in Tablighi Jama'at (TJ), a non-political Sunni Islamic missionary movement.[5] He started attending TJ gatherings in London himself and participated in a forty-day outreach programme which took him to mosques around the UK. Two years later, in 2006, he participated in a four-month programme travelling to India and Bangladesh, living simply and staying in different mosques. It was his first trip overseas without his family and for him it was like a pilgrimage. He was moved by the poverty he witnessed and wanted to engage more in humanitarian work. Back in the UK he took part in Stop the War rallies in London and became politically engaged.

After college Minh had started working in various print shops designing advertisements. He set up his own graphic design company, Shatta Studio, and worked as a freelance designer, with the intention to combine Eastern and Western art in his design. He also taught an evening graphic design class to teenagers at a Turkish community school, went on to work with a refugee community organisation in 2005, where he taught basic computer and job-search skills to refugees predominantly from Somalia and Vietnam, and then to a training company doing similar work. This was the job Minh held when he was arrested in December 2011.

In December 2010, Minh travelled to Yemen with a friend he had met in the UK, seeking to do more to defend Muslims facing persecution. Though his knowledge of the philosophies of the organisation was fairly limited at the time, in January 2011, soon after his arrival, he made an Oath of Allegiance to al-Qaeda in the Arab Peninsula (AQAP) in Arabic, a language in which he was not conversant. He understood from the publicity literature he had seen that they were an 'Islamic army raised to liberate all Muslim countries from injustice and oppression'. While with them, his role was to act as an art assistant for *Inspire* magazine, the al-Qaeda publication, helping design graphics on a couple of occasions. As he became increasingly aware of the political positions of his associates, tensions rose between Minh and the friend he had travelled with, who was less sympathetic to TJ and the political positions that Minh was more endeared to. In court, Minh later told a judge that he wanted to leave Yemen and come back to the UK, and the only way for him to get permission to do so was to agree to a foreign operation. He told Security Services that he had no intention of carrying out an attack, he just wanted to get back home.

On his return from Yemen in July 2011, he was searched by police at Heathrow airport and arrested when they found him to be in possession of a laptop, 7,000 euros, and a bullet. After investigations, he was not convicted and the police released him with a caution. Intelligence on Minh Pham was transferred to the United States. Some months later, in December, he received an order from the home secretary revoking his British citizenship. The deprivation order in his case was unusual, markedly different from all but one or two of the other fifty-three people who have been stripped of their citizenship since 2002, as Minh was in the UK when the deprivation order was issued.[6] This meant that the official removal of his papers would need to be accompanied by the official procedure of removing him. Shortly after receiving the notice, Minh was detained by immigration officials, who initiated deportation proceedings for him to be expelled back to Vietnam.

Appealing to SIAC against his deprivation order in June 2012, Minh was, at first, successful. The court ruled that since the Vietnamese government did not recognise Minh Pham as a national of their state, to deprive him of his British citizenship would make him stateless. But within minutes of SIAC announcing their decision and granting Minh unconditional bail, as he sat in the cells of the court building, he was re-arrested with a warrant that had been issued five weeks earlier on request of the US Department of Justice. They were calling for his extradition in relation to five terrorism charges that the US government alleged he had committed, mostly concerning material support and conspiracy, which carried a maximum penalty of forty years in prison. Minh did not return to his home but was driven straight from the SIAC courts to Westminster Magistrates' Court where he faced extradition proceedings.[7]

In contesting his extradition, Minh's lawyer pointed out that the allegations made by the US would also constitute breaches of UK law, including the Terrorism Act 2000, the Terrorism Act 2006 and the Firearms Act 1968. Still Minh was never charged in the UK. Much of the evidence against him relied on testimony obtained from Ahmed Abdulkadir Warsame, a Somalian who once lived in the English Midlands, and who was subject to extraordinary rendition after being captured in the Gulf of Aden. Ahmed Abdulkadir Warsame was incarcerated on board the USS *Boxer*, known as the 'floating Gitmo', where he was held incommunicado for eight weeks and interrogated under conditions of torture. As with others who have been 'rendered to justice', his interrogation occurred in two parts. In their supporting documentation to the extradition request for Minh, the US Department of Justice submitted to a British court that for approximately the first two months of Ahmed Abdulkadir Warsame's detention on the ship, he was interrogated by non-law-enforcement personnel, and during the last week he was held, was questioned by the FBI. The Department of Justice argued that 'the law enforcement interviews were wholly separate from the prior non–law enforcement interviews'.[8] His legal team contested Minh's extradition to the US because the key witness against him was Ahmed Abdulkadir Warsame, who had agreed to act as a cooperating witness for the US Department of Justice. However, the British High Court ruled that there was insufficient evidence of the conditions under which Ahmed Abdulkadir Warsame was interrogated and that only the information obtained from him by law enforcement and after he had been read his Miranda rights officials would be used.

When Minh was eventually extradited in February 2015, the question of his citizenship was still pending. The initial success of his appeal to SIAC was short-lived when the home secretary, Theresa May argued to the Court of Appeal that even though he was no longer recognised as a Vietnamese national he would still be entitled to the Vietnamese citizenship he was born with. Her appeal was won, and in March 2015 was upheld by the Supreme Court based on legislation passed in 2014 which extended the provisions by which an individual could be stripped of their citizenship. Thus, the court decided that by law Minh was still a Vietnamese citizen even if the Vietnamese state did not recognise him as such because he had acquired nationality elsewhere. Though Minh's lawyers argued that extradition would render him stateless, restrictions under the 2015 Counter-Terrorism Act which limit the right of British citizens to re-enter the country if they have been suspected on engaging in terrorism meant the appeal was denied. Thus the banishment of Minh Pham, and the prospect of the psychological torture he would face once imprisoned, was compounded by a civic and social death resulting from being made de facto stateless.[9] About his removal, the Home Office repeated a statement that has come to be recurrent in connection with terrorism cases: that citizenship is a privilege not a right.

Since the Immigration, Asylum and Nationality Act 2002 came into force, it is estimated that over seventy people were stripped of their British citizenship by 2016, with most of these cases occurring since 2010.[10] Most deprivations of citizenship have occurred when the individuals are out of the country, making it difficult for them to appeal. Some of these men – namely, Bilal al-Berjawi and Mohamed Sakr – were deprived of their citizenship and then subsequently killed by US drones, others were rendered to justice, some were incarcerated in military prisons, and others, such as Minh Pham, were extradited.[11]

The significance of Minh's case was that it exemplified the ideological and legal-technical progression that had taken place over the fourteen-year period since 2001 when calls were fervently made for enhancing state capabilities to enable the deprivation of citizenship and the government recognised its limited capacity for doing so. The relatively quick materialisation of statelessness in Minh's case reflected an advance in the efficiency of such methods, cementing in legal terms what in many ways had already been established through his criminalisation. Yet as Minh's extradition and deprivation of citizenship illuminates the end point of such a process of dehumanisation – and the full weight of state power as it were – the underlying condition which facilitated and legitimated his statelessness is significantly more far-reaching. The point is that citizenship has always been a privilege, not a universal right, its designation favouring white male bodies. Since its inception, the cultural framing and legal recognition of citizenship has been delimited and conditional, and accordingly its withdrawal is also always targeted. The significance here is that, despite international protocols and liberal sensibilities – which sanctify citizenship as a universal, if never fully realised, human right – by defining these standards of humanity against a figure to be excluded as non-human (here, the terrorism suspect) the inherent contradictions are revealed and intensified.

Taking as my starting point the racialised condition of citizenship, this chapter charts the progression of cultural and legal infrastructures allowing for the retraction of citizenship, developments which have been enabled through high-profile terrorism cases.

Citizens and Subjects

Since the formation of the modern state, notions of citizenship, or belonging, have relied upon multiple strategies of racial distinction, privilege and exclusion.[12] The rationale for determining who should or should not be brought into the polity, proffered by key liberal thinkers sets out thresholds for inclusion and exclusion in raced, classed and gendered terms. The universal subject was the propertied white male, a framing contingent on the exclusion of others thought more akin to the State of Nature; recognition of the subject as human was the prerequisite for determining whether citizenship might be granted and what form it would take. As racial hierarchies informed decisions on enfranchisement in European states, they also played a fundamental role in legitimising European colonisation and the civilisationist mode of governance imposed by European powers. Civilisations outside of Europe, the logic proceeded, were not capable of self-governance precisely because they lacked the rational capacity for self-determination. John Stuart Mill, for example, proclaimed that 'the sacred duties which civilised nations owe to the independence and nationality of each other, are not binding towards those to whom nationality and independence are either a certain evil, or, at best, a questionable good'.[13] Over the course of colonial rule, such racial distinctions and gradations were clarified and made more sophisticated so that those deemed to be closer to the Anglo-Saxon race were afforded more privileges than those regarded as being more akin to nature.[14] If Irish and to some extent Scottish people were considered the lesser races of the United Kingdom, for example, they were nevertheless recognised as more capable, more civilised and therefore more entitled than the colonial subjects of Jamaica. The colonial project of marking citizens and subjects relied on processes of dehumanisation. Dehumanisation was the necessary condition for justifying and legitimating unrestrained violence that sustained the political-economic project of empire.

Through the initiation, the duration and the end of formal colonisation, this logic has been continuously reinterpreted, recast in different ways in relation to different categories of racially disavowed humans. In each instance, the disciplinary techniques used to exclude or expel those marked as non-belonging or non-entitled not only enhance state powers to banish, they work sufficiently to reshape the parameters of citizenship and, by implication, notions of democracy more broadly. Where the identified threat of terrorism and the presence of terrorism suspects is used to promote the idea that citizenship ought to be contingent on the character and behaviour of a subject, even based merely on suspicion, in other instances the condition of citizenship is delimited by logics of nativism and indigeneity – whether a subject is considered to rightfully belong to the nation, to be of blood and/or soil. The contrasting rationales serve varying purposes in different moments, but nevertheless all provide legitimating techniques for withholding, and preserving the conditionality of, citizenship. It is indeed, as Giorgio

Agamben indicates, in relation to the position of the 'banned', those subjects categorised as the 'exception' and vulnerable to abandonment, that the status of the political-legal subject-citizen is continuously (re)defined and understood.[15]

Since the granting of citizenship theoretically prohibits, or at least limits, the possibility for abandonment by the state, the quest for self-determination and a meaningful 'universal' citizenship that accompanied the onset of decolonisation presented a new set of problems for the state, disrupting, at least in legal terms, the status differential for which colonisation allowed. As the terms of citizenship in Britain and its empire were reimagined to account for shifting power structures and Britain's altered position in relation to its postcolonial subjects, new categories of citizenship were created, to some extent unsettling the norms of colonial racial hierarchies. Yet if the granting of citizenship was an indication of political recognition, its formalisation in legal terms was accompanied by the development of institutional arrangements to enhance the possibilities of exclusion.[16] The paradox of this moment when legal categories of citizenship were inscribed in British law for the first time is that, as the British Nationality Act 1948 attempted to present some sense of cohesion across the Commonwealth in replacement of the Empire, while theoretically opening up citizenship, the terms of who qualified for citizenship were redefined so as to simultaneously constrain who could gain from its material benefits. The development of citizenship legislation went hand in hand with the expansion of immigration legislation so that the terms set for inclusion were continuously framed by those who were to be excluded.

In the immediate post-war period, the nod to universal suffrage following anti-colonial struggles was accompanied by the political question of how to offer inclusivity while retaining imperial hierarchies of citizenship that limited the entitlements of post/colonial subjects.[17] As postcolonial migration increased to fill post-war labour shortages, along with rising levels of local hostility towards a growing non-white presence, discourses of civilisationism under the Empire were recast in terms of a nativism aligned with the re-envisaged British nation-state. The immigration legislation passed over the course of the 1960s and 1970s, in attempting to curb postcolonial immigration, employed multiple techniques and rationales to restrict the right of black and Asian people to settle in Britain.[18] British nationality was redefined according to ideas of blood and soil. With the Immigration Act 1971 came the racially coded concept of patriality, which meant that only those who could prove their grandparents had been born in Britain would qualify for automatic right of abode.[19] The impact of this legislation was to formally sever the entitlements of postcolonial subjects to British citizenship, as 'New Commonwealth' citizens were reformulated into 'immigrants'. As this worked to significantly restrict levels of immigration and conceptually transform how postcolonial subjects would be legally identified, the effect was to divide families by granting settlement rights to those who had migrated before 1971 while barring spouses and children who had yet to arrive. The British Nationality Act 1981 cemented this distinction further by removing automatic citizenship rights from postcolonial subjects born in Britain and opened up space for future governments to redefine the 'duties' and 'entitlements' of citizenship as they saw fit.[20]

As immigration restrictions curbed postcolonial migration, attention turned towards restricting migration via routes of asylum. Throughout the 1990s, a bill was passed almost every year relating to immigration, nationality and citizenship, with three pieces of primary legislation over this period culminating in the Immigration and Asylum Act 1999.[21] These legislative measures worked through various means to essentially criminalise the very act of seeking asylum, and making the process virtually impossible through lawful procedures. The lack of availability of visas for asylum seekers, the lack of access to passports or other valid travel documentation, disbelief by the Home Office of genuine political asylum status when valid passports were produced on arrival, the criminalisation of using forged identity documents (virtually the only form of travel possible when fleeing a persecuting or failed government), and the criminalisation of those who worked to assist the arrival of asylum seekers in the UK, all contributed to morphing the attempt to claim asylum, nominally a human right, into a rhetoric of 'illegal immigration', thereby precluding at an earlier stage than before any legitimate applications for citizenship.[22]

As the granting of citizenship has been withheld from various racialised populations, it has at the same time remained a precarious status for racial minority populations who have acquired it, positioned as never quite belonging to or *of* the nation. One of the most effective elements of the reframing of citizenship in the context of the War on Terror is that it has combined assertions of bogus asylum seekers with discourses of 'self-segregating' British Muslims. The precarious and conditional nature of citizenship has extended through this connection. The introduction of citizenship tests by the government as a fitting response to riots in 2001 by mostly British-born Pakistani youth, was developed into an entire programme of 'probationary citizenship' with multiple stages, where to fail can leave you, in some circumstances, without the right to reside in the UK at all.[23] In 2007, Gordon Brown proposed that immigrants should pass three stages to become 'full British citizens'. The first stage was to enter as temporary residents; after residing in Britain for five years, they could apply to become a 'probationary citizen'. Approval at this stage would be dependent on evidence of continuing economic contribution and successful completion of the 'Knowledge of Life in the UK' and English language tests. Following a minimum period of one year, those who wish to apply for full citizenship are subjected to a further round of tests to become full citizens or permanent residents. However, those who fail at this stage and did not satisfy the requirements, would 'lose their right to stay in the UK'.[24] This remains the basic template for movement from immigrant status to citizen. At the same time, the grounds for revoking citizenship have been extended on the grounds of national security threats. Perhaps most effective about the reframing of citizenship through the War on Terror is that it has enabled the state to return certain subjects to their dehumanised or colonised state.

From Asylum to Terrorism

Like Minh Pham, Hilal al-Jedda arrived in Britain seeking asylum. He, though, came a little later in life, migrating together with his wife. An accomplished basketball player, he was part of the Iraqi national team until his refusal to join Saddam Hussein's Ba'ath Party made life difficult and he fled the country in 1978. Following periods in the United Arab Emirates and Pakistan, he arrived in Britain in 1992.

The year of Hilal al-Jedda's arrival to the UK was the year that marked the formal creation of a new integrated Europe. Eastern Europe was dealing with the dissolution of the USSR and in the aftermath of the official ending of the First Gulf War, the British military remained enforcing a no-fly zone over Iraq, Hilal's birth place. Shifting borders within Europe and the rising displacement and dispossession that resulted from the expansion of globalised capital and ongoing war saw increasing numbers of refugees arriving in Europe and on Britain's shores. It was around the time of Hilal's arrival to the UK that there began a significant escalation of asylum applications, mostly from war zones and areas under military occupation including numerous countries in Africa (Angola, Ethiopia, Ghana, Somalia, Sudan, Uganda, Zaire), the Middle East (Lebanon, Iraq), Eastern Europe (former Yugoslavia) and Asia (Sri Lanka, India and Pakistan), often places where there had been direct or indirect British involvement. Between 1990 and 1991, the number of asylum applications almost doubled from 26,205 to 44,840, and fluctuated within this range over the course of the 1990s; as this became the main source of immigration over this period, dominant discourses on race, immigration and citizenship centred on the figure of the asylum seeker.[25] Migration for the purposes of asylum outstripped the postcolonial migration that the immigration restrictions of the 1960s and 1970s had worked to curtail, thus becoming one of the principle routes via which citizenship became possible. With many others from Iraq, Hilal was granted refugee status in 1994, gained permanent residency in 1998 and was eventually awarded British citizenship in June 2000.[26]

Although Hilal's arrival to the UK is demonstrative of the predominant route of entry to the UK at the time, his case is also important for illustrating the way in which the discourses and policing approaches towards managing asylum requests have been reconstructed in terms of threats of terrorism. The role of media representation and the political response to the question of asylum is critical to this shift.

In the post-9/11 context, the media began a campaign against the presence of 'Islamic extremists' in Britain. Stories circulated of 'terrorists' on the loose, not least in the aftermath of the arrest of Kamel Bourgass, an asylum seeker, who had fled Algeria some years earlier, who had killed a police officer during an immigration raid on his home and was charged in relation to the 'Ricin plot', an alleged scheme to carry out a bioterrorism attack on the London underground with ricin poison in 2002 which was later found to be unsubstantiated.[27] The moral panic that erupted around national security relied on a racialised trope conflating the 'asylum seeker' with the 'terrorist'. 'How many more terrorists have we let in the country?' the *Daily Mail* asked, claiming that the vast majority of asylum seekers had no proof of identity thus providing 'the perfect cover for terrorists'.[28] The *Sun*'s campaign from 2001 demanding the deportation of Abu Hamza went hand in hand with a campaign demanding 'tougher action' against 'illegal immigrants' more generally. By January 2003, the newspaper claimed that 50,000 readers had already signed in support.[29] Other media outlets joined in; the *Daily Mail*, the *Daily Express* and the *Daily Telegraph* all published similar pieces.[30] The intensity of the panic reached such heights that even David Blunkett, the home secretary at the time, stepped in to ask newspapers not to exacerbate 'fears and concerns', warning that British society was 'like a coiled spring' on the issue of asylum, and that the rising tension might soon lead to vigilante action and 'people taking the law into their own hands'.[31]

The state response to asylum has been widely commented upon for the way in which it dehumanises the subjects characterised as asylum seekers, condensing stories of persecution and oppression while diminishing their agencies of resistance and desires for greater security and material wellbeing.[32] The political response to asylum in the 1990s disconnected from Britain's imperial role much more than in debates on race and immigration in earlier periods, so that rights of asylum seekers to settle in Britain were framed in terms of liberal duties and conventions. Accordingly, obligations to accept asylum seekers were rooted in terms of duties enforced by the UN and international treaties, even as in truth domestic legislation was implemented to work against such duties.[33] This framing limits such racialised humans to not-quite political subjects, outside of fully recognised citizenship and an obligation rather than an active agent.[34] Even as the state pushback against the right to asylum depended on discourses which dehumanised the subject fleeing war, violence and persecution, and which represented them as either without agency, as pitiful and helpless, or as insincere, not endangered but disingenuously fleeing to Europe for a 'better life', such representations are nevertheless confronted by international human rights duties and conventions which nominally stipulate the right for individuals to claim asylum and the corresponding duty of states to uphold such rights.[35] The reframing of the asylum question in terms of securitisation and threats to national security offered an alternative set of narratives for dehumanisation and an alternative route towards realising expulsion. Even the abstract responsibility to protect is thus eliminated: there is a liberal right to seek asylum but there is no liberal right to engage in terrorism. As the asylum seeker is made identifiable and interchangeable with the terrorist, it shifts the terrain upon which the right to enter, the right to citizenship and the right to have rights is debated. Following the 9/11 attacks, the clamp down on asylum seekers came much easier as the threat of asylum morphed explicitly with discourses of terrorism and national security.

Legitimising Statelessness

> SIMON KIRBY (BRIGHTON, KEMPTOWN) (CON): Is this not just about getting rid of very bad people and preventing them from coming back to our country? Is that not the nub of what we are discussing?
>
> THERESA MAY: I am grateful to my hon. friend for putting the matter so succinctly and sensibly. This is about dealing with people whose behaviour is seriously prejudicial to the United Kingdom, and I would have thought that we all wanted to ensure that the Government had the appropriate powers to do that.[36]
>
> *2014*

As part of the media campaign against 'Islamic extremists' in Britain that began in the immediate days after the 9/11 attacks, the British tabloid press became particularly fixated with several British-based Islamic preachers. Abu Hamza, a one-eyed cleric with a hook as a prosthetic hand, took centre stage as the token villain, the domestic Osama bin Laden who had managed to acquire British citizenship. Alarmist headlines personified him as a domestic terrorist, with photographs of his face and hook and provocative cartoons to match. The *Daily Mail* ran a cover story with an image of Hamza and the header 'Hatred UK' under which were listed individuals the paper deemed to be terrorists living in Britain. In the inside pages was an accompanying cartoon showing a bearded, big-nosed man in a turban, standing in front of Whitehall with a placard saying: 'Death to America and Britain!' The caption beneath read: 'Parasite: (Chambers English Dictionary) A creature which obtains food and physical protection from a host which never benefits from its presence'.[37] Other newspapers joined in, with the *Sun* campaigning for Abu Hamza's deportation, asserting that 'Blair's blitz on fanatics should start in Britain'. Numerous letters from readers supported the view, which were in turn endorsed by the paper's editors, who pushed for a government response.[38] Public pressure turned to David Blunkett, the then home secretary, and the Home Office received a raft of letters calling for Abu

Hamza to be deported. Since he was a British citizen this would be difficult, nor could he be indefinitely detained even under the permissions granted in the Anti-Terrorism Crime and Security Act 2001, which had been passed as an emergency measure to target foreign nationals in the initial sweep of post-9/11 arrests. David Blunkett understood that further action needed to be taken.

In February 2002, the Labour government published its principal domestic policy response to growing concerns of global terrorism titled 'Secure Borders, Safe Haven: *Integration with Diversity in Modern Britain*', which intertwined a range of racially charged issues such as asylum, immigration and the integration of British minorities. Laid out here was the plan for updating and extending procedures for depriving an individual of British citizenship which, the documented stated, would be of particular use 'in any case where someone has been granted British citizenship while concealing a material fact such as their past involvement in terrorism or war crimes'.[39] The effect of the power, implemented in the Nationality Immigration and Asylum Act 2002, was to expand the grounds for removal of citizenship to include any person (including birthright citizens) who 'has done anything seriously prejudicial to the vital interests of the United Kingdom or a British overseas territory'.[40] This manoeuvre laid the grounds for a much more expansive and absolute basis upon which a subject could be expelled. Sufficiently vague and all-encompassing in its meaning, this new piece of legislation came to be unofficially known as the 'Hamza amendment' when Abu Hamza became its first target.[41] He was the subject upon which the legislation's efficiency and aptitude was tested when David Blunkett pursued this route in response to media and public alarm at Hamza's continued presence in the UK.[42]

Where the provisions for permitting the removal of citizenship in 2002 appeared to be for the purposes of preserving Britain's imperial interests, by 2006 the terms expanded so deprivation could be ordered simply if it was 'deemed conducive to the public good'.[43] Whether the threshold for this measure had been reached was the judgement of the home secretary, but the definition was expansive enough to be applied for various reasons, notably aligning the threshold for citizenship deprivation with the threshold for deportation. The case of Hilal al-Jedda provided the justification for continued enhancements of this legislation.

In September 2004, after Allied forces had re-occupied Iraq, Hilal travelled back to his country of birth with his four eldest children. Possession of a British passport on being granted citizenship freed up his ability to travel, and from 2000 onwards he had travelled back and forth to Central Asia on numerous occasions, including to Iraq. During a trip to Syria he was apprehended by authorities without explanation and detained for eleven months before he was released.[44] Soon after, Hilal and his wife divorced, and he married a second time in 2001 while in Jordan and became a father again. His four children with his first wife are all British citizens.

En route to Iraq with his family in Autumn 2004, Hilal was arrested and questioned in Dubai by United Arab Emirates intelligence officers, who released him after twelve hours, permitting him and his children to continue their journey to Iraq. Less than two weeks after his arrival, United States soldiers, acting on information provided by British intelligence services, arrested Hilal at his sister's house in Baghdad. The grounds, he learned later, related to his facilitating the travel of another individual to Iraq, who the authorities identified as a terrorism explosives expert, and some other related conspiracy charges. Hilal was taken to Basra in a British military aircraft and then to the Sha'aibah Divisional Temporary Detention Facility in Basra City, a detention centre run by British forces. The precarious and artificial protection offered by his British citizenship is reflected in his incarceration there for three years until December 2007, which was handled by representatives of the Iraqi and British governments and by non-British military personnel and authorised on the basis of intelligence never disclosed to him. Nevertheless, Hilal's British citizenship granted him the ability to appeal against his detention to the European Convention on

Human Rights, which ruled that his rights to liberty and security had been violated as a result.

However, Hilal al-Jedda became another test case for the powers of deprivation of citizenship. A month before his release, then–home secretary Jacqui Smith issued a notification order informing him of her intention to deprive him of his citizenship on the grounds that to do so was 'conducive to the public good'. This was one of the first times that the enhanced deprivation powers, and the lowered threshold for removing citizenship, passed under the Immigration, Nationality and Asylum Act 2006 had been used. It was administered in such a way which meant that Hilal, detained in Iraq at the time, was unable to challenge the notification and one month following, on 12 December 2007, he was officially deprived of his citizenship. When he was released from prison at the end of December, with neither a British passport nor officially recognised Iraqi nationality, he moved to Turkey from where he launched an appeal to regain his British citizenship.

Sixteen months after the notification depriving Hilal al-Jedda of his citizenship had been delivered by the Home Office, the Special Immigration Appeals Commission dismissed his appeal, holding that secret evidence presented by intelligence authorities indicated Hilal had been planning to carry out an attack against coalition forces.[45] Like Minh Pham, Hilal was represented by a special advocate in court and was not privy to the closed evidence which had secured the judgement. On appealing the decision, Hilal's lawyers argued that since he had lost his Iraqi citizenship when he became a British citizen, as stipulated by Iraqi law at the time, to revoke his British citizenship would make him stateless. The Home Office countered that subsequent changes in Iraqi law after the fall of Saddam Hussein meant Hilal could reapply for his Iraqi citizenship, and thus statelessness would be a result of his own doing. After a six-year battle, the Supreme Court eventually ruled in 2013 in agreement with Hilal, deciding that the Home Office's actions would make him stateless and overturned the home secretary's order. Hilal al-Jedda is the only person known to have successfully challenged the loss of his citizenship under the 2006 law, which perhaps reflected the changing political climate in relation to the Iraq War by 2013.[46]

Shortly after the Supreme Court hearing, but before the judgement was announced, the Home Office informed the court that it had discovered that Hilal's Iraqi passport, which Hilal had previously described as fake, was in fact genuine and had been used several times to travel. The Home Office added that it had received reports from the Iraqi government that it regarded him as a citizen and that Hilal's name appeared on its register of citizens. The Supreme Court ruled that it was too late to introduce this evidence. Within three weeks of the judgement, the Home Office issued a second deprivation order on the same national security grounds but this time arguing that they had new evidence to support their case that he had and had used a genuine Iraqi passport. Hilal thus became the first person to have his British citizenship stripped twice; a second appeal process began and is still continuing years later. In the meantime, the government passed a new amendment which would further strengthen their case should their second attempt fail.

On the back of the appeal ruling in relation to the first deprivation order in 2013, Theresa May, then home secretary, began to cite Hilal al-Jedda's case as proof of the need to further revise the law, resulting in the addition of an amendment into the 2014 Immigration Bill. Justifying the amendment, she explained:

The new clause is a consequence of a specific case. The power to deprive on conducive grounds is such that even when I consider the first and arguably the most important part of the test to be met – that it would be conducive to the public good to deprive – I am still prevented from depriving a person of their citizenship if they would be left stateless as a result. That was the point explored in the Supreme Court case of al-Jedda ...

Having studied the Supreme Court determination carefully and considered my options, I asked my officials to explore the possibility of legislating to address the key point identified in the al-Jedda case, namely that our domestic legislation, and the changes brought about in the 2002 and 2006 Acts, go further than is necessary to honour our international obligations in terms of limiting our ability to render people stateless.[47]

The amendment eventually approved and incorporated into the Immigration Act 2014 granted the state additional powers to deprive a person of their citizenship. Its stated purpose was to enable deprivation in 'the most serious cases – such as those involving national security, terrorism, espionage or taking up arms against British or Allied forces ... without regard to whether or not it will render them stateless'.[48] It allowed for the home secretary to deprive naturalised citizens of citizenship on conducive grounds if it was *believed* another citizenship could be acquired – effectively extending the grounds upon which a subject could be made stateless. It is under these same powers that the deprivation of Minh Pham's citizenship was upheld by the Supreme Court in 2015 after he was extradited.

In many ways, the extension of state powers that came with the move to further hollow out the security of citizenship in Britain reflected, in a globalised context, an amplification of imperial governmentality where the granting and recognition of citizenship is characterised by its provisional and insecure terms.[49] The precariousness of citizenship demonstrated through Hilal al-Jedda's case did not begin with the retraction of his British citizenship – his positioning within the global hierarchy of imperial citizenship is critical to the story. The mass deportations, banishments, executions and threats of punishment for non-compliance that were in operation under Saddam Hussein's regime were supported by partial and hierarchised notions of citizenship ingrained in Iraqi nationality and citizenship law.[50] A legacy of British colonial rule in Iraq in the early twentieth century, which had institutionalised sectarian divisions as a way to manage perceived threats from Shi'a populations and thereby consolidate British power, Iraqi law distinguished the nationality of its citizens on the basis of patriarchal lineage, that is, whether the subject was considered to be of Ottoman or Persian descent. Saddam Hussein further embedded this unequal framing of citizenship and its function of expulsion and disqualification. In 1980 his regime passed a decree stating that 'any Iraqi of foreign origin will be stripped of his Iraqi nationality if he is found to be disloyal to the country, the people and the supreme social and nationalistic goals of the revolution'.[51] This decree extended powers set in the 1950s for denaturalising political dissidents (mostly communists) for 'following the order of foreign governments'.

The complicity of Western powers in such hierarchies of citizenship is reflected both in their support for Saddam's regime and in their connected reluctance to recognise and accept those displaced populations fleeing state violence and occupation under his regime as asylum seekers or eligible citizens. Derek Gregory notes that prior to the invasion of Kuwait in 1990 not only had the US administration barely commented on the human rights infractions occurring on a routine basis in Iraq, George Bush, Sr had actively intervened to secure a large loan for Iraq and signed an executive order vetoing economic sanctions which had been passed precisely to protest human rights conditions there.[52] It was at this time, too, that asylum legislation was passed continuously through the 1990s to impede claims to settlement in Britain and that a programme of deportation was intensified.[53]

Asylum, in this context, comes then to represent an inadvertent by-product of imperialist interventions. The arrival of Iraqis to Britain propels to the fore the discrepancy between Europe's liberal commitment to human rights, including the right to seek asylum, and the political backlash against asylum seekers. Access to those liberal principles which arrival on Europe's shores brings for people fleeing war, poverty and despair is of course significant and forms the principle route through which asylum seekers, including Hilal, have been able to successfully obtain residency though this is in practice continuously contested.[54] Where the liberal sensibility calls for a measured response to asylum, the reconstruction of individuals such as Hilal al-Jedda from asylum seeker to terrorism suspect in fact facilitates the return to imperialist hierarchies of citizenship. It simplifies the debate. Accordingly, the global schema of citizenship, with its hierarchies of meaningful citizenship, is more easily retained.

In the parliamentary debate that followed the proposal to allow for deprivation of citizenship even if resulting in stateless-ness, from which I quote the Conservative MP Simon Kirby at the start of this section, the case supporting such a measure was presented in simple, generic terms: 'about getting rid of very bad people', individuals who, criminalised as 'terrorism suspects', should by the same logic not qualify for the same kinds of safe-guards as 'good people'. As this reductive reasoning reasserted the same kind of civilizationist sensibilities of earlier periods, it also denoted something much more significant than the mere banishment of those undesired.

The Privilege of Citizenship

While the act of imposing statelessness is not new, the recent political determination to expand the terms upon which doing so can be legalised brings to the fore questions concerning the role, status and significance of citizenship. The rationale for the deprivation of citizenship and statelessness of terrorism suspects sees such subjects as already outside of the polity, representing threats to 'our way of life'. Their removal in legal terms, then, follows logically. But the discourse that has come to surround terrorism cases of citizenship as a privilege actually forms part of a broader shift that – as legal paper identity has become increas-ingly central to one's existence – positions citizenship explicitly as something to be earned.[55] In British policy, this idea has been materialised through administrative requirements introduced in 2002 which mandated extra thresholds to be met before citi-zenship would be granted. These new prerequisites brought a number of additional demands: if you worked hard enough, if you earned enough money, if you paid your taxes, if you learned good enough English, if you abide by 'our' values, and you wait your turn in orderly fashion, citizenship would be granted.[56] In many ways, this policy change illustrated the broader neoliberal shift that repositioned rights within a capitalist logic in which they were conditional to 'work'.[57] Following the deprivation order against Abu Hamza, David Blunkett told the BBC,

> I want to deal with people who our intelligence and security people believe are a risk to us. If you encourage, support, advise, help people to take up training, if you facilitate them, then of course that takes you right over the boundary. *People have to work to earn citizenship.* They will be proud to have it. I'm proud to have done that.[58]

Blunkett's reference to Hamza was a reminder that as citizenship was there to be gained, it was also there to be lost.

Against the imaginary claim of a universal citizen bearing equal rights and entitlements, the borders of citizenship were being reframed through an economic narrative contingent upon racially inscribed notions of securitisation. The 2002 white paper, *Secure Borders, Safe Haven* introduced a whole new set of measures designed to strengthen the 'value' and 'significance' of British citizenship. In response to the notion of a British citizenship crisis – of not knowing what it meant or how to implement it, linked no doubt to what Paul Gilroy has termed 'postcolonial melancholia' – the reformulation and modernisation of citizenship has essentially been realigned with neoliberal policy agendas, so that while certain forms of citizen (and immigration) have been encouraged, others are constrained.[59] Immigration that is economically beneficial has been promoted by packaging British citizenship in a way that draws upon Britain's imperial brand as a 'stable and attractive place' to live, with a 'buoyant economy', and the home of the 'universal' English language.[60] The additional measures introduced – in the form of knowledge and English language tests, citizenship education and, on receipt, citizenship ceremonies – add to the sense of status as well as assist in the production of docile subjects who would have not only demonstrated an understanding of 'British values' but would have, on completion, sworn allegiance to the Queen.[61]

As this agenda has progressed, the worth of passports and paper identity have significantly increased. Access to a range of different arenas of social and economic life are being gradually attached to proof of nationality or legal residency.[62] As well as fortifying the restrictions on possibilities to work even in temporary and more precarious forms of employment, in Britain the ability to rent a house, access the health service, open a bank account, learn to drive and go to university are all now dependent on proving legal entitlement to reside.[63] This expansion of securitisation means that the border is rather explicitly encroaching into everyday life such that responsibility for border control are not limited to officials working at the border but are filtered down and made the duty of professionals – doctors, landlords, driving instructors, employers, teachers, administrators – and the public at large. As the material necessity of citizenship increases the precarious positioning of those who do not possess it, or whose legal status to remain within a country is limited or conditional, the proliferation of policing and monitoring systems to sustain this system further reinforces material insecurities, particularly for those on the margins. It extends the reach of the securitised state.

This more securitised form of citizenship was bred in the value-laden conditional requirements of David Blunkett's early reforms of 2002, where it was used as part of the disciplinary apparatus for targeting populations labelled as failing to integrate, of not working hard enough to commit to 'British values'.[64] These measures targeted both British (Muslim) citizens and the residency rights of immigrants represented as insincere or 'bogus'. In 2002, citizenship education became a central part of the Community Cohesion programme directed at the marginalised Muslim communities who had been protesting racist exclusion in the 2001 riots, so that levels of English proficiency and knowledge of British civil society and history became yardsticks for measuring (unreachable) levels of belonging.[65] By positioning the civic and human rights of asylum seekers alongside the precarious civic and human rights of British Muslims, broader racial dynamics of citizenship were brought to the fore rearticulating a hierarchy of subjecthood, of whose lives were more recognisable, as more valuable than others.

By this rationale, the acquisition of citizenship was not only attached to fulfilling residency and employment requirements but relinked to the 'character' of a subject. If this was implicit in the political discourse around citizenship, it was rather explicitly materialised in the policy framing for citizenship grants and refusals. Though the consideration of the character of a subject is not a new measure for assessing the granting of citizenship, its re-centring as a threshold requirement is made evident in Home Office statistics on citizenship awards and rejections.

The 'good character' requirement for citizenship was revised in 2009 as part of the reforms brought in under Gordon Brown.[66] His government's *Path to Citizenship* further strengthened the notion that citizenship was something to be earned as new measures established a staged process requiring a demonstration of an applicant's contribution to social and economic life in a number of ways, as well as proving a certain degree of assimilation.[67] As the Immigration Bill passed through parliament, committee members agreed that it was 'prudent to continue to apply the character test ... via discretion [of the Home Office] rather than by establishing specific requirements in primary legislation'.[68] This meant the secretary of state would continue to hold ultimate authority over who should and should not be refused citizenship; it would be a decision made by the executive, not judicial authority.

While the overall numbers of people being granted citizenship has been increasing since 2000, in part because less desirable categories of migrant are prevented by immigration restrictions from reaching the point of eligibility for application as well as government preference for authorised permanent residents to become full citizens, the number of people being refused citizenship on the grounds of 'not good character' has increased to become the principal reason for refusal.[69] There is no official definition of what constitutes 'bad character' though policy guidance specifies it may include 'not abiding by or respecting the law', being associated with war crimes, not having one's 'financial affairs in appropriate order', being involved in 'notorious activities' that 'cast serious doubt on standing in the local community', being dishonest with the UK government, 'assisting in the evasion of immigration control' or having previously been deprived of citizenship.[70] The guidance have been kept sufficiently vague and expansive so that a decisionmaker can still refuse citizenship if they have cause for doubt beyond those listed.[71]

For Muslim applicants, there are material consequences of the connections between the subjective reading of character, commitment to 'British values' and earning citizenship. As the discourse of terrorism has furthered narratives of segregation and discursive connections are made between 'lack of integration' and 'extremism', greater emphasis is placed on communities to self-police, to report suspicious behaviour.[72] There is simultaneously increased pressure from intelligence services for members living in targeted communities to work as informants. There are a growing number of cases in which individuals denied naturalisation have been told that citizenship would be made available to them if they would be willing to cooperate and work for MI5.[73] Similarly, a number of British citizens' passports have been confiscated, a measure used in some ways as a proxy for citizenship deprivation, after they have refused to work for MI5, or have had their passports not returned on that condition.[74] Immigration lawyers report that authorities refuse to renew British passports or grant citizenship to individuals with indefinite leave to remain on similar grounds.[75] The experiences of individuals in high-profile cases, such as Mahdi Hashi, who had reported to the media – before he was deprived of his citizenship, illicitly detained in Djibouti and then rendered to the US – that he had been subject to harassment from MI5 for three years, are reminders of the full force of disciplinary powers available to the state.[76]

Recent challenges to the secrecy around the decision-making process in cases where citizenship is refused on grounds of terrorism or national security–related concerns have revealed that the Home Office supports the coercive practices of the intelligence services in its guidance to its case workers. In some appeals against citizenship refusal heard in the Special Immigration Appeals Commission, lawyers representing those appealing have argued that applicants should be fully informed of the criteria against which they are being judged.[77] After some reluctance, the Home Office disclosed some of the guidelines issued to case-workers, stipulating that a person might meet 'good character' requirements if they had not associated with individuals identified as 'extremists', if they had ceased such association once they 'became aware of the background of these individuals' and, critically, if they had *'presented strong evidence of choosing such associates with the aim of trying to moderate their views and/or influence over others'*. Conversely, applicants should be refused citizenship if they associated with individuals deemed to have 'extremist views' and were aware of this or *'provided little or no evidence to suggest that they were seeking to provide a moderating influence'*.[78] The upshot of this is that if a Muslim person who is identified as associating with another individual identified as 'extreme' refuses to work for the state, this in itself becomes sufficient reason for being refused citizenship.

The full scope of the 'good character' requirements allow for blatant racial sorting and exclusion in other ways, too. Claims of 'deception and dishonesty' in any liaison with a state department forms another sufficiently broad criterion used against those applying for citizenship. Refusal of citizenship on grounds of 'deception' refers to attempts to enter the country using false or misleading documents and/or to access public and social services which one's immigration status prohibits. Since the legal constraints which restrict petitions of asylum make it near impossible to arrive as an asylum seeker without incurring some kind of legal infraction, and the total exclusion from or limited access to basic services such as healthcare and housing for those who are granted asylum mean transgression becomes a necessity for most to survive, the criterion of 'deception and dishonesty' in essence offers a way to exclude from British citizenship large numbers of individuals who have arrived via the asylum route. This is borne out in data.

The individuals who are most frequently subject to refusal of British citizenship on the grounds of bad character originate from countries including Afghanistan, Iraq, Pakistan, Somalia, India, Turkey, Jamaica, Nigeria, Kosovo, Bangladesh, Sri Lanka and Iran.[79] Notably, these are all areas to which Britain has direct postcolonial links or a present military occupation or interest. Immigrants from these countries are also among the most marginalised communites in Britain. When comparing the data from recent years on refusals of citizenship on character grounds with data on asylum applications, a correlation emerges between the countries from which most asylum applicants originate and the nationalities of individuals refused citizenship.[80] Though denial of citizenship by naturalisation does not mean the right of residency is retracted, it does prolong a position of precariousness for those who are refused, sustaining restrictions on freedom of movement for those with no viable passport or the possibility of future deportation.

The expansion of deprivation measures as a disciplinary technique is illustrated further in the cases of a group of British Pakistani men convicted for sex offences in 2015, who were removed of their citizenship on the basis of their convictions.[81] As these cases illuminate the complex but proximate interconnections between racial and gender violence, the broader significance in this instance was their role as a test case for exemplifying how deprivation measures could be imposed beyond national security and terrorism concerns and ordered more routinely.

These multiple forms of citizenship deprivation, suspension and denial indicate the formalisation of a more permanent precarious subject, who can be continuously manipulated for the state's own ends to suit multiple purposes and shifting goals. Since citizenship can work in two directions – it can both be earned and lost – these shifts in the management of citizenship become a way to discipline racially othered populations, for whom now exclusion via patrial clauses, as established in the Immigration Act 1971, does not apply. But more than this, it introduces a more workable permanence to the status of the precarious non-citizen alongside a flexibility in how this arrangement can be administered. The notion that citizenship is 'a privilege not a right', that it is not an 'entitlement', informs popular logics and gains a normative rationale.[82] It requires the institutionalisation and hardening of authoritarian practices for it to be sustained.

The increase in the value of citizenship requires its exclusivity: Abu Hamza and Hilal al-Jedda provided justification for furthering disciplinary mechanisms with which to exclude certain subjects, enabling access to citizenship to retain its restricted status.

The Fate of Minh Pham

Minh Pham entered into a plea bargain weeks before his trial in New York was scheduled to begin. During his sentencing, prosecuting lawyers argued that Minh had also been involved in a never-executed plot to construct and detonate an explosive device at Heathrow Airport after returning to the UK from Yemen in July 2011. His lawyer's objection to these claims was dismissed. Pham was sentenced to forty years in prison, and broke down in tears as the sentence was passed. He is incarcerated in the supermax prison ADX Florence in Colorado and remains stateless, a status that was upheld by the European Court of Human Rights.

4

Courting Human Rights

I mean longer prison sentences, I mean making it easier to deport foreign terrorist suspects back to their own country and I mean doing more to restrict the freedom and movement of terrorist suspects when we have enough evidence to know they are a threat but not enough evidence to prosecute them in full in court. And if our human rights laws stop us from doing it, we'll change the laws so we can do it.

Theresa May, 2017[1]

And that is the thing I hold against pseudo-humanism: that for too long it has diminished the rights of man, that its concept of those rights has been – and still is – narrow and fragmentary, incomplete and biased and, all things considered, sordidly racist

Aimé Césaire, 1972[2]

I know the law is an ass but in this instance it seems to be outrageous.

Peter Bone, MP, 2014[3]

In 1999, when Haroon Aswat was twenty-five, he visited the US for the first time, travelling with an acquaintance, Oussama Kassir, to New York before they journeyed across the US, eventually reaching Bly, Oregon. He was there to teach Arabic and provide religious instruction on the Quran. He would also receive some training in the use of arms, believing it was his religious duty to train for self-defence.[4] Though he had never heard of al-Qaeda at the time, the government would later argue that his attendance at the camp, together with some literature found on the hard drive of his computer some years later, was evidence that he was 'committed to violent jihad'. The literature included a book on survival skills in the event of a nuclear, biological and chemical weapon detonation; *The Anarchist Cookbook*; a hand-to-hand combat instruction manual; *The Close Combat Textbook*; and *The Big Book of Mischief*. Haroon's defence lawyer argued that the book on survival skills was a pamphlet produced by a group called Citizens Defence, a survivalist organisation in operation since 2002; that *The Anarchist Cookbook* was available as a Kindle e-book for $1.99 and had been ubiquitous in the 1970s; the 'hand-to-hand combat instruction manual' referred to *Hand-to-Hand Combat: Krav Maga books and videos*, readily available online as part of Krav Maga Worldwide, which describes itself as, 'the official hand-to-hand combat system of the Israeli Defense Forces, and is widely regarded as the best self-defense system because of its efficient, no-nonsense tactics that emphasise instinctive movements, practical techniques and realistic training scenarios'; *The Close Combat Textbook* was likely another website offering college graduates living in Manhattan lessons in self-defence; *The Big Book of Mischief* dates from 1991 and is a 'treatise' on all types of explosives (mostly homemade).[5] The overwhelming majority of files found on his computer, they noted, were religious videos or CDs promoting prayer and condemning violence.

Haroon had lived his whole life in Britain. Born in Batley, West Yorkshire, he was the son of Indian migrants who had settled in the area in the 1960s. He grew up in a large, extended family and was the third oldest of ten siblings. His father ran a grocery business until he suffered a stroke, and later in life his mother become wheelchair bound after she, too, had a stroke. Haroon enjoyed playing cricket, and left high school with four GCSEs before he went on to study electrical and electronic engineering at college. After working for a few years doing electrical odd jobs, he moved to London at twenty-two.

While in London, Haroon began to suffer from depression. After a few years he moved again, and after his short trip to the US, he travelled to Mecca for pilgrimage in 2000. He subsequently spent time in Pakistan and Afghanistan, where he was involved in teaching Islam. Haroon then relocated to South Africa where he lived for two years, working as a travelling salesman buying and selling religious CDs. During a visit to Zambia in 2005, Haroon was arrested and deported back to the UK where he was re-arrested on arrival, pursuant to a US indictment on charges relating to material support for terrorism for his attendance at the camp in Oregon in 1999.[6] The request was initially dealt with relatively quickly and the home secretary approved the decision by a senior district judge that he should be extradited. Haroon's appeal to the High Court was dismissed and he was subsequently refused permission to appeal to the House of Lords. At around the same time that Babar Ahmad's appeal to the ECHR was submitted, Haroon also appealed to the European Court of Human Rights against the conditions of confinement he faced in the US. When later applications by Talha Ahsan, Abu Hamza, Khalid al-Fawwaz and Adel Abdul Bary were submitted, the Court collected them together and considered them jointly.

Three years into his incarceration, first in Belmarsh and then in Long Lartin Prison, Haroon's mental health began to deteriorate rapidly. He became agitated, would shout and chant, and after refusing to be locked in his cell, was placed in segregation.[7] This led to more singing and chanting and he refused to eat. Haroon's acute psychotic episode was later diagnosed as paranoid schizophrenia. Arrangements were made for his urgent admission to Broadmoor Hospital in March 2008, where he was treated with medication to make him calmer. After some time, Haroon's mental health showed signs of improvement. He could read, watch TV, play pool and attend classes, and mix freely with other patients. Whilst there he completed an Open University course. In November 2011, the First-Tier Immigration and Asylum Tribunal agreed that it would be detrimental for Haroon to be returned to prison but that he should continue to be detained in the hospital equivalent. In a doctor's report on his condition, it was considered that Haroon's mental disorder could be managed by general adult psychiatric services in a local psychiatric hospital but Haroon remained in Broadmoor miles from his family home in West Yorkshire, where he awaited the decision of his extradition appeal to the European Court of Human Rights.[8] Deciding that the gravity of Haroon's mental health condition warranted separate consideration, a year after the ECHR decided that the other five Muslim men could be extradited, in a landmark hearing in 2013 the court eventually ruled that Haroon's extradition would violate his human rights.[9]

Even as the ECHR's ruling was noteworthy for its contrast with its earlier decisions approving extraditions, it nevertheless fed the broader political backlash, such as that which had developed around expelling Abu Hamza. This was, namely, the notion that not only was extending human rights to serious criminals and terrorism suspects a misapplication of a human rights framework that involved unnecessary bureaucracy and over-zealous safeguards, but that a judicial system which allowed decisions by the ECHR to outrank decisions made by its own British courts reflected European encroachment on British sovereignty.[10]

Taking Haroon Aswat's story as a starting point for reflecting on the racialised dimensions and limitations of liberal human rights framework, in this chapter I consider the juxtaposition between the constrained availability of human rights for terrorism suspects on the one hand and the appropriation of terrorism cases to further the general retraction of human rights on the other.

Who Counts as Human?

A couple of years before Haroon's extradition, in December 2011, following a national campaign for Babar Ahmad to be put on trial in the UK, a backbench parliamentary debate took place led by Dominic Raab, a Conservative MP, who had advocated strongly against the terms of Britain's revised extradition arrangements both with other European countries and with the US.[11] Though the public call for action had solidified around Babar Ahmad's case, after a parliamentary debate in his name was initially refused, it was agreed to incorporate it in a wider discussion of extradition arrangements. The issue of extradition was high on the political agenda in part due to a *Daily Mail*–backed campaign that had been lobbying to save Gary McKinnon, a white British male with Asperger's syndrome, from transfer to the US. Gary was accused by the US of hacking into ninety-seven United States military and NASA computers over a thirteen-month period between February 2001 and March 2002, using the name 'Solo'. The US authorities claimed that, after gaining remote access to US military computing networks, he deleted critical files from their operating systems, which shut down a US Army network of 2,000 computers for twenty-four hours, and deleted US Navy weapons logs, rendering a naval base's network of 300 computers inoperable for some time, including after the September 11 terrorist attacks.[12] Gary's defence was that he was looking for evidence of a state cover up of UFO activity. The *Daily Mail* had for some time been lobbying against terms of the extradition treaty, namely for what it saw as unjust infractions on British sovereignty and limitations placed on UK law to 'protect UK citizens'.[13] The reach of its campaign was such that both David Cameron and Nick Clegg had lobbied against Gary's impending extradition in their 2010 election campaigns. A few months after his election, Prime Minister David Cameron went on to raise the issue with President Obama.[14]

The insertion of Babar Ahmad's case into a broader debate around extradition served to obscure its specificities, instead fitting it to suit the more prominent political concern, as summarised in Dominic Raab's opening statement, that 'in taking the fight to the terrorists and the serious criminals after 9/11, the pendulum [had] swung too far the other way'.[15] The key point of contention raised by most of the politicians was that a number of (white) British citizens, such as Gary McKinnon, were subjected to inhumane conditions of confinement and justice devoid of due process, contrary to the principles of 'British justice'. As Dominic Raab put it, 'Gary McKinnon should not be treated like some gangland mobster or al-Qaeda mastermind'.[16] Though Babar Ahmad's case was mentioned occasionally, and Talha Ahsan's case mentioned once, they floated in the background uneasily; Haroon Aswat's case was not mentioned at all. The question of their human rights as 'British citizens' jarred against their designation as 'terrorism suspects'.[17] The implication of Dominic Raab's framing of the debate was to reassert racially coded distinctions, rooted in colonial politics, which determined who counted as fully human.

From both the conservative and liberal ends of the political spectrum, the argument put forward in defence of human rights rested on the assertion that the arrangements allowed for through the US–UK Extradition Treaty 2003 bypassed safeguards built into the justice system. The consequence, David Davis, another Conservative MP, argued, was that it opened up space for 'accidentally punishing the innocent or over-punishing those guilty of minor crimes'.[18] For him it was important to:

> keep in mind that the rather draconian process that we have, which was put in place to defend us against terrorism, does not appear to have had much impact in that respect. In practice, the outcome is much more mundane. The truth of the matter is that we will have far more Gary McKinnons extradited than Osama bin Ladens.[19]

Outside of the parliamentary debate, Liberal Democrat peer and then–Independent Reviewer of Terrorism Legislation Lord Carlile of Berriew QC openly supported the extradition of Abu Hamza, Babar Ahmad and Talha Ahsan, commenting simply that it was 'perfectly reasonable that they should be tried where the crime was aimed', despite decisions over jurisdiction being a contentious issue in every one of these cases.[20] Yet on Gary McKinnon, his view was that 'there is no doubt that Mr McKinnon could be prosecuted in this country, given that the acts of unlawful access occurred within our jurisdiction (i.e., from his computer in North London)'.[21] That Babar Ahmad and Talha Ahsan were also accused of computer-related offences committed from their homes in London did not, according to Carlile, warrant the same defence. It was through distinctions such as these that the rationalisations made in support of or against more draconian judicial arrangements for extradition were exposed for their underlying racialised logics. Seen through the fractured lens of criminalisation, due process and assumptions of 'innocent until proven guilty' were not so applicable to those who had a priori been framed as terrorism suspects. The selective use of this label was perhaps no more obvious than in the charges against Gary McKinnon, which were framed not in terms of terrorism but as computer-related offences.[22]

Mental health played as a racially coded trope here, too, further humanising Gary while further dehumanising Haroon and Talha. One strand of the political discussion surrounding the extradition of Gary McKinnon centred around the justice of criminalising an individual with mental health issues. The 'naivety' attributed to Gary in his search for UFOs, was presented as a trait characteristic of his Asperger's syndrome.[23] His depiction by the *Daily Mail* as a 'harmless computer nerd' whose mental health condition made him highly vulnerable drew from the assessment of medical experts who reported to the High Court that Asperger's syndrome meant Gary was 'vulnerable to the stress of social complexity' and that the conditions of incarceration would mean there was a risk he would 'take his own life'.[24] Gary's diagnosis of Asperger's, indeed, came following his arrest and helped provide an explanation of his behaviour.[25]

Although mental health vulnerabilities further qualified Gary's innocence and solicited empathy for his case, the mental health conditions of the Muslim men were rarely mentioned, and when they were it was often to promote an image of their irrationality and barbaric tendencies. The *Daily Mail*, for example, seemed to only report Talha Ahsan's case in conjunction with Abu Hamza's, as one of the 'other' Muslim men being extradited at the same time, and generally refrained from mentioning that Talha, too, had Asperger's syndrome.[26] Haroon Aswat's case was scarcely reported by the British media, but when it was his paranoid schizophrenia was usually invoked alongside a depiction of him as Abu Hamza's 'aide'.[27] Abu Hamza's own physical disabilities, his prosthetic hand and one blind eye, compounded his villainous status, making him an ideal demonic trope.

The distinctive representations of the men were upheld in the political justifications for differential treatment, resulting in quite different material outcomes. In the House of Commons parliamentary debate, Damien Green, then immigration minister, noted that Gary's case was different from Babar's (and by implications Talha's case). Though Gary had exhausted all his rights of appeal under the UK Human Rights Act 1998, the home secretary, Green argued, had 'a duty not to act in a manner that was incompatible with a person's rights under the European Convention on Human Rights'. It was for her to 'consider whether, as a result of events occurring after the extradition proceedings, it would be contrary to the convention for a person to be extradited' and in Gary's case, there was still a question about whether extradition was 'compatible with Mr McKinnon's convention rights'.[28] The mental health of the Muslim men facing extradition did not warrant the same concern.[29] Four days after Babar and Talha were extradited, Theresa May decided that 'after careful consideration of all of the relevant material ... Mr McKinnon's extradition would give rise to such a high risk of him ending his life that a decision to extradite would be incompatible with Mr McKinnon's human rights'.[30] She withdrew the extradition order against Gary.

Such inconsistencies in the political rationales used in determining when to invoke human rights and when such rights would be excessive or inefficient were not unprecedented or extraordinary. They were, to the contrary, rather consistent with a liberalism characterised by points of exceptions and limits, in which democratic processes and 'rights' can be suspended or withheld.[31] The debate over extradition as a violation of an individual's human rights, in this sense, was another exemplification of the interconnections between liberalism, and its rhetoric of inalienable rights, with structures of racial privilege and exclusion. The political rationalisations of who should be offered the judicial protections of due process, to what extent and how, were rooted in appeals to a liberal framework characterised by its conditional nature, not least in terms of human rights.[32]

The principal critique of the Universal Declaration of Human Rights, established in 1948, from the perspective of the colonised was that the symbolic condemnation of genocide in Europe was still entirely concurrent with ongoing colonial violence across the European empires.[33] Human rights as they were then codified did not extend to colonial subjects, indigenous peoples, or to African Americans bearing the brunt of the racially segregated United States.[34] The Colonial Office in Britain grappled with the extent to which the European Convention on Human Rights could or would apply to the colonies on the basis that the inhabitants of these territories had not yet reached the same stage of development as Europeans.[35] Brian Simpson notes that various solutions were considered such as keeping the rights enumerated to a minimum so as not to recognise political rights, and introducing a special form of colonial applications clause which would permit modifications 'to meet local conditions in underdeveloped territories'.[36] It was this partial application of human rights that informed Aimé Césaire's critique of the Declaration, which for him, as quoted above, was based on a 'pseudo-humanism' that was 'narrow', 'fragmentary', 'incomplete' and 'all things considered, sordidly *racist*'.[37] Césaire's questioning of the notion of universalism in the context of Western imperialism, as Barnor Hesse has highlighted, illuminated the Europeanisation of the contemporary concept of human rights.[38]

At the same time, this falsehood of universality has parallels in the Geneva Conventions and in international humanitarian law. While the human rights offered within the framework of European statehood provided for the individual rights of subjects, developments in international law were intended to extend humanitarian protocols to the law of war. These too, however, depended on recognition of the people involved in war as fully human subjects, and were built on earlier advancements of international law which had framed the protections it offered in terms of a language of civilisation.[39] It was through distinctions between civilised and uncivilised populations within international law that colonial violence was rationalised and sanctioned. When it came to agreeing the terms of the Geneva Conventions, as Laleh Khalili has noted, while 'European powers and the new superpowers [reluctantly] agreed to certain provisions ... the British and French did not necessarily see them as applicable to the colonial wars being fought in Asia and Africa'.[40] When they eventually signed the Convention, they implied that the article for protecting non-combatants would only be in effect should the sovereign so decide, and significant limitations were placed on recognising the rights of rebel forces.[41]

The logics in operation here functioned on two levels: dehumanisation of colonial subjects limited access to individual rights, safeguards and protections that the framework of the Convention of Human Rights was supposed to provide; it also removed the constraints on the kinds of Western state violence allowed in war or as part of counterinsurgency. In many ways, the retraction of human rights that was being lobbied for to facilitate the extradition of these Muslim men continued to work along these two dimensions. These retractions included advocacy against access to individual human rights protections that would otherwise be deemed sacrosanct, and the granting of permission for disciplinary mechanisms that would otherwise be regarded as inhumane. Dehumanisation both watered down civil protections and legitimated the intensification of punishment.

Against the political wrangling over the terms and material conditions of extradition, a number of human rights organisations put forward proposals for legal amendments that would enhance the level of judicial oversight within the extradition process. Employing a similar rationale to that expressed in the parliamentary debate, these recommendations have also been fraught with qualifications and points of exception that permit only a selective application of human rights. Liberty, a national human rights organisation in Britain, raised a number of concerns with the terms of the 2003 Extradition Act.[42] They lobbied against powers which permit requesting countries to indict an individual without providing prima facie evidence, against the removal of the requirement that extraditable offences would also need to be offences in the UK, and against the removal of the forum bar, which stipulated that a UK court could refuse to extradite someone if the offence, or part of it, took place in the UK.[43] For Liberty, a more just process would incorporate some of the 'traditional and important safeguards' historically written into extradition treaties, including the rule of dual criminality (the requirement that the act with which a person is charged is criminal in both the sending and receiving state), the rule of speciality (the requirement that an extradited person cannot be prosecuted in the requesting state for anything other than which he or she was extradited) and perhaps most significantly, the political offence exception, a protection incorporated within extradition treaties since their initiation in the mid nineteenth century to safeguard individuals seeking political asylum against being transferred back to the state from which they fled.

The last point, in particular, has been central to liberal principles of extradition law. Yet within this framework of due process, clear limits are placed on when such principles apply. The extradition of individuals accused of terrorism has proved one such sticking point.

Since their creation, the enactment of legal extradition agreements in Britain have been accompanied by political discussions and parliamentary debates on the right of political offenders to exemption from criminal sanction.[44] The traditional safeguards that Liberty call for a return to reference those historically advocated for by key liberal political commentators, such as

John Stuart Mill, who have lobbied for particular precautions for 'liberal revolutionaries'. In the mid nineteenth century, while the general view was that extradition arrangements should be subject to political offence exception, John Stuart Mill argued further protective measures were required in highly politicised cases to retain judicial authority to scrutinise evidence from requesting states. This, Mill argued, was necessary because political offences were very much more likely to be associated with a 'false case' and that while 'political offences *eo nomine* are not ... included in the Extradition Treaty, ... acts really political often come within the definition of offences which are so included'.[45] John Stuart Mill also suggested that extradition ought to be denied for 'any offence committed in the course of or in furtherance of any civil war, insurrection or political movement'.[46] Moreover, Mill advocated that the political offence exception should include not only acts undertaken in the course of an uprising, but also solicitations to violence expressed during the earliest stages of an uprising if the ultimate purpose of the expressions was to bring about changes in government.[47]

Although John Stuart Mill was very vocal about the need to protect the sanctity of the political offence exception, his position was also qualified by later comments expressing a distinction between the resistance of 'liberal revolutionaries' and colonial subjects. Mill campaigned in parliament for the need to maintain robust protections for political offenders at the same time as Irish counterinsurgency and anti-colonial resistance were escalating and modern discourses around terrorism began to circulate. Fenian efforts to free political prisoners in the Clerkenwell Prison bombing of 1867 Mill regarded not as part of a political movement but as illegitimate violence that did not follow either the laws of war or recognised codes of rebellion. In response to a letter asking him to support amnesty for certain Irish prisoners, Mill, in contrast to his earlier commitment to safeguard political offenders, expressed the belief that 'in rebellion, as in war ... a distinction should be made between fair weapons or modes of warfare and foul ones'.[48]

In their call for the reintroduction of the political offence exception clause, Liberty similarly qualified what would constitute a legitimate political offence, that is distinguishing between 'just violence' from 'terrorism', by noting the difficulties of the definition of 'political offence'. Designed to protect people from punishment on the 'grounds of race, religion, nationality, ethnic origin or political opinion', the concept, Liberty argued, has problems 'especially in relation to terrorism offences'.[49] Liberty's contemporary acceptance of the same distinction as John Stuart Mill's was less categorically marked in terms of colonial distinction, but nevertheless relied on the liberal framing of terrorism in its more recent definition, as being 'more ruthless', 'more destructive and indiscriminating' and no longer confined to targeting 'ministers and heads of State but the population at large'.[50] Their calls for a return to human rights safeguards were careful to delineate the boundaries, constraints and limitations of when and where such provisions might be appropriately applied.

The key difference between debate of these rights in earlier periods at the height of the British Empire and that in the political context in which Liberty were advocating, has been the notable expansion of formal citizenship rights, with the result that they have made the relatively clear distinctions between citizen and subject somewhat greyer. The postcolonial subjects represented as terrorism suspects could also be formal British citizens, not just subjects of the Empire. The sleight of hand operating in contemporary debates is that, as the liberal call for the maintenance of judicial safeguards and protections maintains a qualified 'universal' human rights, (precarious) access to the same systems by those for whom it was unintended has prompted counter calls for greater restrictions. In the name of universalism, the restrictions argued to be necessary for efficient dealings with the terrorist threat, could never (formally) be selectively applied. As David Blunkett aptly retorted to his colleagues in the House of Commons debate, extradition arrangements must (in theory) be applied consistently, not amended each time popular dissent arose:

The Americans quite rightly put to me, 'What about Abu Hamza? Whose hands are going up for a type 1 diabetic who is a double amputee, and for his associate, who is alleged to be bipolar? Who feels they ought to run such campaigns on their behalf to stop extradition?'[51]

Paradoxically, the liberal framing of universal human rights was the very constraint being mobilised to justify the further repeal of judicial protections.

From Rights to Responsibilities

It is becoming more than clear that violating human rights is an inherent and necessary part of the process of implementing a coercive and unjust political and economic structure in the world. Without the violation of human rights on an enormous scale, the neoliberal project would remain in the dreamy world of policy.

Arundhati Roy, 2005[52]

On the eve of Abu Hamza's extradition in October 2012, the media coverage fixated (again) on the failings, limitations and set-backs of the European Court of Human Rights and the European Convention on Human Rights for prolonging the process of extradition.[53] In stark contrast to the political calls for safe-guarding judicial protections in the enactment of extradition, the overriding political narrative surrounding the extradition of Abu Hamza and 'other terrorism suspects' claimed the over-reach of human rights. Labour MP Denis MacShane was interviewed for *Newsnight* and reiterated a sentiment that had been expressed in a number of national newspapers: 'What is the extra protections that terrorists, alleged terrorists – in due course, convicted ter-rorists – have? Why it is that QCs [Queen's Counsel barristers] and judges bend over backwards?'[54] He called for a proper par-liamentary examination of this area of law and courts.

When the European Court of Human Rights ruled in Haroon Aswat's case that extradition to the US would violate his human rights, the judgement helped to confirm the fears expressed by the political class of the misuse of the European Convention. The gravity of Haroon's mental health condition, the court decided, warranted separate consideration, and in April 2013, a year after the court consented to the extradition of the others whose stories I have discussed, it ruled that to extradite Haroon Aswat, given the severity of his schizophrenia, would be a violation of Article 3 of the ECHR, which prohibits torture and degrading treatment. Extradition, they judged, would likely exacerbate his condition.[55] A forensic psychiatrist report submitted to the court indicated that 'participation in occupational and vocational activities at Broadmoor, including attendance at the mosque, had helped prevent any significant deterioration in his mood' and that Haroon would likely relapse if he ceased taking his medication.[56] The court recommended that he remain in the UK.

This provoked some political backlash. Conservative MP Patrick Mercer remarked that Haroon's 'human rights would have been best served by him being in America' where he could 'prove his innocence or otherwise in a trial ... Sending him there would also be wonderful for the human rights of the British taxpayer.'[57] Such sentiments appeared, too, in Theresa May's determination to appeal the court's decision.

Undeterred by the refusal of the court's Upper Grand Chamber to hear an appeal a few months later, Theresa May announced that Haroon's extradition could go ahead regardless.[58] The Home Office noted that they had received 'assurances' which addressed the concerns raised by the ECHR over Haroon's detention in the US and that 'having carefully considered the panel's decision', they had 'informed Mr Aswat's legal team that extradition should proceed'.[59] Subsequent attempts by Haroon's defence team to appeal this decision were unsuccessful as the British High Court was persuaded by US assurances that Haroon would be given the medical support he required.[60] Haroon was ultimately extradited to the US in October 2014.

The ECHR had been clear that the special case for Haroon was a result of his pre-existing mental health condition. It had already decided, when it ruled on the appeals of Babar Ahmad, Talha Ahsan, Abu Hamza, Khalid al-Fawwaz and Adel Abdul Bary, that the other grounds on which Haroon was appealing relating to the conditions of confinement in the US did not constitute a violation of human rights. In the court's ruling on these other five cases, associated only through the fact that all were facing terrorism charges simultaneously in the US, the men's key arguments in defence were that extradition to incarceration in long-term solitary confinement would constitute a violation of Article 3 rights, the provision in the European Convention on Human Rights which prohibits torture and 'inhuman or degrading treatment or punishment'.[61] Specifically, their appeals argued that conditions of confinement in ADX Florence, the US federal supermax prison with (extra-)high-security facilities designed for housing the 'most dangerous' of the domestic prison population, and the prospect of a life sentence without parole would constitute inhumane treatment. Assurances from US authorities guaranteeing the accused due process under the US federal criminal justice system informed the court's decision that any prospective 'ill-treatment' had not met the 'minimum level of severity' to constitute a violation.[62]

The court rationalised its decision in relation to the conditions of confinement, specifically the prospect of long-term solitary confinement, in the following terms:

> It is clear from the evidence submitted by both parties that the purpose of the regime in those units is to prevent all physical contact between an inmate and others, and to minimise social interaction between inmates and staff ... The restrictions are, for the most part, reasonably related to the purported objectives of the ADX regime ... The Court finds that there are adequate opportunities for interaction between inmates. While inmates are in their cells talking to other inmates is possible, admittedly only through the ventilation system. During recreation periods inmates can communicate without impediment ... All of these factors mean that the isolation experienced by ADX inmates is partial and relative.[63]

With regards to the prospect of lengthy incarceration that might otherwise seem 'grossly disproportionate', the court's judgement was that 'while the offences with which these applicants are charged vary, all of them concern involvement in or support for terrorism. Given the seriousness of terrorism offences (particularly those carried out or inspired by al-Qaeda) ... the Court considers that discretionary life sentences would not be grossly disproportionate in their cases'.[64]

According to this decision, communication to other inmates via ventilation systems in toilets or the opportunity of one hour of exercise per day (and not every day) in a 'dog cage', which would be available to inmates only if they were willing to be strip-searched before and after their time 'outside', were sufficient measures for ensuring sensory stimulation as stipulated under human rights conventions.[65] By accepting the assurances of the United States that the extradited subjects would not face the death penalty or be prosecuted before a military commission, and agreeing that the potential for their isolation was 'partial and relative' to the crimes they were being accused of, the ECHR judgement legitimised the extradition of these Muslim men by the British courts by granting that the process was compliant with the framework of human rights.[66] When two years later Haroon Aswat made a final attempt to appeal to the ECHR on the grounds that the assurances from the United States were inadequate, the court dismissed it, ruling that the appeal was inadmissible and the basis for his claim was 'manifestly ill-founded'.[67]

In the same vein, just as the process of extradition of these men relied on assurances by the US government that it would maintain European human rights standards, so, since 2001, has there been analogous diplomacy between British and non-Western governments to facilitate the deportation of foreign national terrorism suspects, a programme later referred to as 'deportation with assurances'. In an almost parallel case some months before it ruled on the extradition cases of Babar Ahmad, Talha Ahsan, Abu Hamza, Khalid al-Fawwaz and Adel Abdul Bary, the ECHR had also ruled on the deportation of Abu Qatada.

A Salafi cleric and Jordanian national, Abu Qatada was one of the people detained in the sweep of arrests following the enactment of the Anti-Terrorism Crime and Security Act 2001 and was held without charge in high-security units for two years before being placed under house arrest. Provisions in the 2001 legislation allowed for the indefinite detention of foreign nationals pending deportation. Since it was implicit that deportation would be difficult to achieve because of the high risk that those detained would be subject to torture in their home countries, the legislation effectively allowed for indefinite incarceration without charge or the prospect of trial. When in 2004 the House of Lords ruled that this was incompatible with Britain's obligations under the European Convention on Human Rights, control orders were introduced under counterterrorism legislation that could be used on both British citizens and foreign nationals, to avoid any accusations of discriminatory treatment. For some of those detained, like Abu Qatada, indefinite detention in prison shifted to indefinite detention in a domestic residence. But the 7/7 attacks in London provided renewed impetus and justification for the enhancement of powers to deport, and this developed into 'deportation with assurances', diplomatic agreements with states (known for their use of techniques of torture) that they would comply with their human rights obligations under international law.[68] With Abu Qatada's case in mind, the British government negotiated one of its first Memoranda of Understanding with Jordan and served him with a deportation order in 2005.[69]

The ECHR was asked to decide whether his deportation and the conditions of confinement that he would likely face if retried for offences he had been convicted of in Jordan in absentia would constitute a violation of his human rights. Again, the court ruled that assurances by the Jordanian government ensured there was no risk or torture or inhumane treatment, noting brazenly that there was 'no prohibition on seeking assurances when there is a systematic problem of torture and ill-treatment in the receiving State'.[70] They did rule, though, that there would be a violation of Abu Qatada's right to a fair trial (Article 6) on account that there was a real risk of evidence obtained by torture of third persons being used at his retrial.[71] On that basis, the SIAC court in Britain determined he could not be removed, but following the negotiation of a separate Mutual Legal Assistance Treaty, an agreement between states to cooperate in the prosecution of crime, which provided greater guarantees of a fair trial, Abu Qatada left voluntarily in 2013.[72]

The political and legal negotiations around protocols, safeguards and diplomatic assurances that would eventually result in extradition or deportation in each of these cases operated almost as a backdrop to the more prominent political concern regarding the powers of the European Court of Human Rights. Though the ECHR's initial decision in Haroon's case and its collective judgement on the cases of Babar Ahmad, Talha Ahsan, Abu Hamza, Khalid al-Fawwaz and Adel Abdul Bary indicated contrasting judgements, the eventual outcomes all the men faced illustrated there were sufficient means of expelling undesired subjects. Indeed, contrary to the hegemonic discourse invoked across the political spectrum which fixated with the ECHR's misdirected application of human rights protections, the deliberations of the ECHR reflected exactly the preservation of liberal constraints on universalism and thresholds for 'rights' that were being called for.[73] The consistent effect of the court has been to mediate and set the parameters of state disciplinary techniques, while also rationalising and legitimising otherwise contested practices.

In this regard, the ECHR's humanitarian interventions within Europe, particularly in its role overseeing the adjudication of terrorism cases, have aligned with a broader approach to military intervention that seeks to co-opt human rights in the martial techniques used to discipline target populations under siege or occupation.[74] The ECHR's deliberations on the conditions of incarceration (such as long-term solitary confinement), acts of deportation, and criminal justice processes to assess whether they meet minimum thresholds of severity to qualify as violations were an exemplification of the collusion between the human rights framework and military and political powers in a process that seeks to determine, as Eyal Weizman notes, the 'lesser evil'. Writ large it reflects a collaboration sometimes referred to as 'humanitarian imperialism', or what Weizman has termed the 'humanitarian present'.[75] The court's rationales in the cases discussed echo the reasoning which has helped to condition military intervention in the context of colonial and imperial occupation, offering justifications in which violence is sanitised, as Weizman notes, through an emphasis on calculated risk and proportionality.[76]

The involvement of human rights experts and organisations in the design and implementation of military interventions has become a defining characteristic of contemporary counterinsurgent operations, serving to help sustain and legitimate them.[77] As the doctrine of human rights is inserted into strategies of preemptive military action, projects of 'nation building' and 'social and economic development' are accompanied by military pacification. The political strategy of offering humanitarian aid and infrastructure as part of such military operations is intended to help pacify civilian populations, while internationally this approach allows the occupying power to maintain an image of superiority in its standards of civilisation.[78] In a similar way that the categorisation, quantification and evaluation of military techniques by human rights arbiters provides a mediating force that legitimises war, the deliberation over and rationalisation of dehumanising methods of punishment by the European Court of Human Rights works to validate disciplinary techniques employed within domestic institutions.

In the domestic setting, then, the ECHR has done much to support the state's War on Terror internationally and domestically. The court's ruling in relation to Abu Qatada offered Theresa May currency to state that 'deportation with assurances enables us to deport foreign nationals suspected of terrorism in compliance with our obligations under the European Convention on Human Rights, the UN Convention on Torture and the International Covenant on Civil and Political Rights'.[79] Some months later, the home secretary launched a review into the practice of deportation with assurances, an appraisal that had been in the pipeline for some time following the election of the coalition Conservative–Liberal Democrat government in 2010. In her review of counterterrorism legislation, Theresa May recommended that the government 'actively pursue deportation arrangements with more countries, prioritising those whose nationals have engaged in terrorist-related activity here or are judged most likely to do so in future'.[80] The case of Abu Qatada would be further drawn upon for this purpose.

It is noteworthy that the relationship between the European Court and the British state security objectives is, however, never definitive but always in flux. Within the British state, the emphasis on the sanctity of human rights, however partially they might be applied in practice, by liberal forums overseeing legislative changes means that the drive to retract human rights safeguards is continuously met by counter criticisms. The UK Parliamentary Committee on Human Rights contested proposals for extending the programme of deportation with assurances in 2006, stating that 'the use of diplomatic assurances against torture undermines that universal legal prohibition, and presupposes that the torture of some detainees is more acceptable than the torture of others'.[81] Equally, while the ECHR can help affirm the state's security agendas in some regards, it can also impede state plans. In this sense, the role of the ECHR is that of an arbiter of state power, sometimes aligning with the British government's securitisation agenda, and sometimes acting as a containing and constraining force.

The position of the ECHR, though part of the broader human rights apparatus, is of course distinct in terms of its role as a judicial authority that is, theoretically, separate from the state. This means that it has licence to work according to its own logic, which does not always coincide with the desires of government. An analysis of the case law decisions of the ECHR in relation to the UK government show that while the court is amenable to lengthy punishment of terrorism suspects within civilian/domestic settings, multiple judgements have condemned the British government for detaining, harming or punishing subjects in settings of war.[82] In consideration of most of the terrorism cases that have been dealt with in Britain that are brought before it, the court has supported the judicial processes of the British judicial system, asserting, as it did in the cases discussed here, that a terrorism offence warranted forms of punishments that might otherwise be regarded as excessive. At the same time, the court has found the UK government in violation of the European Convention on Human Rights in relation to its operations in Iraq on a number of occasions, such as for killing civilians during security operations, for detaining individuals without charge or trial, and for transferring detainees into Iraqi custody.[83] The ECHR's judgements in these cases are often ambiguous, inconsistent and inflected with the arbitrary nature of sovereign power. But where on military intervention, its rulings tend to prioritise the curtailment of violence, its rulings on civilian justice systems are given more latitude. These interventions of the ECHR on British military action overseas has quietly underpinned justifications for Britain's moving away from Europe and has informed the discourse of the Conservative Party, in particular, on the excessive nature of human rights.

Pushing against the encroachment of European jurisdiction on British sovereignty, in 2014 the Conservatives published 'Protecting Human Rights in the UK', a proposal for changing human rights laws that would involve repealing the Human Rights Act 1998 and replacing it with a UK Bill of Rights and Responsibilities.[84] This plan was included in the Conservative Party Manifesto 2015 to break the formal link between Britain and the European Court on Human Rights. Attempting to firm up support for leaving the European Union, or at least to manage grievances, the *Protecting Human Rights* document proposed to cement qualifications to rights. The same principles of the European Convention on Human Rights would be applied, it argued, but the new proposals would also restore 'common sense', limiting access to 'human rights' so that they would not be misused by 'foreign nationals', who might, for example, claim the right to a family life, when issues of 'national security, public safety or the economic well-being of the country' were at stake.[85] Specifically, the proposal for a UK Bill of Rights and

Responsibilities would 'limit the reach of human rights cases to the UK, so that British Armed forces overseas are not subject to persistent human rights claims that undermine their ability to do their job and keep us safe'.[86]

The preservation of sovereignty, David Cameron informed *Sun* readers, was the reason for the need to scrap the Human Rights Act and move towards a British Bill of Rights. 'British Parliament' was to be 'accountable to British people', and 'British judges' would make 'decisions in British courts'.[87] The terms through which this sovereignty would be preserved, it seemed, would maintain the selective application of human rights in order to 'restore the reputation of rights'. It would also, notably, involve reduced state accountability for and greater state protection against the excesses of its humanitarian interventions.

That the legal framework of human rights is available as an institutional point of redress to those who have generally been excluded from its protections complicates the arguments around human rights. In a small way, endeavours to appeal to the ECHR have been reflective of ordinary struggles to make the law, in its interpretation and execution, more accountable, inclusive and universal. From the subaltern perspective, the initial judgement in Haroon's case was testimony to the protections that such judicial infrastructures can at times provide. It was also a reminder of the individualised nature of such provisions. The initial judgement in his case illustrated the possibility of a ruling, on a discrete basis, that contravened the prevailing notions that had informed the judgements in other terrorism cases.[88] The about turn on this decision, which resulted in his extradition regardless, illustrated the limit of human rights protections for those marked as less than human.

In October 2015, a year after he was extradited, Haroon Aswat was sentenced to twenty years in prison for conspiring to provide material support for terrorism, though the requirement stipulated that this be spent in a special psychiatric facility.[89] The judge agreed to the possibility that Haroon be transferred back to Britain to serve his sentence. At the time of writing, he still waits to be returned.

5

On Recognition, Rights and Resistance

You fight oppression wherever it occurs and whatever shape it takes. In other words, you fight for a principle and not for a particular organisation.

A. Sivanandan, 1995[1]

There can be no real peace without justice. And without resistance there will be no justice.

Arundhati Roy, 2005[2]

The cases that I have discussed in this book did not go unchallenged. To the contrary: they provoked vibrant and militant campaigns spanning a range of politics and motivations. Challenging the extension of the security state in this way sometimes entails broad coalitions. At other moments, it requires sharp political focus. About six weeks after the European Court of Human Rights decided that the extradition of Babar Ahmad, Talha Ahsan, Abu Hamza, Khalid al-Fawwaz and Adel Abdul Bary to the United States would not constitute a violation of their human rights, a public meeting took place in central London. It was chaired by Bruce Kent, a former Roman Catholic Priest and British political activist particularly known for his work in the Campaign for Nuclear Disarmament. The meeting was titled 'My Name is Ahsan' in tribute to Talha Ahsan, and a play on the name of the critical Bollywood film *My Name Is Khan*, which told the story of a Muslim man with Asperger's wrongly detained in the US on suspicion of being a terrorist. The meeting was focused on lobbying against the imminent extradition of British citizens Babar and Talha and the white Britons, facing extradition for non-terrorism-related charges, Gary McKinnon and Richard O'Dwyer. Richard was indicted in the US in 2011 for copyright infringement, accused of managing a website which signposted to other sites where pirated media could be downloaded, an act not illegal in Britain.[3] Growing public awareness of and opposition to the US–UK arrangements, which in many ways became more urgent following the ECHR ruling that the extraditions of the Muslim men would proceed, resulted in around 150 people turning up to the venue. The breadth of interest in their cases was reflected in the range of speakers that addressed the meeting: Bruce Kent was accompanied by the human rights lawyer and representative for Babar and Talha, Gareth Peirce; Isabella Sankey from the human rights organisation Liberty; Salma Yaqoob of the Respect Party; the *Guardian* journalist Victoria Brittain; Riz Ahmed, an actor who had performed in *The Road to Guantanamo* and *Four Lions*; Father Joe Ryan from the Westminster Justice and Peace Commission; Talha's brother, Hamja Ahsan; Babar's family; and Richard O'Dwyer's family. The meeting was broadcast on the Islam Channel.

The meeting was in many ways a 'live' version of an earlier petition campaign to halt Babar Ahmad's extradition to the US. Initiated in 2011 by Babar Ahmad's family, following the seventh anniversary of his detention without trial in Britain, the petition rejuvenated his battle for justice, demanding that he be put on trial in Britain. Propelled by the recommendation of the Joint Committee on Human Rights, which had urged the British government to change the law so that extradition could not be granted in cases such as Babar's 'where the UK police and prosecution authorities ha[d] already made a decision not to charge or prosecute an individual on the same evidence adduced by the US authorities to request extradition', the Free Babar Ahmad campaign mobilised the growing public awareness to call for 'British justice for British citizens'.[4] In many ways, this allowed the movement to seize on the growing disquiet around extradition arrangements more broadly. Publicity and meetings across the country increased public awareness to such an extent that just short of 150,000 people would sign the petition, resulting in the reluctant debate in the House of Commons in late 2011 discussed in the previous chapter. The petition in some ways marked a poignant moment in Britain when resistance to anti-Muslim racism had staked its claim against the normative liberal political platform of human rights.

These campaigns for justice brought together political organisations and movements affiliated with the left, including Stop the War, numerous chapters of the Guantanamo Campaign, the Campaign Against Criminalising Communities (CAMPACC), the Campaign for Nuclear Disarmament, Iraqi Democrats against Occupation, and the Troops Out Movement; representatives from a range of political parties, most prominently Salma Yaqoob of the Respect Party, Labour Party MP Sadiq Khan, Green Party MP Caroline Lucas and even Boris Johnson MP of the Conservatives, then also London mayor; high-profile human rights lawyers and organisations such as Liberty and Friends Extradited; organisations working against Islamophobia such as the Islamic Human Rights Commission, CAGE (formerly known as Cageprisoners) and Stop Political Terror; and race equality organisations such as the Institute for Race Relations and JUST West Yorkshire. The strength, and legacy, of this movement lay in its creation of a national and international network that could be tapped to organise against the multiple forms of state violence channelled towards suspect communities and individuals.

There have been a range of ways in which these organisations and affiliations have operated both within a nationalist anti-racist frame and an anti-imperialist one. It is how issues of racism and imperialism have been framed within these grassroots struggles that is the focus of this chapter.

'British justice for British citizens'

In 2012, around the time of heightened mobilisation against the revised extradition arrangements, a campaign developed led by a group of professionals across the UK who mobilised under the slogan 'We are Babar Ahmad'. Bringing together the cases of Babar Ahmad and Talha Ahsan with the profiles of two white British citizens, Gary McKinnon and Richard O' Dwyer, as the 'My Name Is Ahsan' meeting had done, the campaign's key claim was that the extradition treaty had 'robbed British citizens of sovereignty and given the ability to a foreign state to accuse *our* nationals and extradite them' (emphasis added).[5] Eschewing any differentiation between the four men in the form of criminalisation each faced, whether, that is, they were regarded as terrorism or non-terrorism suspects, the campaign instead focused on the similarities of their stories. Gary McKinnon and Talha Ahsan were both represented as suffering from Asperger's syndrome. The gravity of being detained for eight years without trial, as Babar Ahmad had been, was pivotal to the story of injustice they told. Highlighting issues of sovereignty, the campaign's choice to mobilise under the British Muslim identity of Babar Ahmad was no doubt significant for its nod to multicultural Britain, incorporating a more inclusive sense of 'Britishness' in its quest for justice. There was something transgressive about a campaign focused on the upholding of the liberal principles of habeas corpus and the tenets of British justice that was fronted by a Muslim face.

The multicultural nature of this campaign effectively re-humanised some of the individuals who had been consistently demonised in media portrayals of extradition when they concerned Muslims, invariably charged with terrorism. At the same time, however, it relied on a nationalist framing of justice. Where such a framing was effective because it drew on liberal principles connected to rights of citizenship, it was precisely the same framing of nationalism that simultaneously constrained the horizon upon which the nature of the injustice could be effectively articulated and understood.[6] This was apparent, firstly, through the interpretation of the events they protested as a *universal* assault on British sovereignty. The consequence of this was to overlook structures and mechanisms of racial stratification that elevated the value of some lives over others. These structures were integral to justifying the retraction of universal safeguards in the first place and concurrently shaped the value of citizenship that each 'British citizen' was granted. The second issue with this framing is that any acknowledgement made of the racial distinction at work in questions of citizenship was bounded by the constraints of the British nation, so that even when the role of racism was conceded, it was divorced from the underlying concerns of imperialism.

While citizenship provides a conduit through which calls for rights and political recognition are given legitimacy, the limitation of restricting the struggle to the rights of the citizen is that rights belong only to those recognised as 'properly inside' the spatial confines of the state.[7] The rights of citizens are intrinsically dependent on recognition by the nation-state in which one is located. In this way, underlying such demands is the assumption that the same forms of state violence being opposed remain defensible when applied towards those subjects outside of the nation's boundaries, whether residing outside of the nation, in this context the UK, or as an internal denizen marked as an outsider.[8] The liberal construction of citizenship defines the citizen always in relation to an 'other' who is outside of sovereign space and accordingly not recognised as a complete political subject.[9] This emphasis on a friend/enemy or citizen/immigrant distinction indicates that the claim to citizenship is to make a theoretical division between the subject who is to be protected by the state from violence and the subject who is to be the principal target of state violence. In invoking 'British justice for British citizens', even as the campaign's attempt to apply the 'universal' principles of citizenship rights as much to Babar Ahmad and Talha Ahsan as to Gary McKinnon and Richard O'Dwyer transgressed the imagined line between which subjects were recognised as rightful citizens and which were not, the demand nevertheless appealed to a nationalist conceit. To lobby that the state was duty bound to protect its citizens meant mobilisation was necessarily constructed around forms of 'national identity', a strategy which in its most progressive stance sought to broaden the kind of nativism inherent within nationalist positions to incorporate difference and recognise the multicultural nature of contemporary Britain. It was a nativism of the left.[10] The logic of this, however, still required excluding from such protections anyone designated as outside of or beyond the national frontier – not least, here, the non-British citizens also resident in the UK detained for even longer periods without trial and awaiting a similar or worse fate upon extradition to the US.

The limits to nativism, as invoked by the campaign, was not simply that the race-blind approach to justice would exclude from rights to civil protection any denizen subject, but that it overlooked the cultural representations which intersected with legal status to further differentiate between sections of the population. The claim to citizenship rights made by the 'British Justice for British Citizens' campaign was inhibited by the quite distinct processes of criminalisation which assigned the Muslim men as terrorism suspects and the white British men as regular criminal suspects. Since the key justification for laxer extradition arrangements rested on the need to more efficiently address the threat of terrorism, the racialised markings of the terrorism suspect attributed to these Muslim men had a priori fixed them as of the outside, as subjects that needed to be disposed of. British Citizenship for them, in this regard, was to some extent meaningless.

The popular, media and political responses to the differently racialised subjects articulated this distinction quite clearly. Taking up Gary McKinnon's case, the *Daily Mail* had brought national attention to the revised criteria of the US–UK Extradition Treaty 2003 which permitted the US to request an individual for extradition without providing prima facie evidence, only showing cause for reasonable suspicion. The *Daily Mail*'s efforts resulted in both David Cameron and Nick Clegg lobbying against Gary's extradition to the US in their national election campaigns.[11] Once elected, Cameron in his capacity as prime minister raised the issue with President Obama, even reporting in a joint press conference in 2010 that he hoped 'a way through' could be found for McKinnon to be tried in Britain.[12] Cameron's support for McKinnon is a stark contrast to his response following the decision of the ECHR to permit the extradition of Babar Ahmad and Talha Ahsan with the other three Muslim men, saying that he was 'very pleased with the news' and that it was 'very important that the deportation and expulsion arrangements [work] promptly and properly, particularly when people are accused of very serious crimes'.[13] Whereas Cameron's negotiations with Obama also worked in favour of Richard O'Dwyer who was also saved from extradition, the merits of 'British justice' were consistently invoked to *support* the extradition of individuals accused of terrorism. This was evident in the parliamentary debate that followed the petition for Babar Ahmad's trial in the UK, which was only agreed to on the basis that it would be incorporated into a wider debate on extradition. The ensuing deliberation centred on the figure of Gary while it did not similarly use the cases of Babar and Talha as examples in support of change, and the debate played out along the same terms of racial privilege and exclusion that had been left unaddressed in the race-blind struggle for citizenship rights.

The efficacy of divide-and-rule tactics were most visible in their enforcement when ten days after the Muslim men were extradited to the US, Theresa May halted Gary McKinnon's extradition on health grounds. Janis Sharpe, Gary's mother, thanked the 'brave' home secretary and the *Daily Mail* celebrated their victory.[14] Richard O'Dwyer's case ended in November 2012 when he agreed to a 'deferred prosecution' agreement with the US authorities. Richard travelled to the US voluntarily to complete the agreement, paying a small sum in compensation and agreeing not to infringe US copyright laws again. Now with (only) half of the 'British citizens' removed to the US, for some campaigners this represented a measure of justice, while for others the fight became exceedingly more difficult, not least because the individuals for whom they campaigned had halved in number, crossed national borders and been moved Stateside.

In some senses, the campaign for justice for 'British citizens' sat within a broader spectrum of struggles that have disconnected demands for equality in the West from global struggles for justice in the Third World. By mobilising around a nationalist multiculturalist concern, the practice of extradition was framed as if it were solely a domestic governmentality rather than one of many forms of violence employed as part of an imperialist project, of which the War on Terror is indicative. If the protection of Gary McKinnon offered a way for David Cameron to demonstrate his commitment to defending national sovereignty against the imperial weight of the US, the terrorism cases offered an opportunity to demonstrate Britain's imperial might and special allegiance with the US in administering global security operations. The rationale, too, for differential treatment of the Muslim men underscored the connection between the racial exclusionary politics of nationalism and imperialist wars being waged across the global East and South.

Outside of this short-sighted battle for 'British justice', as the campaigns to free Talha Ahsan and Babar Ahmad marched on the struggles in many ways resonated with longstanding domestic anti-racist campaigns that have fought for a more inclusive approach to national cultural representation and recognition of difference.[15] In thus calling for the recognition of Babar and Talha as British citizens, the movements were part of a lineage of anti-racist resistance that since the mid twentieth century has fought for civil rights and greater institutional protections enforced through race equality legislation, campaigns that had lobbied against the divisiveness of immigration policy, against divide-and-rule within the trade union movement, and against a nationalism that provided the breeding ground for racism.[16]

Addressing the connection between Islamophobia at home and the targeting of Muslims in Western foreign policy and military interventions, other campaigns against the extradition of the Muslim men have been framed within more all-encompassing mobilisations against the wars in Iraq and Afghanistan and the practices of rendition, torture and indefinite detention in military prison sites. Building on the tradition of anti-racist movements articulated as part of struggles against imperialism, the campaigns for justice for Babar Ahmad and Talha Ahsan were also taken up by activists with histories of involvement in the Asian Youth Movements of the 1970s and '80s, and the Indian Workers Association, as well as other anti-imperialist labour struggles, which have all recognised the specificity of state violence against forms of political resistance.[17] In this anti-imperialist sense, the struggle for justice for Babar Ahmad and Talha Ahsan was also a struggle for others such as Khalid al-Fawwaz and Adel Abdul Bary, and equally aligned with struggles against Guantanamo, against torture, and against war. One of the key organisations that has lobbied in this vein is the Muslim human rights organisation CAGE.

That Old Sounding Drum

CAGE, initially known as Cageprisoners, was set up in October 2003 with the purpose of raising awareness of the plight of prisoners at Guantanamo Bay and other clandestine sites of detention that were being used to hold Muslims labelled by the US as 'enemy combatants'. Its mission was to represent the 'voice of the voiceless', lobbying against the human rights violations that have become synonymous with such military detention sites.[18] Finding little existing provision among Muslim communities for responding to shifting political events, the organisation began by creating an online information portal detailing all the individuals being detained as part of the War on Terror.[19] CAGE quickly rose to the forefront of organisations protesting the violence and abuses being legitimated through the War on Terror, not least because of its broad scope working internationally with communities affected by the ongoing war. In a similar stance to most other human rights groups, CAGE have maintained its protest in relation to Guantanamo detainees as one of principle rather than in support for individuals per se, arguing that the retraction of rights in these cases, through the neglect of due process and the rule of law, ultimately means a retraction of rights for all.

It is the organisation's sensitivity to the connections between domestic counterterrorism policing and Western imperial ventures overseas that underlie the strength of its work and campaigns. As the War in Terror has progressed, CAGE have continued to document simultaneously the nature and impact of preventive policing programmes in the UK alongside the British government's complicity in rendition and torture. The organisation's affiliation with Moazzam Begg, a former Guantanamo detainee who has acted as their outreach director, has been central to this work, enabling access to people and information otherwise hard to reach. At the same time, CAGE's connections to, and trust from, targeted Muslim populations in Britain – largely established through their casework and advocacy – mean they are one of the few organisations that has been particularly capable of documenting the state interventions that have affected suspect individuals and communities. The narrative of state violence they report is remarkable, not only for the level of detail and insight but for its linking of racial profiling and the criminalisation of Muslim communities domestically with Western foreign policy agendas.

CAGE's critique of the British government's Prevent programme, an initiative set up in 2005 initially as a 'community-led' programme involving the distribution of state resources to Muslim community organisations for the purposes of 'tackling violent extremism' and widely condemned for its institutionalisation of racial profiling, for example, has been forceful for illuminating the shallowness of the epistemological assumptions underpinning some of the scientific elements that have helped to provide the initiative with credibility.[20] As the initiative progressed and was made statutory in 2015, so the policy guidance around it became more rigid, detailed and specific. CAGE's report, *The Science of Pre-Crime*, exposed to the policy world the broad and shallow criteria used for assessing and diagnosing 'radicalised behaviour' amongst Muslims and the lack of rigour in the scientific model 'Extremism Risk Guidance 22+' developed by psychologists, that formed the basis of the guidance upon which assessments of radicalisation are to be based.[21] Noting the flimsy reasoning in which the indicators of risk range, from expressed support for political causes such as Palestine to behavioural changes and increased religiosity, CAGE have also drawn on case studies of the communities they work with, in order to bring to public attention the social and material realities of Prevent as it is administered in practice.[22] Through their work we learn about Muslims who have been questioned about their views on ISIS while visiting their GP, Muslims whose mental health was questioned because they appeared to become more religiously devout, Muslim children who were believed to be on the path to radicalisation because they explained to their teachers their late arrival at school as being the result of morning prayer or who expressed a lack of desire to partake in music lessons.[23]

At the same time, through CAGE's attempts to shift the public discourse around Syria, their challenges against the criminalisation of travel to Syria and their centring of the British state's role in the Syrian War, there has been greater exposure of the arbitrary disciplinary practices imposed against those marked as suspicious, as well as the practices of the intelligence services in their attempts to co-opt young Muslims to act as informants. CAGE has collected the testimonies of individuals on the impact of that harassment and these reports illuminate both in suspect communities in Britain and in arenas of British foreign policy interest, how individuals are pressured to become informants for the purposes of intelligence gathering.[24]

It is arguably precisely because of such interventions that CAGE has become a central target of state condemnation as an extremist organisation misappropriating the premise of human rights for jihadist means. Although neo-conservative civil society organisations such as the Henry Jackson Society and the right-wing media have long denounced CAGE as a 'jihadist front', public opprobrium reached new heights when the then Prime Minister David Cameron named them specifically as an illegitimate organisation in his speech on extremism in 2015.[25] Cameron's reference point was the beheading of an aid worker volunteer, Alan Henning, a man from Rochdale who had been working in Syria as a driver with Rochdale Aid 4 Syria to provide humanitarian relief, and was captured by ISIS in late 2013. The focus was on CAGE's earlier contact with the man charged with Henning's killing, who had been in touch with the organisation for support some time before he had left the UK for Syria; no mention was made of Moazzam Begg's offer to assist in negotiating with Henning's captors in order to secure his release. In a press conference announcing the publication of correspondence they had with him, CAGE representatives pointed out that Mohammed Emwazi, who the media satirised as 'Jihadi John', had been for some time prior to his departure distressed by the harassment he was experiencing from MI5. Indeed, even the *Daily Mail* reported that Emwazi had written to their security correspondent prior to leaving for Syria, telling them 'he was a dead man walking' and indicating that he was suicidal.[26] Cameron's purpose was to seize on the take of the right-wing media, who had misquoted Asim Qureshi, CAGE's research director at the time, to accuse the organisation of defending Emwazi as 'extremely gentle'. Cameron scolded the National Union of Students (NUS) for aligning with CAGE (which they had done through work on lobbying against Prevent), an organisation he claimed had told people to '"support the jihad" in Iraq and Afghanistan', thus giving weight to broader narratives which have positioned CAGE as unapologetic advocates of terrorism.[27]

Beyond the spectacle of this particular episode, just as the exhibition of extraditing the Muslim men earlier discussed overshadowed the rising use of authoritarian techniques for managing populations, so the vilification of CAGE too eclipsed other political manoeuvrings; two elements that are of particular note. The first is that it acted as a smoke screen for the British state's escalation of counterterrorism operations both abroad and at home. Namely, Britain's military involvement in Syria was being escalated at the same time that the domestic counterterrorism programme, Prevent, was being intensified. David Cameron had earlier expressed a need 'to do more' in Syria, such as augmenting Britain's involvement.[28] His reassurances that this would only be done with approval of the House of Commons were proven false when, a few days before making his speech on extremism, it was reported in the media that Cameron had been aware UK personnel were already involved in carrying out air strikes over Syria despite a lack of authorisation by Parliament.[29] It was following this press revelation that Cameron identified CAGE as an extremist organisation.

Around the same time that British intervention was growing in Syria, dissent was rising against the statutory implementation of Prevent, which placed a legal duty on public institutions to monitor students for signs of potential radicalisation and was being rolled out across schools, colleges and universities over the summer of 2015. The vilification of CAGE, and the association of the NUS with them, helped to legitimate this agenda. Malia Bouattia, the then black student officer of the NUS and also vilified as being a terrorist sympathiser for speaking against Zionism, noted this connection and responded that David Cameron's attack on the student union allowed him to avoid any engagement with the 'lists of grievances' against British domestic and foreign policy, not least that the Prevent programme was the 'greatest threat to civil liberties in a generation'.[30]

The second element is that, in positioning CAGE in the context of a general assault on extremism within UK Muslim communities, Cameron reified an essentialist reading of political dissent within Muslim quarters as being tied to innate culturalist tendencies, reducing all protest of state actions to adherence to irrational and extreme versions of Islam that were antithetical to liberal values. The criticism of CAGE was not that through their advocacy of terrorism suspects the organisation took a misguided approach to human rights that risked sullying the sanctity of human rights overall – a critique made of other human rights organisations – but that CAGE themselves were sympathetic to and supportive of 'threatening' Islamic ideologies that were at odds with more progressive liberal values. The accusations were, like those of Andrew Gilligan who wrote in the *Telegraph*, that CAGE were 'part of a closely connected network of extremists relentlessly ... lying to young British Muslims that they are hated and persecuted by their fellow citizens in order to make them into supporters of terror'.[31] Like the individuals for whom they advocated, CAGE, too, were guilty by association, portrayed as terrorism suspects.

But the disdain of CAGE as a human rights organisation has not only come from the right. It has also been routinely voiced from the liberal/left end of the political spectrum, who have expressed the view that CAGE is a reactionary organisation operating in the vein of religious fundamentalism. The nature of this critique varies. There are those following a more traditional liberal line who argue that human rights are hard won, and engagement in war means there are exceptions to the application of human rights (a view also expressed by conservatives).[32] In contrast, those further on the left who adhere to the notion that the universality of human rights ought not to be compromised argue that adherence to extreme forms of religion should not be supported as a right when it compromises other liberal principles and rights.[33] Across these positions there remains a consensus that a Muslim rights organisation aligned with and rooted in Salafi Islam *by definition* contravenes universalist principles of human rights – not least in relation to issues of gender equality, a position which has formed the principle attack from these quarters.

This liberal/left critique is as much aimed at human rights organisations such as Amnesty International for campaigning alongside CAGE and/or in the name of terrorism suspects, for compromising what are presented as sacrosanct liberal principles and the project of global feminism. In 2010, in an exchange that has since become deeply scrutinised and prolifically debated, Gita Sahgal, head of the gender unit at the London base of Amnesty International, gave an interview to the *Sunday Times* in which she asserted that the human rights organisation was undermining its own record of championing women's rights by collaborating with CAGE. Specifically, her critique centred on Amnesty's association with CAGE's Moazzam Begg, whom she referred to as 'Britain's most famous supporter of the Taliban.' Sahgal's view was that Amnesty was 'risking its reputation' as defender of universal human rights by campaigning against torture alongside him, and that while she recognised it was worthwhile to hear his experiences of incarceration at Guantanamo Bay, 'it was absolutely wrong to legitimise him as a partner'.[34]

It is of note that classifying CAGE as an organisation whose agenda lay outside a truly inclusive and progressive human rights framework entailed simultaneously positing a revisionist account of liberal universalism, which supposed that liberal human rights have generally always been universally available, and were now suddenly at risk of being compromised. Max Farrar, for example, argued that in contrast to CAGE representatives, 'Liberty and Amnesty staffers stand full square for universal human rights and the values associated with those declarations and the relevant laws'.[35] In a similar vein, the writer Rahila Gupta suggested Amnesty had 'betrayed its own history' such that it would be a 'long time' before it recovered 'from this blow to its reputation'.[36] The historical amnesia here not only overlooked Amnesty's own periodic reluctance to fully recognise certain subjects, not least political prisoners such as Nelson Mandela, it also necessitated an uncritical acceptance of the sincerity of liberal institutional framings of international human rights.[37] The disavowal of CAGE as a legitimate rights organisation required a concurrent re-writing of the history of the liberal human rights framework, disregarding its conditionalities, namely the civilizationist notions that determined who might be considered sufficiently human.[38] In addition, what proceeds without acknowledgement in such a position is that it is precisely because of the limits inherent to liberal universalism that an organisation such as CAGE gains such popular appeal, and comes to perform a necessary and critical service, for Muslim subjects experiencing the sharp end of state violence.

This dismissal of CAGE's work by certain sections of the left has not been without its critics and there have been numerous defenders of the organisation, also on the left, who have pointed to the lack of empirical evidence supporting the range of allegations against them, highlighting the hypocrisy of some of the accusations. Tom Mills, Narzanin Massoumi and David Miller note that the prevailing criticisms of CAGE centre on the figure of Moazzam Begg and his political affiliations pre and post incarceration in US military detention sites as well as his endorsement of 'defensive jihad'.[39] Mills, Massoumi and Miller point out that none of the allegations against Begg involve physical violence, and that the right to defensive jihad, as the right to 'violent resistance to invasion or oppression', is aligned with human rights as set by international law, a point that was also made by the management of Amnesty International.[40] They note the double standards invoked in the vilification of Begg, arguing against some of the comparisons such attacks make between jihadi political movements and fascism, and against the kind of proscriptions placed on the thought and dialogue of Muslim political subjects which are never placed on the thought or expression of neo-con or left-wing revolutionaries. Critically, they draw attention to the left's commitment to a secularist politics that prohibits them from viewing CAGE as anything other than a culturalist organisation, thus undermining their human rights work.

Such a culturalist reading is, of course, not insignificant in a political context that declares multiculturalism dead and 'Muslim culture' as the antithesis of the 'liberal values' of equality and freedom. Indeed, it is in exactly such terms that the disdain of CAGE from the left has been framed, as when Max Farrar claims CAGE 'is not committed to human rights law but to Sharia Law'.[41] Similarly, when Nick Cohen expressed his disdain for Amnesty's actions, his critique was that Amnesty's 'managers must believe at some level that messianic religion is not a threat to the liberal values of feminism, anti-racism and freedom from tyranny they think they hold'. To Cohen they seemed oblivious to the fact that 'the Islamists they embrace aren't nice metrosexuals who support women's rights and want an end to bigotry'.[42]

But there is also an additional point to be made regarding the constraints of a debate about the credentials of a particular organisation, when it comes to form the central concern in a wider struggle that is ultimately aimed at seeking to challenge state violence. Whereas a positivist approach that emphasises the importance of evidence in ascertaining guilt or innocence is useful for gaining wider traction among policy and popular audiences, since it rests on determining the purity of the target under suspicion, its usefulness as a device for grappling with and addressing mechanisms of state violence is limited. If part of the defence of CAGE is to forefront how particular organisations become targets within the rubric of state violence against suspect communities, the point of debate ought to be less whether such an organisation represents or displays actions or behaviours of 'fundamentalism', and more the disciplinary actions that are legitimated and obscured within a frame that a priori constitutes such an organisation as exceptionally heinous.

The response across the spectrum of the liberal/left prompts us to ask whether it is ever possible for such a non-western, non-secularist organisation to be recognised by the human rights framework and its supporters as being aligned with their project of human rights. At the same time, as gender equality is used as the criteria by which calls for cultural recognition are dismissed, rallies against Islamophobia often neglect the particular gendered dimensions that inflect the racist assaults and disciplinary actions of the state. As the mainstream left/liberal position invokes gender rights disregarding the culturalist forms of racism it stokes, the critical left response highlighting the operation of Islamophobia does so in a frame that is negligent to the genuine issue of gender.[43] The commitment to gender and race (religious/cultural) equality play out in the debate between these two positions as if they only exist in binary opposition to each other. The consequence is to remove from the debate any meaningful attempt to deal with real intersections of race and gender through resistance.

Making Space for Feminism

> A feminism which fights simultaneously for a society free of slut-shaming and victim-blaming; as well as for a society wherein wearing the hijab or burka or any form of covering or religious covering by choice would not make you a target or marginal-ise you. A feminism which fights against rape being used as a weapon of war; but also fights for a world wherein we do not war. A feminism which fights against the sexualisation of female bodies but also for greater space for female sexuality. A feminism for all people, but a flexible and active feminism. A critical and radical feminism.
>
> The Brown Hijabi, 2015[44]

In a discussion of the increasing numbers of women drawn to the rhetoric of ISIS and travelling to Syria, Rafia Zakaria notes how ISIS play on the racism and alienation that young women in the West experience in their day-to-day lives. By present-ing their political project as a 'post-national', 'post-racial' and 'just' alternative to Western societies, ISIS market themselves as offering, even if misleadingly, a way out of the violence and alienation of patriarchal practices at home.[45] With this latest shift in focus of the War on Terror towards Syria, the state's appro-priation of feminism and its related representation of Muslim women's bodies has been reformulated. In the early years of the War on Terror, military intervention was largely framed as a civilising mission intent on saving brown women. The domi-nant discourse, and one that continues on some levels, was of submissive Muslim women oppressed by the barbarism of a pre-modern culture. As more women have joined ISIS, hegemonic discourses have veered towards representing their sexuality as a lethal weapon. The rhetoric of 'jihadi brides' invokes a different kind of race-gendered representation of Muslim women as oversexed and hypersexualised, with equal potential as Muslim men for being the purveyors of violence. This way of portraying a weaponised sexuality has had material consequences as women increasingly become the target of state violence. The number of women arrested for terrorism-related offences more than doubled in Britain between 2014 and 2015, and there are growing numbers of stories of women, suspected of supporting or engaging in terrorism-related activity in some form, having their children taken from them as part of pre-emptive policing strategies.[46] Mark Rowley, the Assistant Commissioner for Specialist Operations of the Metropolitan Police Service and chair of National Police Chiefs' Council Counter-Terrorism Coordination Committee, reported in 2016 how national security issues were increasingly being dealt with in family court and that between 2015 and 2016 care proceedings had been initiated for children of up to fifty families.[47] The call for anti-imperialist struggles to address the way in which state oppression operates through the intersections of race and gender within has become ever more pressing.

The complex and multifaceted way in which race and gender are invoked through state violence targeting Muslim women, however, has been relatively marginalised within the liberal secular feminist movement, where emphasis has instead been on a critique of religious extremism, referred to in terms of 'fundamentalism', for its infractions on gender rights. This position has been criticised by other sections of the left for its alignment with the anti-Muslim racism of the state.[48] The contention here is an overlap between the way in which feminists appropriate the concept of fundamentalism to disavow mobilisation around religious identity and the state's use of the term to dismiss political dissent among Muslim communities. Accordingly, one of the by-products of the War on Terror for cultural discourse in the West has been a revival of discussions debating gender versus multiculturalism.[49]

It is this debate which underpinned the fallout between Gita Sahgal and Amnesty International. Sahgal's public objection to Amnesty's partnership with CAGE via Moazzam Begg was made through an interview with *the Sunday Times*, a newspaper owned by Rupert Murdoch with a centre-right readership that had a month prior attempted to present CAGE as an extremist organisation associated with a failed plane bomber.[50] The interview appeared to serve a particular editorial line and was conducted by a journalist who claimed to specialise 'in exposing shortcomings, crime and corruption in the Muslim community', reporting frequently on the pathological tendencies of Muslims.[51] The particular Sunday Times article, as did the subsequent commentary across the media, established an association between Begg and other 'terrorism suspects' stating that he had 'championed the rights of jailed al-Qaeda members and hate preachers'. Sahgal was quoted as referring to Begg as 'Britain's most famous supporter of the Taliban', and someone she later said, while sitting next to him in a BBC radio studio, she felt 'profoundly unsafe' talking to.[52]

Putting aside the gratuitousness of her description, the pertinent point raised by Sahgal and expressed from other quarters of the left, alludes not only to negotiating positions of difference within political struggle, but the way in which a struggle against injustice in one domain could overlook, and thus disavow, other forms of oppression sometimes worsened as a result. This media storm, though focused on individuals, is significant for the way in which it exemplifies a set of positions prolifically debated in relation to the question of gender, race and imperialism.[53] Sahgal's critique was not simply an expression of a personal political perspective but representative of a broader liberal secularist feminist critique, which has been articulated fervently by organisations such as Women Against Fundamentalism.

Formed in the late 1980s in response to religious protests of the publication of Salman Rushdie's *Satanic Verses*, the organisation was part of a movement challenging conservative patriarchal elements of religious communities, not least for the way in which such elements hinder gender equality.

In the tradition of international resistance politics, which aim to connect the local with the global, WAF's critique aims to challenge both the fundamentalist factions of anti-imperialist movements – pointing out that to resist the violence of state power is not necessarily to offer a progressive alternative – and to challenge how fundamentalism presents itself via domestic anti-racist movements, thus obstructing women's equality at the local level. Yet even as this position has made important contributions to the politics of resistance struggles, it has nevertheless proved susceptible to performing some of the behaviours that it has vehemently criticised. There are two particular ways in which this is most pertinent. First, in relation to the question of solidarity in struggle, and second, in relation to the question of cultural essentialism. I unpack each of these in turn.

Feminist objection to the coalition between a liberal human rights organisation and a human rights organisation aligned with political Islam in many senses stems from a broader, well-established feminist critique. Namely, such an objection is rooted in opposition to constructions of false universalisms within resistance movements, a construction which assumes that experiences of exclusion and oppression across multiple contrasting subject positions can be equated.[54] Expounded particularly by Third World feminists, this is a political analysis developed in response to reductive framings proffered by Western feminists and male-centred anti-racist movements which gloss over, fix and/or homogenise the experiences of women of colour so that either global class distinctions go unacknowledged and/or the full complexity of intersecting forms of power manifested through the multiple domains of religion, race, gender, class and caste are erased. Intersectional feminists counter this, arguing that the framing of movement struggles requires the recognition and acknowledgement of difference, including the power differentials that are inevitably manifested in coalitions.[55] In this regard, we might read Sahgal's objection as a valid question pertaining to the position of gender rights within the struggle against imperialist violence, as a question concerning the ethics of who we choose to stand with in mobilising against injustice, and what our choice of alliances means for the gains and set-backs along the way.

The problem with this deliberation around what form solidarity might take is that the question is channelled in one direction only, so that the principal concern is the appropriateness of alliances with 'fundamentalist' factions. Yet in publicly disavowing Islamic-rights organisations that are also being targeted by the state, the same kinds of questions are not posed as to how alliances are then made by default with state powers. Is it legitimate for the fight for gender equality to assist, even if inadvertently, with the justification of state violence against suspect individuals and communities? And how does a struggle against 'fundamentalism', conceived of in this way, affect the gendered positions of women within suspect communities? Without sufficient consideration of these questions too, what begins as a valid engagement with the politics of gender within anti-racist and anti-imperialist movements loses credibility.

A second point of inconsistency pertains to a now well-rehearsed critique of multiculturalism. In line with more progressive approaches to thinking about anti-racist politics, the issue of concern raised by feminist movements attempting to address fundamentalism is the operation of essentialist notions of culture that are sometimes appropriated by pro-multiculturalist and anti-racist lobbies.[56] The allocation of government resources for 'multicultural' projects has helped to cement fixed and often reductive identities that inhibit recognition of complex, and thus 'fully human', subjects, instead reifying notions that certain cultural behaviours and tendencies belong to particular ethnic and racial groups. In the 1980s and '90s, these state-managed approaches to multiculturalism surfaced to, at times, pacify anti-racist struggles and move attention away from the material problems of racism and injustice. The uncritical acceptance of cultural stereotypes by certain factions of the left and within minority communities undermines any engagement with fundamental issues such as patriarchy within communities.[57] Cultural authenticity gets played out in such a way as to side-line gender issues. The key argument advocated by feminists resisting fundamentalism is that conservative religious leaders are often identified by the state as the leaders of minority communities, determining the parameters of what constitutes cultural tradition, disallowing for the heterogeneity within those communities and modes of resistance by them against hegemonic conservative proscriptions. The assertion put forward by feminists against fundamentalism is that 'women's demands for freedom and equality are seen as being outside "cultural traditions" ... and therefore not legitimate'.[58] An open-minded reading of such an argument might note that their point is to caution against the limits of identity politics.

There is much to be said for the ways in which the project of state multiculturalism has worked to pacify resistance against state racism by buttressing patriarchal practices at the community level. But in pointing to the negative consequences of cultural essentialism, particularly in terms of the impact on funding for women's organisations and services, the narrative constructed around religion within minority communities often invokes the same kind of essentialism that the protagonists lobby against. Nira Yuval-Davis notes how multiculturalist programmes provided an increase in funding for religious schools and a simultaneous decrease in funding for women's services, such as refuges, arguing that religious school systems also usually equate to pressure for children to attend single-sex schools, especially for girls.[59] Against feminist arguments which have shown the benefits of single-sex schools for girls' education in the mainstream public and private systems, Yuval-Davis' view here is that in religious schooling the same assumptions of a 'structure and curriculum similar to those of a mixed school' do not apply because their 'purpose is clearly to bring up girls to be dutiful wives and mothers'.[60] Problematically, this kind of assertion is premised on the same sorts of racial/religious stereotypes of Muslim communities that are in continuous circulation, particularly as they relate to depictions of Muslim women as pathologically submissive and without agency, in need of rescue. Since her claim is, indeed, contradicted by statistics that show some Muslim girls schools rank among the highest achieving in the country, its credibility is called into doubt while the question of how to struggle against the intricate relationship of race and gender oppression remains insufficiently addressed.[61] This type of secularist anti-racist feminist politics fails to speak to the gendered forms of oppression experienced by Muslim women through the interplay among race, religion, gender and imperialism in contemporary global politics.

As the increasingly harrowing climate of state-sanctioned Islamophobia serves to diminish space available for addressing gender oppression and dilute complex questions of gender equality, a point noted by a number of feminist scholars, the intersections of race, gender and imperialism remain the very issues of concern for young feminist activists trying to figure out what a radical feminism in this context might look like.[62] Some of the particular concerns they raise draw attention to the ways in which the War on Terror has inflicted insidious violence in the most intimate familial spaces. Expressions of political difference are relegated to symptoms of family dysfunction and a failure of parenting, in which, as Gargi Bhattacharyya observes, the 'status of women and attitudes toward sexuality play a central role in the narrative'.[63] The targeted policing of Muslim women involves the scrutiny of motherhood, a strategy that has long been in use against suspect communities, as well as calls on mothers (and wives, sisters and sometimes daughters) to perform duties of surveillance within their families and communities and report signs of extremism and radicalisation, to play their role in counterterrorism policing.[64] Such a practice is a critical element of the tapestry of state violence and illuminates the intricacies of criminalisation which manipulate affective relations as tools of enforcement and simultaneously demonise Muslim women through their relations with Muslim men.[65] The radical feminism best equipped to address this complexity is one as Suhaiymah Manzoor-Khan notes, required to 'fight on all fronts', and 'sometimes fight for seemingly opposite things because different people are oppressed in different ways'.[66]

And You'll Never Walk Alone ...

In April 2016, twenty-seven years after the event, Justice for Hillsborough campaigners spoke at an arts and activism festival in London, rejoicing in the victory that had finally come when an inquest verdict one month earlier ruled that the ninety-six people who had died at the Hillsborough football stadium during a match in 1989 were unlawfully killed. Movingly narrating the unrelenting and far-reaching nature of state violence, Sheila Coleman and Becky Shah, two of the campaigners, spoke of the contempt with which Liverpool football fans had been treated, the victim-blaming that had followed, the multiple police and institutional cover-ups that had prevented an honest set of accounts from being publicly reported, and the complicity of the most powerful media outlets in perpetuating discourses that pathologised the Liverpudlian working class.[67] Becky Shah told the audience about the striking similarities in the methods of state violence in the policing tactics and police personnel used at Hillsborough with those used against the miners' strikes of the early 1980s, in Northern Ireland, and against individuals who had died in police custody.

The forum for the talk was *DIY Cultures*, an arts-based resistance festival that had been organised by Hamja Ahsan, who had led the Free Talha Ahsan campaign for his brother. It was one of a number of events and protest meetings that Hamja had organised where the injustices of counterterrorism policing were platformed alongside other campaigns against police and state violence. In this sense, the fight for Talha's freedom took a visionary approach towards what it meant to struggle against injustice. Reclaiming the humanity of Talha Ahsan also meant fighting against multiple forms of state oppression, a powerful rejoinder to the divide-and-rule strategies of the state.

At other meetings, the Free Talha Ahsan campaign has spoken alongside campaigners such as Janet Alder, who has fought to raise awareness of deaths in police custody, starting with calls for police accountability following the death of her brother Christopher Alder, one such victim. The Free Talha Ahsan campaign has also joined the Institute for Race Relations in campaigns drawing on the histories of anti-racist struggle in Britain and centring police brutality against black and Asian communities. Commitment to anti-racist justice activism allowed Hamja to establish transatlantic connections, building solidarity with US-based campaigns against unjust imprisonment, the use of solitary confinement and prison abolition. Prompted by the 30,000-prisoner hunger strike in California in 2013, Hamja founded a London chapter of the Stop Isolation campaign.[68] Recognising that the persecution of Muslims in the War on Terror bridged the histories of racism and of imperialism, the Free Talha campaign also connected their struggle with those of Irish resistance fighters who had felt the full weight of earlier counterterrorism legislation and policing, and meetings were held with Gerry Conlon, one of the Guildford Four wrongfully imprisoned in 1974 for an IRA bombing and whose conviction was overturned fifteen years later. The Free Talha Ahsan campaign worked with human rights organisations such as Liberty, and in the US, the Centre for Constitutional Rights in New York, No Separate Justice, Solitary Watch, the Black Panthers, Robert King, and Ojore Lutalo, influenced by the Black Liberation Army.

The holistic, systemic continuities between oppressions and forms state of violence are brought into sharp focus through the human rights lawyers and activists whose work has involved advocating on behalf of a number of these different struggles. The barrister Pete Wetherby, who fought for the Justice for Hillsborough campaign also lobbied against the extradition of Talha Ahsan; the solicitor Gareth Peirce, who represented many of the Muslim men extradited to the US, was known for her expertise in human rights and hitting back against counterterrorism because of her advocacy on behalf of many accused and wrongly convicted of Irish Republican Army-related activity. The intersections between forms of injustice are quite clearly apparent to those marked as suspect communities, too. It is perhaps by building upon such interconnected, analytical campaigns of resistance that future struggles for justice depend.

Conclusion

This Be the Answer

Because if you need me to prove my humanity,
I'm not the one that's not human
Suhaiymah Manzoor-Khan, 2017[1]

We teach life, sir.
Rafeef Ziadah, 2015[2]

In the run up to the June 2017 national election, the *Daily Mail* published another of many articles aimed at discrediting the leader of the Labour Party, Jeremy Corbyn, this time by drawing attention to his support for Babar Ahmad and Talha Ahsan in the weeks before their extradition.[3] The article quoted Corbyn in an interview on the Islam Channel, where he connected the tradition of civil rights struggles in the US with the campaigns for justice for Babar and Talha, 'The great tradition of civil liberties campaigning in the USA particularly by the black community, I hope they are going to get behind Babar and Talha and say, "Hang on, these guys haven't done anything wrong."' For the *Daily Mail*, this statement reaffirmed yet again Jeremy Corbyn's extremist tendencies.

A week earlier, in the aftermath of the bombing of Manchester Arena at the end of an Ariana Grande concert, the local newspaper, *Manchester Evening News*, contextualised the incident by reminding readers that the last time Manchester had faced a terrorism-related national security incident was when Abid Naseer had been arrested on suspicion of plotting an attack on the Trafford Centre.[4] While the city grieved for the twenty-two people who had been tragically killed, counterterrorism police carried out multiple raids across the city over the subsequent weeks. In some of the arrests that followed, individuals who had been identified as suspicious were confronted with tear gas and controlled explosions to blow off their front doors. Some weeks later it was quietly reported that all twenty-two people who had been arrested in these operations were released without charge.[5]

Both newspaper articles exemplified the rhetorical force that terrorism cases such as those I have discussed in this book continue to hold. The policing response to the Manchester Arena bombing and later in London in the aftermath of another attack on London Bridge were more demonstrations of the ongoing trend of policing to produce culprits.[6] Strengthening the security apparatus, not least through the passage of more counterterrorism legislation, would provide the necessary additional power for those in authority to preserve the wellbeing of the nation.[7] The full spectacle of arrest and capture that immediately followed the two attacks, however, alluded to something more complex. SAS-style counterterrorism officers clad in grey Kevlar body armour and furnished with a range of weapons – sniper rifles, automatic assault rifles, handguns, submachine guns and tasers – supported by further backup from the military were indications of the macho, penetrating authoritarianism inherent in the level of power the state had already awarded itself. Even as Theresa May declared 'enough was enough' in a bid to marshal renewed vigour for tackling terror, the general public sense of the anti-extremism drive she laid out was all rather familiar and all rather fatigued.[8] Yet beyond the rhetoric and the spin, beyond the momentary spectacles of arrests, the fuel was gathered for sustaining an intensified authoritarianism that has become the defining feature of the advancing War on Terror.

The key ingredients for this recipe – race, criminalisation, and securitisation – are the fundamental substance of this book. The purpose has been to illustrate the continuation and reconfiguration of colonial disciplinary techniques, as well as their growing institutionalisation within the British security state. At its most extreme, the enhancement of securitisation has expanded state capabilities for expulsion of individuals who were already on the margins. The development and expansion of prisons has been supplemented with escalating use of deportation and of legislative powers to deny citizenship and deprive it from those who have it. It is the employment, adaptation and augmentation of legal, judicial and policing apparatus in the realisation of these processes which I have endeavoured to illuminate. The War on Terror has, in essence, cultivated the use of authoritarian practices in the West that have been well documented in use in sites of colonial and imperial occupation, now inflected with new technologies of imprisonment and drone warfare.

While the stark reality of expulsion in each of the cases I have presented is noteworthy for showcasing the full intensity of state power, it is the securitising conditions, the processes, logics and rationalisations that underpin the possibility of expulsion which have much wider resonance and a more enduring impact. That is, these individual expulsions are part of the wider production, legitimation and maintenance of authoritarianism.

In many ways, the form and detail of securitisation that the terrorism cases in this book have exposed reflect the law and order state 'several stages further on' from the 'more-than-routine use of the repressive legal instruments of the state' that Stuart Hall and his colleagues identified in its initial stages in the 1970s.[9] Their assertion then was that this was 'something approaching the progressive corruption of the legal apparatus in the interests of political necessity, and the steady erosion of civil liberties'.[10] As this trend has progressed, the privileged claims to liberal democracy that has been Europe's defining feature, and its mark of contrast and separation from post/colonial states, have been weakened and made messier and more complex. The spatial dislocation between European liberalism and colonial authoritarianism has fissured.

The intensification of securitisation in response to the production of racially dehumanised subjects has exposed the authoritarian elements of the state – an authoritarianism that continues to be intensified.

In the Anglo-American imagination, the abuses of authoritarianism are typically associated with the histories of the other Europe – Francoist Spain, De Gaullian France and most vividly Nazi Germany. With the defeat of the latter in the Second World War, the triumph of liberalism over fascism fostered the notion that the moral superiority of liberalism, with its commitment to benevolent universalism, had been vindicated. Liberalism had seen to the victorious overthrow of Europe's dictatorial regimes, and the principles of democracy, sovereignty and equality had conquered totalitarian excess. Critiques of this insincere distinction point to the false dichotomy that hid the continuities between the liberal and authoritarian regimes of rule.[11] Arguing against this disconnect, the critical interventions of figures such as Aimé Césaire and the early work of Hannah Arendt illustrated the cultivation of Nazism in Europe's colonies of Africa and Asia, contradicting claims of the relative morality of liberalism.[12] The key problem of Hitler's Germany, Césaire noted, was that 'he applied to Europe colonialist procedures which until then had been reserved exclusively for the Arabs of Algeria, the "coolies" of India, and the "niggers" of Africa'.[13] The techniques of social exclusion, segregation, demonisation, marginalisation and annihilation that were administered under the legal and policy provisions of Nazi rule were all quite familiar within the political context of European colonies. As Barnor Hesse and Salman Sayyid succinctly note, 'In many ways what was radical about fascism was not its precise meaning, but its dislocation of the Europe/Empire divide: fascism was colonialism re-applied to Europe'.[14]

The significance of the War on Terror is that it has elaborated on this relationship, acting as a legitimating ideological force for extending and normalising totalitarianism and in so doing exposing the reliance of liberalism on its own authoritarian facets. In the early years of the War on Terror, Angela Y. Davis remarked on signs of 'an impending fascist policies and practice', the early indications of which were shown in the 'torture neglect and depravity meted out to people in Guantanamo' and the broader erosion of civil liberties and democratic rights through legislation.[15] The expansion of counterterrorism legislation in Britain served the same purpose, which have since become an almost normalised feature of government.

Race and bureaucracy, two of the elements Hannah Arendt identified as integral to the development of authoritarian imperialism, continue to be central components of its contemporary expression.[16] The creation and pursuit of exceptional spaces – whether sites of colonial occupation, slave plantations, prisons in all their variations, or concentration camps – are spaces where disciplinary technologies of surveillance and control have been tried, tested and developed.[17] The justifications for such spaces and the technologies used within them have been characterised by racial delineation of targeted populations that degrades or outcasts those marked in some form or another, whether attributing to such groups a lack of civilisation, a status of non-belonging or a tendency to criminality.[18] As the security state has grown and developed to meet the needs of the advancing global neoliberal political economy, the intricate connections between race and securitisation have continued to evolve alongside. The turn towards, and expansion of, law and order as a system for governing society has been a deeply racialised project in which the impact of the growth of the security arms of the state has been disproportionately felt, and resisted, by racially marginalised communities.[19]

The manipulation and appropriation of the law to enhance, sustain and legitimate state power is a key component of the realisation of authoritarianism, and the cases I have focused on here have been riddled with examples of it in action. It is not so much that the law is suspended but that the separation between the judicial and executive arms of the state is progressively eroded. Judicial institutions and arrangements, which are in principle independent of the executive, are adapted and reshaped to accommodate growing executive power. Administration and bureaucracy proceed as the way forward.

The cases I have discussed throughout the book have illuminated multiple particular expressions of authoritarianism in the current moment. The racialised system of overt and covert surveillance that has been expanded in the name of counter-terrorism policing is one of this authoritarianism's principle elements. The increased criminalisation that has come with enhanced securitisation is characterised by its emphasis on pre-emptive policing, so that it has become legitimate for people to be guilty of 'crimes' they are yet to commit. Such systems of policing based on suspicion, vague intelligence and racial profiling entail a move away from open, evidence-based and independent criminal justice systems, and a move towards increasing use of administrative systems that operate without juries and are designed to be sympathetic to state interests. The growing use of secret courts and secret evidence remains racially marked by their disproportionate application in allegations of criminalised activities which are themselves racialised – terrorism, immigration and gang and drug-related cases – and so illustrate the expansive institutionalisation of racial states of exception. Whereas secret courts represent the harsher end of this practice, the institutionalisation of mass surveillance through the Prevent programme has normalised a system of bureaucratic, clandestine policing, performed not only by the police but by the public and professionals, that is, by society as a whole.

The extension of powers that enable the state to more freely deprive citizenship illuminates starkly the growth of executive power. The entire procedure for deprivation of citizenship is initiated by and centred around decisions made by the secretary of state and reliant on information offered by the intelligence services, and the specific reasons for any verdict are typically not divulged to those receiving the deprivation order. The suggestion that this process reflects a return to medieval practices of banishment is insufficiently attentive to the colonial continuities

I am suggesting are at play here, though the observation does reflect the explicit, unforgiving and totalising nature of the act.[20] The reliance on executive power to administer various processes for deprivation and deformation of citizenship – processes which range from exclusion orders to passport removals – obscure them from scrutiny and interrogation. Again, their selective application to racially marginalised sections of the population proceeds in line with features of fascist/colonialist rule.

The despotic decision-making procedure for deprivation of citizenship has filtered into the bureaucratic administrative systems for citizenship applications, too. The process for deciding who ought and ought not be granted citizenship is a closed one, in which the full criteria against which decisions are made are not disclosed publicly and the guidance listing criteria by which applicants are judged is not exhaustive, so the decision maker has discretion to decide beyond the set criteria.[21]

Finally, calls by government and sections of the (mostly right-wing) media to withdraw from the European Convention on Human Rights reflects the ultimate retreat from supra-national judicial oversight of government action. The ambivalent role of the ECHR in relation to terrorism cases notwithstanding, the desire by certain sections of the British state to move away from external judicial oversight is part of the same logic underpinning the expansion of secret justice. Namely, it reflects a realignment of judicial procedures in favour of state protection. In the same way that secret courts and secret evidence protect the government from public revelations that it has been complicit in practices that contravene standard democratic principles, such as involvement in torture and clandestine detentions, part of the desire to circumvent the ECHR is to impede judicial checks that constrain and admonish the state for its disciplinary excess. The push for increasing state protection through a retreat from international assessment is not so much because the state itself is under threat but more to guard against the fracturing of the illusion of sacrosanct democracy as practice. The retreat from the constraints of judicial oversight allow for the increasing reliance on authoritarian practice to remain in the shadows.

The use of no-jury secret courts with secret evidence, banishment orders made by executive decision, the implementation
of covert surveillance systems targeting suspect communities,
the retraction of rights of appeal against judicial and executive
decisions all reflect elements of despotic government that liberal
thinkers such as John Stuart Mill identified as a 'legitimate
mode of government' for 'dealing with Barbarians'.[22] Thus, the
authoritarian elements inherent to liberalism are exposed.[23]

Against this, Theresa May's call for greater securitisation in
the summer of 2017 following the attacks in Manchester and
London did not, notably, hold the same populist appeal that it
has typically had. The cultural counterweight of the response
after the Manchester bombing in the form of blood donations,
food donations, free taxi rides, hit-backs against attempted
incursions of the English Defence League, vocal public support
for civil liberties and *universal* human rights and calls for
less austerity and more equality, were all signs of hope. Signs,
perhaps, of future changes to come.

And So We March ...

The systems of dehumanisation that are both relied upon and
produced through authoritarianisms, even as they are over-
whelmingly stifling, are never totalising. During the Free Talha
Ahsan campaign meetings, readings of Talha's poetry, himself
an acclaimed poet, not only penetrated the political space with
cultural expression – and, indeed, exemplified the importance
of the cultural form for the political movement – they brought
Talha's voice into meetings in which he could not be physically
present. They brought his thoughts to the discussions, debates,
strategising and organising for justice. 'This Be the Answer', was
Talha's poetic response to the police officers who had yelled
at Babar Ahmad during his arrest, asking 'Where is your God
now?'. His reply to their question framed many of the campaign's meetings:

A Prisoner on his knees
scrubs around a toilet bowl
and the bristles of the brush
scuttle to and fro
as a guard swaggers over
to yell rather than ask

Where is your God now?

And the prisoner still on his knees
his brush still cleaning answers:

He is with me now, gov.

My God is with me now
hearing and seeing,
whilst your superiors
when they see you, do not look at you
and when they hear you, do not listen to you.[24]

The incessant dehumanising in the form of a question, perhaps one of the most mundane features of twenty-first-century state extremism, is nonetheless one that activists resist. Rafeef Ziadah, a Palestinian activist and poet, eloquently illustrates the unfaltering resistance against just this tactic when she corrects a journalist's pathologising question, 'Why do Palestinians teach their children to hate?' with her poem 'We Teach Life, Sir'.[25] Suhaiymah Manzoor-Khan, a blogger and activist, too, movingly uses poetry, reminding the world to see Muslim humanity not when they see traits of relatability or likeability, but when they do not, in a plea for rehumanisation against the limited frames that recognise only the normative human being.[26] The shrewd observations of both poets show the spectre of dehumanisation as something produced through the gaze of the dehumaniser. It is not a status that exists a priori; it is a status that is made. The resistance of their poetry is its power for recuperating the humanity of Muslims, Palestinians, oppressed peoples.

An expression of other truths, poetry offers currency to those whose ability to speak out in dissent is otherwise constrained, those who, as Arundhati Roy notes, are not voiceless but 'deliberately silenced or purposely unheard'.[27] But more than this, the power of poetry comes through its ability to serve justice when justice is denied in the formal institutional spheres where it is conventionally sought. Poetry, as the cultural counterpart of political organising, provides an antidote to the authoritarian tenets of the state.

My own involvement in these campaigns was really the germinating ground for initiating the research that resulted in this book. When Babar's case first came to my attention, I was haunted by the police brutality that had marked his body. Images of scars, bruising and bleeding on his face, arms, shoulders, back, wrists and feet circulated by his campaign portrayed the aesthetic of state violence. They tallied with the stories, too often repeated and long fought against, of violence and deaths in police custody. Of detention without charge, of immigration incarceration, of surveillance, harassment, of stops and search. These stories have been the key focal points of anti-racist struggles. They are reminders of the persistence of the sharp end of state racism, the recognition of which is habitually side-lined in favour of more acceptable popular debates on race that choose instead to address the merits and material realities of the multicultural without regard for the structural. These stories are reminders that racism has not been reduced to a fraction of what it once was; institutional racism in and beyond the police is still alive and well. The images of assault on Babar Ahmad's body took us back. We were returned to the 1970s. We were returned to the colony. We were returned.

But to speak in terms of a return is naive, not quite right. State violence perpetually floats in the background. It was growing. It was hardening. It was protected by the illusion of equality. It was different.

State violence depended again on criminalised bodies, racialised criminalised bodies. It produced these bodies and disciplined them. In this disciplining we were (re)learning that the struggle for full rights and recognition had not yet been won. Not only this, but that the goal posts were moving further away. Citizenship did not guarantee rights to a fair trial. It did not guarantee due process. It was itself not guaranteed. It had to be earned by brown and black subjects, continuously. In an instant, it could now be taken away.

But the implication of these terrorism cases, the perpetration of state racism through the criminalisation of and violence against brown and black people, now marked as terrorism suspects, has not always been easy to convince others of. The familiar and recognisably grotesque tropes of state racism remain the spark incidents for protest and mobilisation. The Home Office sponsored 'Go Home' immigration vans, vehicles bearing the slogan 'Go home or face arrest' driven round neighbourhoods with high ethnic minority populations to demonstrate the government's tough stance on immigration, and a mimicry of the racial slurs of the 1960s, '70s and '80s, being one such example. These moments of mass protest are important, but mobilisation against counterterrorism is less forthcoming, harder to gain support for. The backlash and accusations against Malia Bouattia during her year as the first black female Muslim NUS President is perhaps the most high-profile exemplar of a broader indifference to the demonisation, vilification and dehumanisation of Muslims in recent times.[28] Charges of antisemitism, and labels of 'terrorist sympathiser' were some of the responses to her championing the Students Not Suspects campaign and mobilising against Prevent.

Anti-imperialist campaigners protest and present critiques and strong objections to reactionary insurgent movements, including those that have erupted across the Muslim world. They understand that a comprehensive analysis of these movements requires a criticism of the state violence, enshrined in racism, that helps to breed and sustain them.

And so the campaign for justice for Babar Ahmad and the campaign for justice for Talha Ahsan were, for me, broad anti-racist campaigns, part of the tradition of anti-racist and anti-imperialist struggles that have been led by postcolonials in Britain, which in its peak periods of history have been formidable. Many of the meetings I spoke at, organised by Hamja Ahsan, were part of this tradition.

My small contribution to these struggles, and my offering here, was to take up paper and pen, to draw on the library and other scholarly resources to which I had access, in order to retell stories that tend not to be told and are known only to those who already know. My aim was to try and offer some of the complexity that human stories have, but also to make connections between the micro and the macro, between the individual and the general. I wanted to write against the binary of 'innocence versus guilty', but felt compelled equally to acknowledge injustice when it was apparent.

Paper and pen were used to write to prisoners, too. It was one of the ways in which my activist work informed my intellectual work. I learned much from their responses: I learned of the intricacies of the daily regimes of prison life, of the despair that carceral conditions impose, of the hope and humour that prisoners retain, of their sharp insight in articulating oppression and of their vanguard position in shaping resistance. I learned much more than I offered.

What I gathered from all of these sources of knowledge, I have tried to bring together and make sense of here. For all the shortcomings, oversights, misunderstandings and miscalculations that may well be features of my own sense-making, I have been driven in this project by that which drives many 'scholar activists', succinctly articulated by Sivanandan: 'The function of knowledge is to liberate, to apprehend reality in order to change it'.[29]

Acknowledgements

In the introduction to *Policing the Crisis* Stuart Hall and colleagues humbly note that the book had been 'longer in preparation than its ultimate quality deserves'. They explain this is partly 'because it was written while other things – working, teaching, research – had to be done' but also 'because the book has been researched, written, argued over, revised, edited and *lived* with as a piece of collective work'. Though I cannot lay claims to joint authorship in the same way or to the foresight of that iconic book, the observation is one I identify with. This book, a long time in writing, has been lived. Its central contentions continuously debated, contested, rethought and revised. With it, my own intellectual and political insights have grown, altered and deepened in ways I hadn't anticipated when I began. It was a journey travelled with a collective without which there would be no book and to whom I am indebted.

First and foremost, I am thankful to all those political prisoners and their families who were willing to speak with me in some way or another despite the constraining circumstances which often inhibited what could be said. I am particularly grateful to Babar Ahmad for the knowledge and insight he imparted while in prison and when he returned, and to Talha Ahsan whose perceptive understanding of events and poetic flair significantly enhanced parts of the book.

Equally, to the human rights lawyers, activists and advocates who were interviewed both during 'official meetings' and in ongoing conversations, taking time from their busy schedules to impart the wisdom that comes from the day to day graft they do. I have learned much from them. There are multiple people connected to this world who both provided access to 'interviewees', and enhanced my knowledge and stimulated my thinking. I am especially thankful to Hamja Ahsan, Muhammad Rabbani, Arnaud Mafille, Arzu Merali, Amanda Weston, Simon Cox, Khadija Naeem and Ian Patel. Stateside, Arun Kundnani, Jeanne Theoharis and Aviva Stahl facilitated introductions with activists and scholars in the US and also offered hospitality, warmth, solidarity, and thought-provoking conversation.

The intellectual space to begin thinking through this work came during a fellowship in 2012–13 with the Center for Race and Gender in the Social Sciences at Duke University. I am thankful to Kerry Haynie, in particular, for the opportunity and for the friendship and support he offered throughout. There, thanks to Frances Hasso and Duke Islamic Studies Center, I presented some of this work in its earliest stages and was overwhelmed by the perceptive comments of Frances, Sally Deutsch, Charlie Kurzman, Laurie McIntosh, Aarthe Vadde, Jeanette Jouili and Eduardo Bonilla-Silva, who took the time to engage.

Later, funding came in 2015 from the Economic and Social Research Council through a Future Research Leaders Award, which enabled me to expand the *Deport, Deprive, Extradite* project and pursue other mechanisms of expulsion and marginalisation further. Thanks to Gurminder Bhambra and Vron Ware who supported the project from the outset; the advisory board for the project – Arun Kundnani, Amanda Weston, Ian Law, Simon Cox, Vron Ware, Asim Qureshi and Paul Wiles – who have given their time as and when needed; and most of all, thanks to Kasia Narkowicz, who has worked with me for the second part of the project, allowing the research to continue and progress, offering endless support throughout.

Acknowledgements

I have been fortunate to have many intellectual interlocutors who have helped me articulate and clarify ideas, challenged my thinking, and read proposals and drafts. Thanks to David Theo Goldberg, who supported my work from its infancy when others were less open-minded, and to Vijay Prashad, who helped clarify some of the problems and articulate solutions. For invitations to present some of this work in its earlier stages, thanks to David Miller, Narzanin Massoumi and Tom Mills, to Gargi Bhattacharyya and Aaron Winter at UEL, to Say Burgin in Leeds, to Therese O'Toole in Bristol, and to Kalpana Wilson and Nadine El-Enany at Birkbeck. To friends who are always thinking with me, thanks to Necla Acik-Toprak, Christian Klesse, Joanna Gilmore and Waqas Tufail. Special thanks to Vallu, who carefully read through drafts and whose brilliance comes with a listening ear and sturdy shoulder, and to Virinder Kalra, whose belief, support and patience has sustained.

Much gratitude to all at Verso for helping me bring this book into the world. Particular thanks to Duncan Ranslem for overseeing the production, Angelica Sgouros whose impeccable copy editing was second to none, and most of all, to my editor Rosie Warren, who has never faltered in her enthusiasm for the project and whose support, patience, feedback and encouragement helped me write a better manuscript.

Sitting in the background against all this is my formidable and forever-loving family. To my parents, Sushela Kapoor and Surinder Kumar Kapoor, the most generous, kind and nurturing, to Shefali, my best friend, to my brother, cousins and wider clan, and mostly to my nanee, Santosh Ohri, our rock, foundation, and comfort blanket through all weather. This book is dedicated to her.

Notes

Introduction

1 Talha Ahsan, *This Be the Answer: Poems from Prison*, Edinburgh: Radio Ramadan Edinburgh, 2011.
2 *Lotfi Raissi v Secretary of State for the Home Department* [2008] EWCA Civ 72 (CA(Civ Div)).
3 Gordon Rayner and David Williams, 'Terror Instructor: Algerian Living in Britain Accused of Teaching Hijackers to Fly', *Daily Mail*, 29 September 2001.
4 Ibid.
5 Andy Gardner and Shekhar Bhatia, 'America at War: Britain's Escape', *Sunday Mirror*, 23 September 2001, 4–5; Daniel McGrory and Dominic Kennedy, 'Dozens of terrorists on run in Britain', *Times*, 28 September 2001.
6 Richard Alleyne, John Steele and Sarah Womack, 'Pilot 'taught four of US hijackers'. Algerian fights to stay in Britain', *Daily Telegraph*, 29 September 2001, p.1.
7 *Bary and Ors v Secretary of State for Justice and Anor* [2010] EWHC 587 (HC(Admin)).
8 *Lotfi Raissi v Secretary of State for the Home Department* [2008], EWCA Civ 72 (CA(Civ Div)) para. 144.
9 Ibid., para. 48.
10 David B. Ottaway and Joe Stephens, 'In Case of Algerian Pilot, Much Uncertainty; Officials Back Away from Early Assertions that Raissi Trained Four September 11 Hijackers', *Washington Post*, 18 December 2001, A14.
11 Al-Fawwaz [2001] UKHL 69, 17 December 2001.

12 Victoria Brittain, 'Egypt Puts British Justice to Shame', *Guardian*, 20 April 2011.

13 *Lotfi Raissi v Secretary of State for the Home Department* [2008] EWCA Civ 72 (CA(Civ Div)), s144; Al-Fawwaz [2001] UKHL 69. Seven years after Lotfi's acquittal he was exonerated by a British court of appeal when he successfully challenged the British Home Office (if not the FBI). The judges acknowledged that the extradition proceedings had been used as a means of keeping Lotfi in custody while inquiries were pursued in the US, and decided that the manner in which extradition proceedings had been effected, including the denial of bail based on allegations which were unfounded in evidence, had amounted to an abuse of process. Lotfi was awarded £2 million in compensation. The US upholds an international warrant for his arrest.

14 Benjamin Weiser, 'Egyptian Gets 25-Year Term in 1998 Embassy Bombings; Judge Calls Plea Deal Generous', *New York Times*, 6 February 2015. Khalid al-Fawwaz was sentenced to life.

15 Sean O'Neil, '"I Am a Victim of My Nationality and My Religion. I Am a Victim of September 11": Lotfi Raissi, Accused of Training the New York Hijackers, Tells of His Nightmare in Prison', *Daily Telegraph*, 15 February 2002, 13.

16 David Blunkett, House of Commons Debate, 15 October 2001, vol 372, c924.

17 Stuart Hall, *Race, the Floating Signifier. Transcript*, Northampton, MA: Media Education Foundation; Hannah Arendt, *Origins of Totalitarianism*, London: Harcourt, 1968.

18 Saskia Sassen, *Expulsions: Brutality and Complexity in the Global Economy*, Cambridge, MA: The Belknap Press of Harvard University Press, 2014.

19 Grahame Allen and Chris Watson, 'UK Prison Population Statistics', *House of Commons Library Briefing Paper SN/SG/ 04334*, 20 April 2017. The total prison population for the UK at the beginning of 2017 is estimated at around 95,000 people.

20 Ibid., 13–14.

21 Matthew J. Gibney, 'Asylum and the Expansion of Deportation in the UK', *Government and Opposition*, 43(2), 146–67, 2008; Scott Blinder and Alexander Betts, 'Deportations, Removals and Voluntary Departures from the UK: Briefing Paper', *Migration Observatory*, 19 July 2017.

22 See Ian Cobain, 'Obama's Secret Kill List – The Disposition Matrix', *Guardian*, 14 July 2013.

23 There has been some protest regarding the erasure of judicial safeguards in extradition arrangements, but the process of removal itself, even when the basis for indictment by, and transfer to, the US is weak, has received relatively little contestation from human rights organisations, particularly in terrorism-related cases.

24 Gargi Bhattacharyya, *Dangerous Brown Men: Exploiting Sex, Violence and Feminism in the War on Terror*, London: Zed, 2008, 78; David Theo Goldberg, *The Racial State*, Chichester: Wiley Blackwell, 2002.

25 I use 'Muslim' here as a political category to incorporate the range of subjects racialised as Muslim, not so much in terms of a religious subjectivity or identity.

26 Christian Joppke, 'Terror and the Loss of Citizenship', *Citizenship Studies*, 20(6–7), 728–48, 2016, 728.

27 Chetan Bhatt, 'Human Rights and the Transformation of War', *Sociology*, 46(5), 813–28, 2012.

28 Jeremy Scahill, *Dirty Wars: The World is a Battlefield*, New York, NY: Nation Books, 2013; Arun Kundnani, *The Muslims Are Coming*, London: Verso, 2014.

29 See, for example, Scott Poynting and Victoria Mason, '"Tolerance, Freedom, Justice and Peace"?: Britain, Australia and Anti-Muslim Racism Since 11 September 2001', *Journal of Intercultural Studies*, 27(4), 365–91; S. Sayyid and Abdoolkarim Vakil (eds), *Thinking through Islamophobia: Global Perspectives*, New York, NY: Columbia University Press; Liz Fekete, 'Anti-Muslim Racism and the European Security State', *Race and Class*, 46(1), 3–29.

30 Tufyal Choudhury and Helen Fenwick, 'The Impact of Counter-Terrorism Measures on Muslim Communities', Equality and Human Rights Commission, research report 72, 2011.

31 Robert. S. Leiken, 'Europe's Angry Muslims', *Foreign Affairs*, 84(4), 120–35, 2005; Marc Sageman, *Leaderless Jihad: Terror Networks in the Twenty-First Century*, Philadelphia, PA: University of Pennsylvania Press, 2008; Tufyal Choudhury, *The Role of Muslim Identity Politics in Radicalisation*, London: Department of Local Communities and Government, 2007; C. McCauley and S. Moskalenko 'Mechanism of Political Radicalisation: Pathways Toward Terrorism', *Terrorism and Political Violence*, 20(3), 415–33, 2008.

32 Ruth Wilson Gilmore, *The Golden Gulag: Prisons, Surplus, Crisis and Opposition in Globalizing California*, Oakland, CA: University of California Press, 2007.

33 David T. Goldberg, *The Racial State*.

34 Laleh Khalili, *Time in the Shadows: Confinement in Counter-insurgencies*, Stanford, CA: Stanford University Press, 2013; Avery Gordon, 'Abu Ghraib: Imprisonment and the War on Terror', *Race and Class*, 2006, 48(1), 42–59.

35 There are resonances here with the thesis of Stuart Hall and his colleagues in Stuart Hall, Chas Critcher, Tony Jefferson, John Clarke and Brian Roberts, *Policing the Crisis: Mugging the State and Law and Order*, London: Macmillan, 1978.

36 See, for example, David E. Pozen, 'The Mosaic Theory, National

Security and the Freedom of Information Act', *Yale Law Journal*, 115(3), 2005, 628–79; Justice Report, *Secret Evidence*, London: Justice, 2009. I also experienced restrictions myself in attempts to collect data for this research, and the same has also been reported by journalists and other academic researchers doing similar work.

1. Making Non-Humans

1 Tony Blair, Speech to Parliament, 4 October 2001.

2 Edward W. Said, *Culture and Imperialism*, London: Vintage, 1994, 375.

3 Frantz Fanon, *The Wretched of the Earth*, London: Penguin, 2001 [1961], 32.

4 Robert Verkaik, 'Exclusive: How MI5 Blackmails British Muslims', *Independent*, 21 May 2009.

5 Alice Ross, 'Stripped of his UK Citizenship, Now Mahdi Hashi Is in Solitary Confinement in New York', *Bureau of Investigative Journalism*, 19 April 2014.

6 Dick Marty, 'Alleged Secret Detentions and Unlawful Inter-State Transfers of Detainees Involving Council of Europe Member States', Parliamentary Assembly, Council of Europe, 12 June 2006.

7 Ibid., 1–2.

8 Law in Action, 'Deprivation of Citizenship', BBC Radio 4, 12 March 2013.

9 Djibouti hosts the largest American permanent military base in Africa, Camp Lemonnier, which is home to more than 4,000 personnel as well as the Combined Joint Task Force-Horn of Africa. Camp Lemonnier is the centrepiece of a network of around six US drone and surveillance bases stretching across the continent. Due to its strategic location, Camp Lemonnier also serves as a hub for aerial operations in the Gulf region.

10 *USA v. Mahdi Hashi*, submitted affidavit ECR 99-2, 16 September 2014.

11 Hashi submitted in his affidavit that he believed these personnel to be members of the Joint Special Operations Command or CIA.

12 *USA v Mahdi Hashi*, submitted affidavit ECR 99-2, para.8, 16 September 2014.

13 *USA v Mahdi Hashi* 2014 WL 8877777

14 *USA v Syed Hashmi*, Affidavit of Syed Fahad Hashmi, ECF 72 paras. 4-11, 12 January 2009.

15 Ibid. para 16.

16 MACLC, CLEAR and AALDEF, *Mapping Muslims: NYPD Spying and Its Impact on American Muslims*, New York, NY: CUNY School of Law, 2013, 8.

17 Arun Kundnani, *The Muslims Are Coming*, London: Verso.

18 MACLC, CLEAR and AALDEF, *Mapping Muslims*; Jeanne Theoharis, 'My Student, the "Terrorist"', *Chronicle of Higher Education*, 3 April 2011.

19 However, this particular group was never officially declared to be a terrorist organisation in the US.

20 Laura L. Rovner and Jeanne Theoharis, 'Preferring Order to Justice', University of Denver Sturm College of Law, Legal Research Paper Series, 2012, Working Paper No. 12–18.

21 Arun Kundnani has noted that they were more akin to radical activists than terrorists. See Arun Kundnani, *A Decade Lost: Rethinking Radicalisation and Extremism*, London: Claystone, 2015.

22 Laura Rovner and Jeanne Theoharis, *Preferring Order to Justice*.

23 US Attorney Southern District of New York, 'United States Announces First Extradition from United Kingdom on Terrorism Charges', press release, 26 May 2007.

24 George W. Bush, *Public Papers of the Presidents of the United States: Book II – July 1 to December 31*, 2006, Washington, DC: United States Government Printing Office.

25 G. Miller, 'Plan for Hunting Terrorists Signals US Intends to Keep Adding Names to Kill Lists' *Washington Post*, 23 October 2012.

26 See Ian Cobain, 'Obama's Secret Kill List – The Disposition Matrix', *Guardian*, 14 July 2013.

27 Ibid.

28 Laleh Khalili, *Time in the Shadows; Confinement in Counterinsurgencies*, Stanford: Stanford University Press, 2013; Jayne Mayer, 'The CIA's Travel Agent', *New Yorker*, 30 October 2006.

29 Research by the Rendition Project has identified more than 130 people captured in this way from a total of eighteen countries including Pakistan, Georgia, Djibouti, South Africa, Somalia, Mauritania, Indonesia, Thailand and Macedonia. Often for each individual a number of transfers are involved to multiple different detention sites and there remain a number of people captured in this way who are unaccounted for. See the Rendition Project, therenditionproject.org.uk, and Crofton Black, 'CIA Torture: What Happened to the 119 Detainees?', *Bureau of Investigative Journalism*, April 2015. The report notes thirty-nine people were picked up in Pakistan.

30 Christopher H. Pyle, *Extradition, Politics and Human Rights*, Philadelphia, PA: Temple University Press, 2001, 144. It is frequently used by the US both to seize its own citizens who have fled elsewhere and to retrieve outsiders deemed to pose a threat. Vocativ, 'More than 900 Fugitives Were Extradited to the US Last Year', 9 August 2013. Reports by the US Department of Justice indicated that as of November 2000 the Office of International Affairs had 3,636 extradition cases pending, 'approximately

1,100 cases where fugitives wanted by foreign governments were believed to be in the United States and approximately 2,500 cases where fugitives wanted by the United States were believed to be in foreign countries' (Department of Justice, *Review of the Office of International Affairs' Role in the International Extradition of Fugitives*, Report no I-2002—008, March 2002). This is a significant increase from the 1970s. Prior to the 1970s, the United States received fewer than a dozen extradition requests a year. By 1978 it was receiving about one hundred and by 1989 it had grown to 239. About one third of these requests involved white collar crimes such as embezzlement and banking fraud, another third involved drug trafficking, and the remaining third involved crimes of violence included those deemed acts of terrorism and war crimes. (Christopher H. Pyle, *Extradition, Politics and Human Rights*, 143; David Lauter 'There's No Place to Hide', *National Law Journal*, 26 November 1984, 1.28). From the British perspective, the US accounts for more extradition requests to the UK than any other nation, and requests have continued to rise markedly since the 2003 US–UK Extradition Treaty came into force. Of the 198 people requested by the US for extradition from Britain between 2001 and 2015, nine were for terrorism offences.

31 Laleh Khalil, *Time in the Shadows*; David Theo Goldberg, *The Racial State*, Oxford: Wiley Blackwell, 2002.

32 David Wagner, 'Obama's Failed Promise to Close Gitmo: A Timeline', *Atlantic*, 28 January 2013.

33 Micah Zenko 'Obama's Embrace of Drone Strikes Will Be a Lasting Legacy', *New York Times*, 12 January 2016. Full data on drone strikes is being compiled by the Bureau of Investigative Journalism: see Alice K. Ross and Jack Searle, 'Get the Data: What the Drones Strike', 23 May 2014.

34 Reports indicate fifty-eight drone strikes were ordered under Bush's administration, killing an estimated 500 people (recorded officially as a mixture of terrorists and civilians) in Yemen, Pakistan and Somalia; under Obama's administration, between 2009 and 2015, there were over 500 strikes killing as many as 4,333 people. Jack Serle, 'Obama Drone Casualty Numbers a Fraction of Those Recorded by the Bureau', *Bureau of Investigative Journalism*, 1 July 2016.

35 Greg Miller, 'Obama Preserves Renditions as Counter-Terrorism Tool', *Los Angeles Times*, 1 February 2009.

36 Avery F. Gordon, 'Abu Ghraib: Imprisonment and the War on Terror', *Race and Class*, 48(1), 2006, 42–59.

37 RT, '"Don't Interact, Don't Talk, They Are Not Humans' – Gitmo Guard's Basic Orders', *Information Liberation*, 23 May 2013.

38 Dick Marty, *Secret Detentions and Illegal Transfers of Detainees Involving Council of Europe Member States: Second Report*,

Parliamentary Assembly, Council of Europe, 7 June 2007; *Al Nashiri v Poland* Application no. 28761/11 (ECtHR 24 July 2014); *Husayn v Poland* Application no. 7511/13 (ECtHR, 24 July 2014).

39 The Rendition Project, 'Rendition', therenditionproject.org.uk.

40 Babar Ahmad, 'The Babar Ahmad Story', media brief produced on 15 February 2016 which he sent to the author.

41 Syed Talha Ahsan, 'Written Evidence of Syed Talha Ahsan EXL0067 – Submission to House of Lords Select Committee on the Extradition Law 2014', 5.

42 When Las Casas asked of the natives of the New World, 'Are they human?' he established what would become a central theme and rationale underpinning the development of the racial project which accompanied European exploration, expansion and colonisation from the fifteenth century onwards. This quest to decipher between the human and non-human and then to justify differential treatment accordingly played a fundamental role in the colonial project, informing as it did techniques and strategies of governance in the colony as well as the political debates legitimating this order of events in the metropolitan centre. Race-thinking effectively produced what Paul Gilroy refers to as 'infrahumanity', beings not quite human, located somewhere on the spectrum between animal and human and below the threshold of civilisation. Paul Gilroy, *Between Camps: Nations, Cultures and the Allure of Race*, Cambridge, MA: Harvard University Press, 2000.

43 Angela Y. Davis makes this point in relation to the criminal. See Angela Y. Davis, 'Race and Criminalization: Black Americans and the Punishment Industry' in Wahneema Lubiano (ed.) *The House that Race Built*, New York, NY: Vintage Books, 1997.

44 Rex A. Hudson, *The Sociology and Psychology of Terrorism: Who Becomes a Terrorist and Why?*, Washington, DC: Federal Research Division, Library of Congress, 1999, 3.

45 Ibid., 33.

46 Jasbir Puar, *Terrorist Assemblages: Homonationalism in Queer Times*, Durham NC: Duke University Press, 2007.

47 Jerrold M. Post, 'Current Understanding of Terrorist Motivation and Psychology: Implications for a Differentiated Antiterrorist Policy', *Terrorism*, 13(1), 1990, 65–71.

48 Arun Kundnani, *The Muslims Are Coming*.

49 Institute for Economics and Peace, *Global Terrorism Index 2016: Measuring and Understanding the Impact of Terrorism*, New York: IEP.

50 Theresa May, 'PM Statement Following London Terror Attack: 4 June 2017', Prime Minister's Office, 4 June 2017.

51 Mahmood Mamdani, *Good Muslim, Bad Muslim: America, the Cold War and the Roots of Terror*, New York, NY: Pantheon

Books, 2004; Edward W. Said, *Orientalism*, London: Penguin, 2003; Arun Kundnani, *The Muslims Are Coming*.

52 Edward W. Said, *Orientalism*.

53 Theresa May, 'PM Statement Following London Terror Attack: 4 June 2017'.

54 See Scott Poynting and Victoria Mason, 'The Resistible Rise of Islamophobia: Anti-Muslim Racism in the UK and Australia Before 11 September 2001', *Journal of Sociology*, 2007, 43(1), 61–86.

55 Community Cohesion Independent Review Team, *Community Cohesion: A Report of the Independent Review Team Chaired by Ted Cantle*, London: Home Office, 2001.

56 Tony Blair, PM Press Conference, 5 August 2005.

57 O. Wright, 'David Cameron: We must End Muslim "Segregation" to Tackle "Scourge" of Extremism', *Independent,* 20 July 2015.

58 Nazia Parveen, 'Small Part of Manchester that Has Been Home to 16 Jihadis', *Guardian*, 25 February 2017.

59 Amy Martin, *Alter-Nations: Nationalisms, Terror and the State in Nineteenth-Century Britain and Ireland*, Columbus, OH: Ohio State University Press, 2012.

60 Gerry Kearns, 'Bare Life, Political Violence and the Territorial Structure of Britain and Ireland', in Derek Gregory and Allan Pred (eds), *Violent Geographies: Fear, Terror and Political Violence*, Oxon: Routledge, 2007, 7–36.

61 Christopher Pyle, *Extradition, Politics and Human Rights*.

62 Catherine Hall has noted that the Irish both could and could not expect the same rights that had been extended to the working-class male head of household. See Catherine Hall, Keith McClelland and Jane Rendall, *Defining the Victorian Nation: Class, Race, Gender and the Reform Act of 1867*, Cambridge: Cambridge University Press, 2000.

63 Amy Martin, *Alter-Nations*, 108.

64 Stephen Morton, *States of Emergency: Colonialism, Literature and Law*, Liverpool: Liverpool University Press, 2012.

65 Susan Carruthers, 'Two Faces of 1950s Terrorism: The Film Presentation of Mau Mau and the Malayan Emergency', *Small Wars and Insurgencies*, 6(1), 1995, 17-43.

66 Gareth Peirce, *Dispatches from the Dark Side: On Torture and the Death of Justice*, London: Verso, 2010.

67 Amy Martin, *Alter-Nations*; Stephen Morton, *States of Emergency*.

68 Rex A. Hudson, *The Sociology and Psychology of Terrorism*, 12.

69 Bouthaina Shaaban, 'The Rise of ISIS and Other Extremist Groups: The Role of the West and Regional Powers', *Counterpunch*, 29 January 2016; Tom Mills and David Miller, 'Religion Radicalization and the Causes of Terrorism', in J. Lewis (ed.) *Cambridge Companion to Religion and Terrorism*, Cambridge: Cambridge University Press, 2017.

70 Edward W. Said, *Culture and Imperialism*.

71 Angela Y. Davis, '"There is an Unbroken Line of Police Violence in the US that Takes Us All the Way Back to the Days of Slavery"', *Guardian*, 14 December 2014; Stephen Morton, 'Terrorism, Orientalism and Imperialism', *Wasafiri*, 22(2), 2007, 36–42.

72 Tim Dunne, 'Liberalism, International Terrorism and Democratic Wars', *International Relations*, 23(1) 2009, 107–14.

73 Talal Asad, *On Suicide Bombing*, New York, NY: Columbia University Press, 2007; Michael Walzer, *Arguing about War*, New Haven: Yale University Press, 2004.

74 Paul Wilkinson, *Terrorism versus Democracy: The Liberal State Response*, third edition, Oxon: Routledge, 2011, 4; Walzer, *Arguing about War*.

75 See, for example, Antony Anghie, *Imperialism, Sovereignty and the Making of International Law*, Cambridge: Cambridge University Press, 2005; Nasser Hussain, *The Jurisprudence of Emergency: Colonialism and the Rule of Law*, Ann Arbour, MI: University of Michigan Press, 2003.

76 Talal Asad, *On Suicide Bombing*, 20.

77 Judith Butler, *Frames of War: When Is Life Grievable?*, London: Verso, 2010, 156.

78 A distinction which some have indicated has intensified with the enhancement of technological capabilities for warfare. Gregoire Chamayou, for example, notes how one of the key objectives of military intervention in twenty-first-century wars has been to ensure the protection of US (or NATO) military personnel over the lives of the civilians they are ostensibly intervening to protect, regardless of whether this also means more civilians are killed as a result. In so doing, 'just warfare' becomes 'war without risk'. The decision for NATO aircraft to fly above 15,000 feet in their intervention in Kosovo in 1999 meant they would be protected from enemy aircraft defences. Differential representations are exemplified both through the ways in which targets are identified by NATO military forces and through the rationale that is used to determine who counts as a civilian and who a combatant, with reports that the US generally records all military-age males in a strike zone as 'militants'. Gregoire Chamayou, *A Theory of the Drone*, New York, NY: The New Press, 2015, 129; J. Becker and S. Shane, 'Secret "Kill List" Proves a Test of Obama's Principles and Will', *New York Times*, 29 May 2012.

79 Judith Butler, *Frames of War*, 156.

80 Jeanne Theoharis, *My Student, the "Terrorist"*.

81 Rovner and Theoharis, *Preferring Order to Justice*.

82 US Attorney's Office, 'Three Members of Al Shabaab Plead Guilty to Conspiring to Provide Material Support to the Terrorist Organization', press statement, 12 May 2015.

83 He is due for release in 2020 and has been moved to a minimum-security prison.

84 The Family of Fahad Hashmi, *Post-Sentencing Statement*, National Coalition to Protect Civil Freedoms, 10 June 2010.

85 Benjamin Weiser, 'Ex-Brooklyn College Student Admits Conspiring to Help Al Qaeda', *New York Times*, 27 April 2010.

2. Blind Justice and Blinding Crime

1 Arundhati Roy, *The Ministry of Upmost Happiness*, London: Hamish Hamilton, 2017, 281.

2 John Fahey, 'Officers Beat Me, Says Al Qaeda Suspect', *Independent*, 5 May 2011.

3 Khalida Yusuf, 'A Counter-Productive Extradition Policy – The Effect of the Babar Ahmad Case in Radicalising Muslims in Britain', London: Free Babar Ahmad Campaign, 2006.

4 The final charges were somewhat different than those Babar initially faced. In October 2004, a federal grand jury in Bridgeport, Connecticut, returned an indictment against him alleging he committed four felonies between 1997 and August 2004, which included 'conspiracy to provide material support to terrorists; providing material support to terrorists; conspiracy to kill, kidnap, maim or injure persons or damage property in a foreign country; and money laundering' with specific allegations that in the years 1997–2000 Babar furnished support for the Mujahideen in Chechnya and for the Taliban in Afghanistan. *Babar Ahmad and Haroon Rashid Aswat v Government of the USA* [2006] EWHC 2927 (HC(QB Div)). It is of note, of course, that Chechen rebel fighters were given US military support and training at this time and members of the Taliban had also been trained and equipped by the US in the 1990s, historical observations that support the argument I make in Chapter Two.

5 Khalida Yusuf, *A Counter-Productive Extradition Policy*, 7–8.

6 The demand for an 'Independent Police Complaints Commission' itself comes out of inquiries into racial violence of the police, and thus in many ways is a product of the racialised criminal justice system. The Lord Scarman Inquiry into the Brixton riots in 1981 and the Stephen Lawrence Inquiry in 1999 into the police response to the murder of Stephen Lawrence called for an independent police complaints commission.

7 Fiona Murphy, Babar Ahmad's lawyer, reported that the judge in the trial, Mr Justice Eady, had ordered the Met Commissioner to disclose the history of complaints by black and Asian men against some of the officers involved in the raid. 'That order was never

complied with – and several mail sacks of complaint dockets were mislaid within the Met'. See Fiona Murphy, 'Babar Ahmad's Principled Stand Shames the IPCC', *Guardian*, 5 June 2011.

8 'Babar Ahmad Police Officers Not Guilty of Assault', BBC News, 3 June 2011.

9 Prior to Babar's trial, a black police officer had raised a complaint against PC Mark Jones for assaulting two British-Arab youths, which resulted in a court case against him. Jones was acquitted as 'a decent officer' (Dominic Casciani, 'Acquitted PC Was 'a Decent Officer', BBC News, 3 November 2009). Subsequently, it was reported that PC Mark Jones and five other white police officers, all members of the Territorial Support Group, sued Scotland Yard for racial discrimination claiming that they were 'sacrificed on the altar of political correctness'. They suggested they had only been charged because the force was scared of being called 'institutionally racist' if they did not accept the complaint of a black officer against a white officer ('White Policemen "Sacrificed on Altar of Political Correctness by Met Police"', *Telegraph*, 27 November 2010).

10 Mike Brogden, 'An Act to Colonise the Internal Lands of the Island: Empire and the Origins of the Professional Police', *International Journal of the Sociology of Law*, 15, 1987, 179–208; Georgina Sinclair and Chris A. Williams, '"Home and Away": The Cross-Fertilisation Between "Colonial" and "British" Policing, 1921–1985', *Journal of Imperial and Commonwealth History*, 35, 2007, 221–38; Paul Dixon '"Hearts and Minds"?: British Counter-Insurgency from Malaya to Iraq', *Journal of Strategic Studies*, 2009, 32(3), 353–81.

11 Paddy Hillyard, *Suspect Community: People's Experience of the Prevention of Terrorism Acts in Britain*, London: Pluto, 1993.

12 Graham Ellison and Conor O'Reilly, 'From Empire to Iraq and the "War on Terror": The Transplantation and Commodification of the (Northern) Irish Policing Experience', *Police Quarterly*, 11, 2008, 395–426.

13 The Terrorism Act 2000, for example, which expanded the definition of terrorism, was designed to effectively simultaneously police the political events of Northern Ireland with growing concerns related to Islamic and other political movements elsewhere. Benefiting from Britain's reputation as an experienced hand in all matters terrorism, Britain's legislative model's ready availability in the aftermath of the 9/11 attacks, and the UN Security Resolution 1373 adopted on 28 September 2001, which obliged member states to 'legislate separate criminal offences proscribing terrorist acts under domestic law', meant its provisions were re-imported into terrorism legislation across much of Britain's former empire including Pakistan, Malaysia, Kenya, Grenada, Canada, Australia,

Bahamas and Tanzania. See Kent Roach, 'The Migration and Derivation of Counter-Terrorism' in Genevieve Lennon and Clive Walker (eds), *Routledge Handbook of Law and Terrorism*, Oxon: Routledge, 2015, pp.68-84.

14 Ben Bowling, Alpa Parmar and Coretta Phillips, 'Policing Ethnic Minority Communities' in Tim Newburn (ed.) *Handbook of Policing*, Devon: Willan Publishing, 2003, 528–55.

15 Kenneth Newman, for example, who began his career by joining the Palestine Police in 1946, later became Chief Constable of the Royal Ulster Constabulary in the 1970s, having also been a Commander in the Metropolitan Police. Less than a year after the 1981 riots in British cities, Newman returned to London as commissioner of the Met Police and oversaw the production of a secret handbook called *The Public Order Manual*. This guide called for the end of 'policing by consent' and advocated instead a policing strategy based on the RUC and the paramilitary Royal Hong Kong Police. See Jane Bennett, 'One of a Long Line of Barbarians', *Fight Racism! Fight Imperialism!*, 5 April 2017.

16 Liz Fekete, 'Total Policing: Reflections from the Frontline', *Race and Class*, 54(3), 65–76, 2013.

17 Lord Carlile of Berriew QC, *Report on the Operation in 2007 of the Terrorism Act 2000 and of Part I of the Terrorism Act 2006*, Independent Reviewer of Terrorism Legislation, June 2008, 10.

18 David Anderson QC, *The Terrorism Acts in 2015: Report of the Independent Reviewer on the Operation of the Terrorism Act 2000 and Part 1 of the Terrorism Act 2006*, December 2016, 69.

19 Paddy Hillyard, *Suspect Community*; On how the process of surveillance plays an important role in actually constructing a suspect community, see Jordan T. Camp and Christina Heatherton, 'Total Policing and the Global Surveillance Empire Today: An Interview with Arun Kundnani' in J. T. Camp and C. Heatherton (eds), *Policing the Planet: Why the Policing Crisis Led to Black Lives Matter*, London: Verso, 2016, 90–1. On the range of total policing, see Gareth Peirce, *Dispatches from the Dark Side*, London: Verso, 2010; Liz Fekete, 'Total Policing'; Frances Webber, *Borderline Justice: The Fight for Refugee and Migrant Rights*, London: Pluto, 2012. On the use of deportation, see Corporate Watch, *Collective Expulsion: The Case Against Britain's Mass Deportation Charter Flights*, London: Corporate Watch, 2013; Mary Bosworth, Ines Hasselberg and Sarah Turnbull, 'Imprisonment in a Global World: Rethinking Penal Power' in Y. Jewkes, B. Crewe and J. Bennett (eds) *Handbook on Prisons*, second edition, Oxon: Routledge, 2016, 698–711.

20 The category of 'dangerous offenders' has been explicitly referred to in the Criminal Justice Act 2003, Criminal Justice and Immigration Act 2008 and Criminal Justice and Court Act 2015.

'Dangerous offences', as defined in 2003, range in gravity from murder, kidnap and manslaughter to crimes that do not involve direct or serious harm to people, such as having intercourse with an animal and exposure.

21 Statewatch, 'Anti-Terrorist Stop and Searches Target Muslims, but Few Arrests', *Statewatch Bulletin*, 13(6), Nov.–Dec. 2003.

22 Statistics published in 2016 indicate that the use of stop and search proscribed under various criminal and counterterrorism legislation has been in decline over preceding years.

23 It is of note that while funding for the civilian police force has been cut since 2010, resulting in a sizeable reduction of community police officers, the proportion of resources committed to counterterrorism policing has grown. See Rowena Crawford, Richard Disney and David Innes, *Funding the English and Welsh Police Service: From Boom to Bust?*, Institute for Fiscal Studies, November 2015.

24 Chief Inspector M. J. Keene, 'The Metropolitan Police Special Patrol Group', *Police Journal*, 40(4), 1967, 155–62.

25 Fiona Murphy, 'Babar Ahmad's Principled Stand Shames the IPCC'. In October 2015, the London High Court ruled that PC Mark Jones had assaulted and racially abused two Arab teenagers with techniques similar to those that had been used on Ahmad. He no longer works for the Met Police.

26 Paul Lewis and Mathew Taylor, 'Scotland Yard Riot Squad Faces Call to End "Culture of Impunity"', *Guardian*, 6 November 2009. The systemic nature of this kind of violence is reflected in the broader figures reporting deaths in police custody and the enduring lack of accountability for these. Between 1991 and 2014, the Institute for Race Relations reported 509 black and ethnic minority people had died in suspicious circumstances while in state detention: 348 had occurred in prison, 137 in police custody and 24 in immigration detention, yet not a single officer has ever been prosecuted. When incidents of assault and harassment are added to these figures, the picture is bleaker still.

27 IPCC, *Metropolitan Police Service Territorial Support Group: A Review of Complaints Data and IPCC Cases 2008–2012*, London: IPCC, June 2009.

28 An internal investigation into his death showed that the Special Patrol Group headquarters had a hoard of unauthorised weapons, including various illegal truncheons and knives, two crowbars, a whip, a three-foot wooden stave, and a lead-weighted leather stick.

29 Cage, StopWatch and Liberty, for example, have raised human rights concerns in relation to the use of Schedule 7 stops. It is of note that Liberty's one case study for its campaign is its use against David Miranda, the partner of journalist Glenn Greenwald, who exposed the United States and British global surveillance programs

in 2013, despite this being a measure disproportionately impacting black and Asian Muslims.

30 House of Lords, *Constitution Committee – Fifteenth Report. Fast-track Legislation: Constitutional Implications and Safeguards*, Session 2008–09, 17 June 2009, para. 67.

31 Paddy Hillyard notes in relation to the 1974 provisions that since arrests could be made without suspicion and every nine out of ten resulted in no charge, the point of this practice was not really to prosecute but to use these interventions as opportunities for intelligence gathering. Paddy Hillyard, *Suspect Community*; Graham Ellison and Jim Smyth, *The Crowned Harp: Policing Northern Ireland*, London: Pluto Press, 2000. It is estimated that only 0.2 per cent of those stopped in 2015 were arrested. Benjamin Politowski, 'Terrorism in Great Britain: The Statistics', *House of Commons Briefing Paper*, no. 7613, 9 June 2016.

32 Helen Wallace 'The UK National DNA Database: Balancing Crime Detection, Human Rights and Privacy', *EMBO Reports*, July 2006, s26–s30; Home Office, *National DNA Database Strategy Board Annual Report 2012–13*, London: Home Office, 2013. Prior to 2012, DNA samples and records could be permanently retained from anyone arrested, regardless of whether or not they were charged or convicted. This changed following the Protections of Freedom Act 2012, following which it was reported that over 1.7 million DNA profiles taken from innocent adults and from children had been removed from the DNA database and that 7,753,000 DNA samples have been destroyed.

33 The Home Affairs Committee, *Select Committee on Home Affairs – Second Report 2006–07*, London: House of Commons, 2007.

34 The Equality and Human Rights Commission called for a race equality impact assessment to be carried out in response, speculating about three concerns in particular: firstly, that race patterns on the database could strengthen the tendency for racial profiling, stereotyping black men as suspects for particular types of offence; secondly, that the stigma of extreme overrepresentation would have unknown social consequences; and thirdly, that samples/profiles could be sold to commercial companies carrying out research to link 'criminogenic genes' with race.

35 James Brokenshire, House of Commons Debate, 16 October 2013, vol. 568, c776w.

36 Brian Brady, 'Police Told to Explain Use of Unregulated DNA Database', *Independent*, 9 June 2013; National DNA Database Ethics Group, *Ethics Group: National DNA Database Seventh Annual Report 2014*, 24 March 2015.

37 Alastair R Macgregor, *Further Report by the Biometrics Commissioner on Issues Raised in His 2015 Annual Report*, London: HM Government, May 2016.

38 Lewis Carroll, *Alice's Adventures in Wonderland and Through the Looking Glass*, New York, NY: Cosimo Classics, 2010 [1865], 45.

39 Interview with Talha Ahsan conducted by the author, September 2015.

40 A stall distributing leaflets and literature promoting the teachings of Islam, which in itself has become a criminalised activity through counter-terrorism legislation. They have also been used as an avenue for sting operations, as, for example, in the Munir Farooqi case. In 2008, the North West Counter Terrorism Unit launched an operation where two undercover officers faked their conversions to Islam after repeatedly approaching the Da'wah stalls that Munir ran in Manchester. They used the operation to spy on the local Muslim community and would later portray the stalls as recruiting grounds for terrorism.

41 *USA v Syed Talha Ahsan*, submitted memorandum ECF No. 179, 16 June 2014.

42 The arbitrary nature of state power is illustrated when Talha Ahsan's case is compared with Ahmad Faraz, a British-based bookseller who ran a bookshop and acted as distributor of Azzam Publications. He was prosecuted in the UK. At first, he received a five-year sentence but was eventually acquitted on appeal. At the initial stage of Faraz's conviction, Azzam Publications were regarded as publishing historical documents rather than terrorism materials.

43 The charges of conspiracy to provide and providing material support equated to a maximum sentence of eighty to one hundred years in prison.

44 Interview with Talha Ahsan conducted by the author, September 2015.

45 Indeed, this was assisted by the European Court of Human Rights' (unexpected) decision to rule on all five cases simultaneously.

46 Jeanne Theoharis, 'My Student, the "Terrorist"', *Chronicle of Higher Education*, 3 April 2011.

47 *Abu Hamza v USA*, [2008] EWHC 1357 Civ (HC(Admin)).

48 When preparing for his defence, Babar would later discover that even this was not the case: the server was actually hosted in Illinois. This discovery was significant in diminishing the prosecution's case against him.

49 Gareth Peirce, Babar Ahmad's defence lawyer, argued that if the case had been tried in the UK, charges would likely have been dropped.

50 Babar Ahmad, 'My Unjust Extradition After Eight Years in Detention Without Charge', *Guardian*, 4 October 2012.

51 This is an argument made consistently in appeals against extradition in these terrorism cases.

52 Hamza initiated an appeal against extradition on the basis that

the offences of which he was accused were all matters that could be tried in Britain, because at least part of the evidence against him had been obtained through means of torture, and because his health conditions meant that incarceration in long-term solitary confinement would violate his human rights. His medical complaints included

> 'type 2' diabetes and raised blood pressure, for both of which he is prescribed medication, extensive psoriasis, hyperhydrosis (excessive sweating provoked by a neurological condition) which requires him to shower and change his clothes at least twice daily, blindness in the right eye, with poor vision in the left, and bilateral traumatic amputation of the distal third of both forearms for which prostheses are fitted. The stumps in both arms are subject to regular outbreaks of infection'.
>
> (*Abu Hamza v USA and the Secretary of State for Home Department* [2008] EWHC 1357 Civ (HC(Admin), para. 7).

53   *Abu Hamza v USA and the Secretary of State for the Home Department* [2008] EWHC 1357 Civ (HC(Admin), para 26).

54   The collaborative process in policing has continued apace. In 2014 it was reported that specialist counter-terrorism FBI officers would be working in British airports to monitor suspect passengers as well as investigate 'terror hotspots' across Britain. Asserting that British authorities were not doing enough to stem the flow of individuals travelling to join the Islamic State of Iraq and Syria, their role was to be dual purpose: to concurrently liaise with the Metropolitan Police SO15 Counter Terrorism Command and MI5, British intelligence services, as well as conduct their own parallel investigations and recruit their own informants within Britain and Europe more widely. A US intelligence source reported to the media that their contribution was to 'bring to the table advanced monitoring capabilities and terrorist-tracking and identification techniques which have been tried and tested'. C. Wheeler and A. Bassey, 'FBI Agents to Guard UK Airports Against Jihadi Fanatics', *Express*, 24 August 2014.

55   Theresa May, 'Speech to Conservative Party Conference', Birmingham, 9 October 2012.

56   See Angela Y. Davis, *Abolition Democracy: Beyond Empire, Prisons and Torture*, New York, NY: Seven Stories Press; Avery F. Gordon 'Abu Ghraib: Imprisonment and the War on Terror', *Race and Class*, 48(1), 2006, 42–59.

57   Since the 1980s–90s onwards, the number of US prisons and the size of the prison population has drastically increased, and the US now hosts the largest prison population in the world. Across the country as a whole, there are approximately 2 million people in prison or jail, around 5 million people on probation or parole,

and a further 65,000 imprisoned under immigration authorities and the office of the US Marshals. More than 60 per cent of the prison population are people of colour. See Ruth Wilson Gilmore, *Golden Gulag: Prisons, Surplus, Crisis and Opposition in Globalizing California*, Berkeley: University of California Press, 2007; Avery F. Gordon, *Abu Ghraib*. For global prison population totals, see International Centre for Prison Studies.

58 Avery Gordon, *Abu Ghraib*; Stephen C. Richards, 'USP Marion: The First Federal Supermax', *Prison Journal*, 88(1), 2008, 6–22.

59 Ray L. Levasseur, 'Trouble Coming Everyday: ADX One Year Later' in D. Burton-Rose (ed.), *The Celling of America: An Inside Look at the US Prison Industry*, Monroe, ME: Common Courage, 1998, 206–11; Avery F. Gordon, *Abu Ghraib*.

60 Daniel McGowan, 'Exposing "Little Guantanamo": Inside the CMU', New York, NY: ABCF-NYC, 2009.

61 It is reported that the small numbers of non-Muslim prisoners are referred to by guards as 'balancers' because they are there to balance out the racial make-up of the prisoners to deflect from potential law suits.

62 *USA v Abid Naseer*, [2011] EW Misc 4 (MC).

63 Nisha Kapoor, 'On the North West Ten: Postcoloniality, the British Racial State and the War on Terror', *Identities: Global Studies in Culture and Power*, 20(1), 2013, 61–76.

64 Of the twelve arrests made, one of the men was released within a short time without being taken into custody, a second was a UK national, a third was an Afghan national and the remaining nine individuals were of Pakistani nationality.

65 The Assistant US Attorney for the Eastern District of New York, Jeffrey Knox, stated, 'Communications in the e-mails about weddings, marriage, girlfriends, computers and weather were [seen as] codes that referred to attacks, bomb ingredients travel documents and target sites' (*USA v Abid Naseer*, [2011] EW Misc 4 (MC), para, 1. There was speculation that Huma was code for hydrogen peroxide, Foiza was code for fertilizer, friends' names were code for the operatives, and marriage dates in the emails were an indication of the scheduled attack. The justification for these rationalisations were again set out in the closed judgement.

66 Lord Carlile of Berriew QC, *Operation Pathway Report Following Review*, Independent Reviewer of Terrorism Legislation, October 2009.

67 *Abid Naseer, Ahmad Faraz Khan, Shoaib Khan, Abdul Wahab Khan and Tariq Ur Rehman v Secretary of State for the Home Department* [2010] SIAC SC/77/80/81/82/83/09, para. 15, emphasis added.

68 Lord Carlile of Berriew QC, *Operation Pathway Report*, 3.

69 It would subsequently come to light that the massacre of Sikh

separatists occurred with full knowledge and involvement of the British government. See Georgia Graham, and Dean Nelson, 'Britain "Backstabbed" Sikhs by Advising India on 1984 Golden Temple Raid', *Telegraph*, 14 January 2014.

70 When it was first introduced, the bill was praised by members on all sides of the House for its progressive approach to the issue. Justice note that one Opposition MP remarked that it was 'not a contentious piece of legislation', while another predicted that it would lead to 'a process whereby human rights will be placed at the heart of all our immigration and asylum legislation'. Justice, *Secret Evidence*, London: Justice, 2009, 40–41.

71 The first case before SIAC came in 1999 when a man, Mr Rehman, was accused by the secretary of state of being involved with Markaz Dawa al-Rishad (MDI), regarded as an Islamic terrorist organisation. The secretary of state argued that MDI had ties to Lashkar Taiyyaba (LT), a resistance group fighting against the Indian occupation of Kashmir, and that Mr Rehman had been involved in fundraising and recruitment on LT's behalf. Although the secretary of state did not allege that Rehman's activities were directed anywhere other than at the Indian part of Kashmir, he was accused of being 'partly responsible' for an increase in the number of British Muslims undergoing military training abroad and that 'the presence of returned jihad trainees in the UK may encourage the radicalisation of the British Muslim community'. Justice, *Secret Evidence*, 43.

72 Ibid., 72.

73 *Ajouaou and Others v Secretary of State for the Home Department* [2003] SIAC SC/1/2002, para. 81. The Court of Appeal likewise has upheld that SIAC could lawfully consider evidence obtained by torture.

74 Justice, *Secret Evidence*, 52.

75 Justice, *Secret Evidence*.

76 Ibid; Nisha Kapoor and Kasia Narkowicz, 'The Character of Citizenship: Denying the Rights of Asylum Seekers and Criminalising Dissent', *Open Democracy*, 20 May 2017.

77 *Roberts v Parole Board* [2004] EWCA Civ 1031 (CA(Civ Div)).

78 *Guardian News and Media, Ltd v AB CD*, [2014] EWCA Crim (B1).

79 Interview with human rights barrister conducted by the author, 20 January 2016.

80 Whereas around 97 per cent of federal criminal cases are resolved through plea bargaining, the rate is around 85 per cent for terrorism cases. Baher Azmy, Sally Eberhardt, Pardiss Kebriaei, Arun Kundnani, William Quigley, Laura Rovner, Saskia Sassen and Jeanne Theoharis, *Evidence from US Experts to the House of Lords Select Committee on Extradition Law*, written evidence (EXL0049), 12 September 2014.

81 *Abid Naseer, Ahmad Faraz Khan, Shoaib Khan, Abdul Wahab Khan and Tariq Ur Rehman v Secretary of State for the Home Department* [2010], SIAC SC/77/80/81/82/83/09. Abid Naseer was sentenced to forty years.

82 Andrew Buncombe, 'Abid Naseer Trial: Documents Recovered from Compound of Osama bin Laden Can Be Used as Evidence, Court Rules', *Independent*, 20 February 2015.

83 *USA v Abid Naseer*, trial transcript, ECF 429, p.2109, 20-21, 16 March 2015.

84 *USA v Syed Hashmi*, emergency motion to prohibit Attorney General from restricting defense counsel's access to defendant and infringing on defendants constitutional rights, ECF 20, 15 November 2007; Laura L. Rovner and Jeanne Theoharis, *Preferring Order to Justice.*

85 *USA v Babar Ahmad and Syed Talha Ahsan*, transcript of sentencing hearing, ECF 220, p.49, 22-23, 16 July 2014.

86 Arun Kundnani and Jeanne Theoharis, 'Breaking the Spell of the Official Terrorism Narrative', *Guardian*, 23 July 2014.

87 Both men were, for example, removed of their passports for some time after their return, and there was some attempt to place a notification order on Talha Ahsan, a form of control order which would stipulate he report periodically at a local police station and report to them every time he stayed away from home. He successfully appealed against this.

3. Deforming and Depriving Citizenship

1 Home Office, 'British Citizenship is a Privilege Not a Right', statement on 22 December 2013.

2 A. Sivanandan, *A Different Hunger: Writings on Black Resistance*, London: Pluto, 1982, 107–8.

3 *B2 v Secretary of State for the Home Department*, [2012] SIAC SC/114/2012.

4 *B2 v Secretary of State for the Home Department*, [2013] EWCA Civ 616 (CA(Civ Div)).

5 Tablighi Jamaat believes that Muslims are in a constant state of spiritual Jihad in the sense of a fight against evil; the weapon of choice is Da'wah (proselytisation) and the battles are won or lost in the 'hearts of men'.

6 Victoria Parsons, 'What Do We Know About Citizenship Stripping?', *Bureau of Investigative Journalism*, 10 December 2014.

7 The specific charges stated in the US indictment are (1) conspiracy to provide material support for a terrorist organisation; (2) providing and attempting to provide material support for a terrorist

organisation; (3) conspiracy to receive military-type training from a foreign terrorist organisation; (4) receipt of military-type training from a foreign terrorist organisation; and (5) possessing, carrying and using a firearm.

8 *Pham v USA*, [2014] EWHC 4167 (HC(QB Div)), para. 15.

9 It was determined in the Court of Appeal that while the law did not permit the secretary of state to make an individual de jure stateless, she could make them de facto stateless. This means that a subject cannot be made stateless if this would result in them not having a nationality of any state (de jure stateless) but can be made stateless if it is determined that they have a nationality under the law of a state but are nevertheless denied protection of the government of that state (de facto stateless). See *B2 v Secretary of State for the Home Department* [2013] EWCA Civ 616 (CA(Civ Div)).

10 Victoria Parsons, 'Theresa May Deprived 33 people of British Citizenship in 2015', *Bureau of Investigative Journalism*, 21 June 2016.

11 Victoria Parsons, 'What Do We Know About Citizenship Stripping?'.

12 See David Theo Goldberg, *The Racial State*, Oxford: Wiley Blackwell, 2002; Paul Gilroy, *Between Camps. Nations, Cultures and the Allure of Race*, London: Penguin, 2000; Charles W. Mills, *The Racial Contract*, Ithaca, NY: Cornell University Press, 1997.

13 John Stuart Mill, *Dissertations and Discussions: Political, Philosophical, and Historical*, vol. 3, 252–3, 1874.

14 Catherine Hall, 'The Nation Within and Without' in Catherine Hall, Keith McClelland and Jane Rendall, *Defining the Victorian Nation: Class, Race, Gender and the Reform Act of 1867*, Cambridge: Cambridge University Press, 179–232, 2000; Amy Martin, *Alter-Nations*.

15 Giorgio Agamben (trans. by Daniel Heller-Roazen), *Homo Sacer: Sovereign Power and Bare Life*, Stanford, CA: Stanford University Press, 1998, 106; Jayan Nayar, 'Thinking from the Ban?: Rebellious Third Worlds and Theory,' *Legal Studies Research Paper* 2010–23, 2010, 5.

16 Hannah Arendt, *Origins of Totalitarianism*, London: Harcourt, 1968. Paul Gilroy makes the point that this figure is of course a racialised human, see Paul Gilroy, *Darker than Blue: On the Moral Economies of Black Atlantic Culture*, London: The Belknap Press of Harvard University Press, 2010, 82.

17 Kathleen Paul, *Whitewashing Britain: Race and Citizenship in the Postwar Era*, Ithaca, NY: Cornell University Press, 1997.

18 Ian MacDonald and Nicholas Blake note that 'one of the difficulties of describing the operation of UK immigration law is that everyone in the field knows that the original purpose of the Commonwealth Immigrants Act 1962 was to stop and if possible

reverse coloured immigration to the UK. That policy was continued by the 1971 Act [which they note remains the cornerstone of
UK immigration law]. Yet no government is prepared to admit this
so' (p. 17). Ian A. MacDonald and Nicholas J. Blake, *MacDonald's
Immigration Law and Practice in the United Kingdom*, fourth
edition, London: Butterworths, 1995.

19 Paul Gilroy, *There Ain't No Black in the Union Jack*, London:
Hutchinson, 1987; A. Sivanandan, 'Race, Class and the State: The
Political Economy of Immigration' in *Catching History on the
Wing. Race, Culture and Globalisation*, London: Pluto, 65–89,
2008, essay first published in 1976.

20 CARF Collective, 'Background-British Racism', *Race and Class*,
23(2–3), 232–44, 1981.

21 Alice Bloch, *The Migration and Settlement of Refugees in Britain*,
Houndmills: Palgrave, 2002.

22 Arun Kundnani, *The End of Tolerance: Racism in Twenty-First
Century Britain*, London: Pluto, 2007.

23 Lord Denham, *Building Cohesive Communities: A Report of the
Ministerial Group on Public Order and Community Cohesion*,
London: Home Office, 2002.

24 Home Office UK Border Agency, *The Path to Citizenship: Next
Steps in Reforming the Immigration System*, London: Home
Office, 2008.

25 Alice Bloch, *The Migration and Settlement of Refugees in Britain*,
44; Home Office, 'Asylum Statistics United Kingdom 1997', *Home
Office*, Issue 14/98, 21 May 1998.

26 *Al-Jedda v United Kingdom*, Application no. 27021/08, (ECtHR,
7 July 2011).

27 Newspaper headlines reported the discovery of a 'factory of death',
that mass death had been planned and that poison gangs were on
the loose. Physicians were warned to watch out for signs that their
patients had been poisoned by ricin. Charles Clarke drew on the
case to justify the need for ID cards. The story went global. In
Ireland two months after the arrests it was announced that anti-
terrorist police and military intelligence were on full alert for fear
that the plotters would spread across the waters. Arrests in France
and Spain became similarly linked despite elusive connections.
See Liz Fekete, 'Anti-Muslim Racism and the European Security
State', *Race and Class*, 46(1), 2004, 3–29. The case was also used
internationally, as part of the argument put forward by Colin
Powell to the UN for rationalising the US invasion of Iraq. For a
period of three years, despite government officials having access
to information to the contrary, the public were led to believe that
ricin had been found in a Wood Green flat occupied by a group
of men accused of being part of an al-Qaeda cell. Ten men were
eventually charged; the charges against four were dropped, and

five were acquitted. There was no 'ricin ring', nor was ricin ever produced there.

28 Steve Doughty, 'Just How Many Have We Let In?', *Daily Mail*, 16 January 2003, 6.

29 Alan Travis, 'Blunkett Vigilante Warning', *Guardian*, 24 January 2003; 'Asylum Meltdown', *Sun*, 20 January 2003.

30 See, for example, Charles Moore, 'The Reign of Terror or the Rule of British Law? The Murder of DC Oake Shows it is Time to Tear Up Agreements that Stop Us Deporting Bogus Asylum Seekers', *Daily Telegraph*, 16 January 2003, 24; Max Hastings, 'We British Need a New Human Right: The Denial of Entry to This Country to Those Who Wish Us Evil', *Daily Mail*, 17 January 2003, 12; Oliver Letwin 'How Blunkett Must Tackle the Crisis of Illegal Immigrants; Terror Threat Grows in Asylum Shambles', *Daily Express*, 20 January 2003, 12.

31 Alan Travis, 'Blunkett Vigilante Warning', *Guardian*, 24 January 2003.

32 Nicholas De Genova, 'The Crisis of the European Border Regime: Towards a Marxist Theory of Borders', *International Socialism: A Quarterly Review of Socialist Theory*, Issue 150, 2016, www.isj.org.uk.

33 Up until 2001, most Iraqi asylum seekers had been recognised as genuine in Britain. In 2000, only 14 per cent were not classified as in need of asylum or temporary protection. With an election looming and increased pressure to crack down further, Tony Blair campaigned on the promise that he would halve the number of people claiming asylum over the following six months. By February 2001, 78 per cent of Iraqis were refused all forms of protection. See Arun Kundnani, *The End of Tolerance*, 109.

34 Hannah Arendt emphasised this point in reference to the positions of twentieth-century refugees, noting that 'the world found nothing sacred in the abstract nakedness of being human'. Hannah Arendt, *Origins of Totalitarianism*, 299.

35 Imogen Tyler, *Revolting Subjects: Social Abjection and Resistance in Neoliberal Britain*, London: Zed, 2013.

36 House of Commons Debate, 20 January 2014, vol. 574, col. 1049.

37 Michael Seamark, 'Hatred UK: Damning Dossier Reveals How Fanatics, Some Wanted for Murder, are Preaching Anti-Western Hatred from Britain – and in Some Cases We're Subsidising Them', *Daily Mail*, 20 September 2001.

38 'Blair's Blitz on Fanatics Should Start in Britain', *Sun*, 20 September 2001.

39 Home Office, *Secure Borders, Safe Haven: Integration with Diversity in Modern Britain*, London: Home Office, 35.

40 Nationality Immigration and Asylum Act 2002, legislation. gov.uk.

41 Amanda Weston 'Deprivation of Citizenship – By Stealth', *Institute of Race Relations*, 9 June 2011.

42 This amendment came into force on 1 April 2003 and on 4 April 2003 the home secretary gave notice to Hamza of his intention to deprive him of his citizenship. At this time, the provision was still suspended pending appeal meaning that Hamza remained a British citizen throughout the judicial process and challenge to his appeal. Hamza eventually won his appeal on the grounds that to deprive him of his citizenship would make him stateless. But in 2004 the government repealed the section of the legislation which continued British citizenship pending appeal of a decision to withdraw it. The repeal was passed under the Asylum and Immigration Act 2004 which, Amanda Weston notes, was not explicitly about nationality, making the provision even less likely to be noticed or debated, with no reference in Hansard at all.

43 Amanda Weston, 'Deprivation of Citizenship – By Stealth'.

44 *Al-Jedda, v Secretary of State for Defence* [2005] EWHC 1809 (HC (Admin)).

45 *Al-Jedda v United Kingdom*, Application no. 27021/08, (ECtHR, 7 July 2011).

46 More deprivation orders were made over the period that Hilal al-Jedda's case was being decided, particularly after 2010. See Alice Ross, 'Deprivation of Citizenship: What Do We Know?', Social Policy Research Centre, Middlesex University, 2014.

47 Theresa May, Hansard Debate on Immigration Bill, 30 January 2014, col. 1040–41.

48 Immigration Act 2014, s66(3), notes, para. 405.

49 Colin Mooers, *Imperial Subjects: Citizenship in an Age of Crisis and Empire*, London: Bloomsbury, 2014.

50 Zainab Saleh, 'On Iraqi Nationality: Law, Citizenship and Exclusion', *Arab Studies Journal*, 21(1), 2013, 48–78. She notes how the first Iraqi Nationality Law of 1924 drafted by British officials undermined the notion of equal citizenship by categorising Iraqi citizens on the basis of citizenship they had held under Ottoman rule and whether they were considered 'Ottoman' or 'Persian' citizens (p. 49).

51 Quoted from Zainab Saleh, *On Iraqi Nationality: Law, Citizenship and Exclusion*, 69.

52 Derek Gregory, *The Colonial Present*, Oxford: Blackwell, 2004, 161.

53 Alice Bloch, *The Migration and Settlement of Refugees in Britain*; Bridget Anderson, Mathew J. Gibney and Emanuela Paoletti, 'Boundaries of Belonging: Deportation and the Constitution and Contestation of Citizenship', *Citizenship Studies*, 2011, 15(5), 543–5.

54 Bridget Anderson et al., *Boundaries of Belonging*.

55 Grégoire Chamayou, *Manhunts: A Philosophical History*, Princeton, NJ: Princeton University Press, 2010.

56 Similar sentiments were expressed in the United States by the Obama administration. See Barack Obama, 'Earned Citizenship', White House, 29 January, 2013.

57 See Conservative Party, *Protecting Human Rights in the UK: The Conservatives' Proposals for Changing Human Rights Laws*, London: The Conservative Party, 2014.

58 'Cleric Stripped of Citizenship', BBC News, 5 April 2003, emphasis added.

59 Bridget Byrne, 'A Local Welcome? Narrations of Citizenship and Nation in UK Citizenship Ceremonies', *Citizenship Studies*, 16 (3–4), 2012, 531–44; Paul Gilroy, *Postcolonial Melancholia*, New York, NY: Columbia University Press, 2005.

60 Home Office, *Secure Borders, Safe Haven: Integration with Diversity in Modern Britain*, 4.

61 It is of note that David Cameron struggled to complete questions from this test. Nicholas Watt, 'David Cameron Fluffs Citizenship Test on David Letterman's Late Show', *Guardian*, 27 September 2012.

62 Recognition of its increased necessity and worth is reflected in the rise in applications for naturalised citizenship in recent years. See Home Office, *Immigration Statistics. Citizenship Tables Table cz_01: Citizenship Applications, Grants and Refusals*, 2015, Home Office, 2016.

63 See Home Office, *Immigration Bill: Part Three – Landlord Immigration Checks and Access to Services*, Home Office, 2013.

64 Imogen Tyler, *Revolting Subjects*; Derek McGhee, *Security, Citizenship and Human Rights: Shared Values in Uncertain Times*, Basingstoke: Palgrave, 2010.

65 Arun Kundnani, *The End of Tolerance*.

66 Borders, Citizenship and Immigration Act 2009, s47.

67 Home Office UK Border Agency, *The Path to Citizenship*.

68 Phil Woolas, House of Commons Debate, 16 June 2009, vol. 494, col. 135.

69 Scott Blinder 'Naturalisation as a British Citizen: Concepts and Trends', The Migration Observatory at the University of Oxford, 8 August 2016; for details of cases, see Deport Deprive Extradite website, dde.org.uk.

70 UK Visas and Immigration Nationality Instructions, 'Chapter 18 Annex D: The Good Character Requirement', Home Office, 3–4.

71 Ibid.

72 Oliver Wright 'David Cameron: We Must End "Segregation" to Tackle "Scourge" of Extremism', *Independent*, 20 July 2015; Therese O'Toole, Nasar Meer, Daniel Nilsson DeHanas, Stephen H Jones and Tariq Modood, 'Governing Through Prevent?:

Regulation and Contested Practice in State–Muslim Engagement', *Sociology*, 2016, 50(1), 160–177.

73 The stories of these individuals have been collected through interviews as part of the wider Deport Deprive Extradite research project.

74 In these cases, the subjects are usually British-born and have no alternative citizenship they can claim.

75 Interviews with immigration and human rights lawyers conducted by the author between 2015-2016.

76 Nisha Kapoor, 'The Tale of the Two Disappeared: Racism, Resistance and Fighting for the Right to Life' in D. Naik and T. Oldfield (eds), *Critical Cities: Ideas, Knowledge and Agitation from Emerging Urbanists*, vol. 5, 2017 forthcoming.

77 *ARM v Secretary of State for the Home Department* [2016], SIAC, SN/22/2015.

78 Ibid., para 33.

79 Freedom of Information Response from the Home Office, FOI Reference 26908, 25 April 2013.

80 Home Office, *Immigration Statistics. Asylum Data Table as_01, 'Asylum Applications and Initial Decisions for Main Applicants by Country of Nationality 1984-2015'*, Home Office, 2016.

81 *Ahmed and Others (deprivation of citizenship)* [2017] UKUT, 00118 (IAC).

82 This sentiment has been rehearsed across Western states – in Australia, Canada, US as well as Britain – see Audrey Macklin, 'Citizenship Revocation, the Privilege to Have Rights and the Production of the Alien', *Queen's Law Journal*, 40(1), 2014, pp.1–54.

4. Courting Human Rights

1 Theresa May, 'Speech at Election Rally' Slough, 6 June 2017.

2 Aimé Césaire, *Discourse on Colonialism*, London: Monthly Review Press, 1972, 3.

3 Peter Bone, MP, in response to a *Daily Mail* story about Abu Hamza's family receiving housing benefit. See Ian Drury and Richard Marsden, 'Nick Clegg Launches Extraordinary Defence of £1.25million Taxpayer-Funded House for Hate Preacher Abu Hamza's Family', *Daily Mail*, 21 May 2014.

4 *Haroon Rashid Aswat v USA*, Reply to Government's Sentencing Memorandum on Behalf of Haroon Rashid Aswat, ECF 507, 15 October 2015.

5 Ibid., p.7. 'Krav Maga Worldwide™', the defence noted, 'offers the highest caliber of Krav Maga self-defense instruction to

thousands of people, including law enforcement agencies and military units across the globe'. The corporation markets itself as 'the largest reality-based self-defense organization in the world' and as 'the original leader of the Western Krav Maga movement'. Krav Maga also has hundreds of training centres throughout the world, including some in New York City.

6 *Haroon Rashid Aswat v USA*, Reply to Government's Sentencing Memorandum on Behalf of Haroon Rashid Aswat, ECF 507, 15 October 2015.

7 *Haroon Rashid Aswat v USA*, Psychiatric Court Report on Haroon Rashid Aswat, ECF 497–2, 2 October 2015.

8 *Haroon Aswat v Secretary of State for Home Department* [2014] EWHC 1216 (HC(Admin), para 15.

9 *Aswat v United Kingdom* Application no. 17299/12 (ECtHR, 16 April 2013).

10 Christopher Hope, 'European Judges' Ruling on Qatada "A Threat to Our National Security": Reaction', *Daily Telegraph*, 7 February 2012; James Slack, 'Europe's War on British Justice: UK Loses Three Out of Four Human Rights Cases, Damning Report Reveals', *Mail Online*, 14 March 2012; *Newsnight*, 22:30 5 October 2012, BBC2 England, 30 mins; David Cameron, 'British Decisions ... British Judges', *Sun*, 15 June 2015, 8.

11 House of Commons Debate, 5 December 2011, vol. 537, cols 82–130.

12 *Gary McKinnon v USA* [2007] EWHC 762, (HC(Admin)).

13 See Geoffrey Robertson, 'Cameron and Clegg Must Now Do Their Moral Duty and Save Gary McKinnon', *Daily Mail*, 27 May 2010.

14 Jo Adetunji, 'Gary McKinnon Campaigners Praise PM for Raising Hacker's Case with Obama', *Guardian*, 21 July 2010.

15 Dominc Raab, House of Commons Debate, 5 December 2011, vol. 537, col. 82.

16 Ibid., col. 84.

17 Nisha Kapoor, 'Extraordinary Extradition' in Nisha Kapoor, James Rhodes and Virinder S. Kalra (eds) *The State of Race*, Basingstoke: Palgrave, 2013, 181–202.

18 David Davis, House of Commons Debate, 5 December 2011, vol. 537, col. 93.

19 Ibid., c91.

20 Matthew Holehouse, 'David Cameron Frustrated at Wait to Send Abu Hamza to US', *Daily Telegraph*, 10 April 2012.

21 James Slack and Michael Seamark, 'An Affront to British Justice: Gary McKinnon Extradition CAN Be Stopped, Says Lib Dem QC', *Mail Online*, 31 May 2010.

22 *Gary McKinnon v Government of USA*, [2007] EWHC 762, (HC(Admin)).

23 Michael Seamark and James Slack, 'Betrayal of a Naive Hacker: Why Are Our MPs Doing Nothing to Help Asperger's Victim Gary?', *Daily Mail*, 3 July 2009.

24 *Gary McKinnon v Secretary of State for the Home Department*, [2009] EWHC 170, HC(Admin)), para. 12.

25 Ibid. The selective use of mental health to explain criminal behaviour here echoes its appropriation in the cases of white terrorism suspects who are frequently labelled as 'lone wolves' with psychotic tendencies in contrast to Muslim terrorists whose behaviour is attributed to a (collective) innate ideology.

26 A LexisNexis search of all articles in the *Daily Mail* on Talha Ahsan between 2006 (when he was arrested) and 1 January 2017 shows that of the sixty-six articles published that referenced him, only two mentioned that he had Asperger's. One of these articles was written by David Bermingham, one of the 'Natwest Three' extradited to the US in 2006 on fraud-related charges.

27 Some examples include: Daniel Bates, 'British Man Described as "Abu Hamza's Personal Assistant" is Sentenced to 20 Years in Prison After He Tried to Set Up a Terrorist Training Camp in America', *Daily Mail*, 17 October 2015; Harriet Alexander, 'Abu Hamza's Ally Haroon Aswat SENTENCED to 20 years by New York Court', *Telegraph*, 17 October 2015.

28 Damien Green, House of Commons Debate, 5 December 2011, vol. 537, col. 129.

29 Unreported in the debate was that lawyers had also expressed concerns about the mental health deterioration of Abu Hamza. A consultant psychiatrist gave his opinion to the Home Office that this decline was attributable to sleep deprivation for eight years, recommending that Abu Hamza be given an MRI scan, which his lawyer, Alun Jones QC, reported that the Home Office ignored. Alun Jones, *BBC Newsnight*, 5 October 2012.

30 Theresa May, House of Commons Debate, 16 October 2012, vol. 551, col. 164.

31 David Theo Goldberg, *The Racial State*, Oxford: Wiley Blackwell, 2002.

32 Barry Hindess 'Citizenship and Empire' in Thomas Blom Hansen and Finn Stepputat (eds), *Sovereign Bodies, Citizens, Migrants and States in the Postcolonial World*, Princeton, NJ: Princeton University Press, 2005; Barnor Hesse and S. Sayyid 'The Postcolonial Political and the Immigrant Imaginary' in N. Ali, V. S. Kalra and S. Sayyid (eds), *A Postcolonial People; South Asians in Britain*, London: Hurst, 2006.

33 Katy Sian, Ian Law and S. Sayyid, *Racism, Governance and Public Policy: Beyond Human Rights*, Abingdon: Routledge, 2013.

34 Barnor Hesse, 'Im/plausible Deniability: Racism's Conceptual Double Bind', *Social Identities: Journal for the Study of Race,*

Nation and Culture, 10(1), 2004, 9–29; Paul Gilroy, *Postcolonial Melancholia*, New York, NY: Columbia University Press, 2005.

35 Laleh Khalili, *Time in the Shadows: Confinement in Counter-insurgencies*, Stanford, CA: Stanford University Press, 2013, 230. To preclude the universalisation of rights being demanded by anti-colonial resistance struggles when the Convention was implemented in the colonies, its force was typically constrained by numerous administrative safeguards that would limit its effect. It was also predictably suspended everywhere Britain fought a counterinsurgency. A. W. Brian Simpson, *Human Rights and the End of Empire: Britain and the Genesis of the European Convention*, Oxford: Oxford University Press, 2004; Karel Vasak, 'The European Convention of Human Rights beyond the Frontiers of Europe', *International and Comparative Law Quarterly*, 12(4), 1963, 1,206–31.

36 Note by Colonial Office in CAB 134/385 IOC (47) 246 in A. W. Brian Simpson, *Human Rights and the End of Empire*, p.491.

37 Aimé Césaire, *Discourse on Colonialism*, 3.

38 Barnor Hesse, *Im/plausible Deniability*, 19. An alternative trajectory of human rights which are more holistic and begin from the standpoint of the disavowed has been discussed by Paul Gilroy, *Darker than Blue: On the Moral Economies of Black Atlantic Culture*, London: The Belknap Press of Harvard University Press, 2010.

39 Antony Anghie, *Imperialism, Sovereignty and the Making of International Law*, Cambridge: Cambridge University Press, 2004.

40 Laleh Khalili, *Time in the Shadows*, 229.

41 Ibid. Laleh Khalili notes that since the British did not ratify the conventions until 1957, they were immaterial to its counterinsurgent wars in Malaya, Cyprus and Kenya (pp. 229–30).

42 Liberty, 'Liberty's Response to the Home Office Review of Extradition Legislation', London: Liberty, 2010.

43 Ibid. When the Extradition Treaty 2003 was passed, all EU and twenty-four other designated countries, including the US, South Africa, Israel, Canada, New Zealand and Australia, were granted the privilege of not having to present prima facie evidence. The forum bar was reintroduced in 2013 following the outcome of the Gary McKinnon case.

44 Christopher H. Pyle, *Extradition, Politics and Human Rights*, Philadelphia, PA: Temple University Press, 2001. Christopher Pyle notes that the UK, slow to join the extradition movement that had begun during the mid nineteenth century, had ratified only three extradition treaties by 1870. One of the reasons for this, as explained by General John T. Coleridge in 1870, was that 'they might be required to surrender political offenders, and violate the

rights of political asylum always afforded here to political refugees' (p. 84).

45 John Stuart Mill, House of Commons Debate, 1866, third series, vol. 184, col. 2,024.

46 Ibid., col. 2,115.

47 Christopher H. Pyle, *Extradition, Politics and Human Rights*, 88.

48 John Stuart Mill, 'Letter to Josiah Sherman', 8 February 1869 in Francis E. Mineka and Dwight N. Lindley (eds) *The Collected Works of John Stuart Mill, Volume XVII*, London: Routledge and Kegan Paul, 1972, 1,559.

49 Liberty, 'Liberty's Response to the Home Office Review of Extradition Legislation', 9.

50 Ivor Stanbrook and Clive Stanbrook, *Extradition: Law and Practice*, Oxford: Oxford University Press, 2000, 76.

51 David Blunkett, House of Commons Debate, 5 December 2011, vol. 537, col 89.

52 Arundhati Roy, *An Ordinary Person's Guide to Empire*, New Delhi: Penguin, 2005, 332.

53 See, for example, *Newsnight*, 22:30 5 October 2012, BBC2 England, 30 mins.

54 Denis MacShane, *BBC Newsnight*, 5 October 2012. Discussion on the programme and in press also connected the issue of policing terrorism with the excesses of European sovereignty over Britain. Conservative MP Mark Reckless argued on the same programme that, even though the European Convention on Human Rights had been incorporated into domestic law, the rulings of British courts were secondary to judgements from Strasbourg. He expressed his upset in terms of the undermining of British sovereignty and the acquiescence to Europe 'to rule on something that our own courts have already determined on the basis of that International law'.

55 *Haroon Aswat v United Kingdom*, Application no. 17299/12 (ECtHR, 16 April 2013).

56 Ibid., para. 51.

57 He went on to state that 'this foreign court should not be stopping us from getting him out'. Anil Dawar, '"Human Rights" Judges Stop UK Sending Hamza Aide to the US', *Express*, 17 April 2013.

58 Tom Whitehead, 'May Pledges to Send al-Qaeda Suspect to US despite Human Rights Ruling', *Daily Telegraph*, 13 September 2013, 13.

59 Ibid.

60 With this assurance, the British high court gave the go ahead for Haroon to be extradited, despite admitting that 'there are still detailed gaps about the precise circumstances in which the claimant would be detained in MCC', including whether he would be housed in a single cell, and if so, for how long inevery twenty-four

hours would there be opportunities and of what kind for contact with others. See *Haroon Aswat v Secretary of State for Home Department* [2014] EWHC 1216, (HC(Admin)), para. 33.

61 There were three cases to which the six men were associated. See *Babar Ahmad and Others v United Kingdom*, Applications nos. 2 4027/07, 11949/08, 36742/08, 66911/09 and 67354/09, (ECtHR, 10 April 2012).

62 Ibid., 63.

63 Ibid., 68–9. The court also noted that

> although it is of some concern that outdoor recreation can be withdrawn for periods of three months for seemingly minor disciplinary infractions, the Court places greater emphasis on the fact that, according to Mr Milusnic, inmates 'recreation has only been cancelled once for security reasons and that the periods of recreation have been increased from five to ten hours per week (p. 69, para. 222).

64 Ibid., 76.

65 Baher Azmy, Sally Eberhardt, Pardiss Kebriaei, Arun Kundnani, William Quigley, Laura Rovner, Saskia Sassen and Jeanne Theoharis, *Evidence from US Experts to the House of Lords Select Committee on Extradition Law*, written evidence (EXL0049), 12 September 2014.

66 The political motives underlying the judgement are worth noting. Facing increasing pressure from the British government and the media who continuously invoked the misuse of the convention by 'terrorists' as reason to withdraw from the European Convention as well as direct intervention from the United States, the judgement was delivered one month after a closed conference in Washington between European Court judges and US Supreme Court justices, where the parallels in 'rights protection' across the Atlantic were discussed. Ian Patel notes that the

> closed-door conference – *Judicial Process and the Protection of Rights: The US Supreme Court and the European Court of Human Rights* – brought together members of the Strasbourg Court with Supreme Court justices Stephen Breyer, Samuel Alito, Anthony Kennedy and Sonia Sotomayor. Also present were the UK government's in-house legal counsellor, Derek Walton, who was representing the UK in Ahsan's ECHR case, and the vastly influential Harold Koh, who was serving as Obama's appointed legal advisor to the State Department.
>
> (Ian Patel, 'The Impossible Injustice of Talha Ahsan's Extradition and Detention', *New Statesman*, 21 February 2013.)

67 *Haroon Aswat v United Kingdom*, Application no. 62176/14, (ECtHR, 6 January 2015), para. 36.

68 Britain is not the only Western state to adopt such a practice but, as Mariagiulia Giuffré points out, it 'has been the only EU Member State formalizing bilateral diplomatic assurances for national security related deportations in the structure of standardized blanket Memoranda'. Mariagiulia Giuffré, 'An Appraisal of Diplomatic Assurances One Year after *Othman (Abu Qatada) v United Kingdom* (2012)', *International Human Rights Law Review*, 2, 2013, 266–93.

69 Victoria Brittain, 'I Know Abu Qatada – He's No Terrorist', *Guardian*, 7 July 2013. The UK established memoranda of understanding (MOU) with Jordan (2005), Lebanon (2005), an exchange of letters providing assurances with Algeria (2006), Ethiopia (2008) and Morocco (2011). A 2005 MOU made with the Gaddafi regime in Libya was discontinued in 2011. See Aisha Maniar, '10 Years of Deportation with Assurances: A National Security Imperative?', *One Small Window*, 4 September 2015.

70 *Omar Othman v United Kingdom*, Application no. 8139/09 (ECtHR, 17 January 2012), para, 193.

71 Ibid.

72 He was put on trial in Jordan and acquitted when it was decided that evidence that had been obtained via torture could not be used against him.

73 Pre-empting a judgement that would support the men's appeals, *Sun* called on Britain to defy the court and said Tory MPs had 'finally lost patience' with it. One MP, Chris Heaton-Harris, was reported as telling the paper, 'We should tell [the court] to stick their judgment where political correctness doesn't shine – and send Hamza to the US to receive justice.' This early version of the paper published before the final ruling had been made (and subsequently changed when it had) was exposed in an editorial in *Guardian*, editorial, 'Abu Hamza: Europe's Judgement Call', *The Guardian*, 10 April 2012.

74 See Eyal Weizman, *The Least of All Possible Evils: Humanitarian Violence from Arendt to Gaza*, London: Verso, 2011; Colin Mooers, *Imperial Subjects: Citizenship in an Age of Crisis and Empire*, London: Bloomsbury, 2014; Gregoire Chamyou, *A Theory of the Drone*, New York, NY: The New Press, 2014.

75 Eyal Weizman, *The Least of All Possible Evils*, 4.

76 Ibid.

77 Laleh Khalili, *Time in the Shadows*; Eyal Weizman, *The Least of All Possible Evils*; Colin Mooers, *Imperial Subjects*.

78 Colin Mooers, *Imperial Subjects*.

79 Theresa May, 'Ministerial Statement: Independent Review of the Deportation with Assurances (DWA) Policy', Home Office, 21 November 2013.

80 HM Government, *Review of Counter-Terrorism and Security*

Powers: Review Findings and Recommendations, London: Home Office, 2011, 35.

81 Joint Committee on Human Rights, *The UN Convention against Torture, Nineteenth Report*, Session 2005–6. These objections were not sufficient to halt the passing of the measure in this case.

82 European Court of Human Rights, *Press Country File The United Kingdom*, HUDOC, March 2017.

83 Ibid., 3.

84 Conservative Party, *Protecting Human Rights in the UK: The Conservative's Proposals for Changing Britain's Human Rights Laws*, London: The Conservative Party, 2014.

85 Ibid., 2.

86 Ibid., 7.

87 David Cameron, 'British Decisions … British Judges'.

88 *Babar Ahmad and Others v United Kingdom*, Application nos. 24 027/07, 11949/08, 36742/08, 66911/09 and 67354/09, (ECtHR, 10 April 2012).

89 *Haroon Rashid Aswat v USA*, Sentencing Transcript, ECF 523, 3 December 2015.

5. On Recognition, Rights and Resistance

1 CARF (Campaign Against Racism and Fascism) Collective, 'Fighting Our Fundamentalisms: An Interview with A. Sivanandan', *Race and Class*, 36(3), 1995, 73–81, p.79.

2 Arundhati Roy, *An Ordinary Person's Guide to Empire*, New Delhi: Penguin, 2005, 331.

3 Gary McKinnon was charged with seven counts of fraud and computer-related charges and Richard O' Dwyer was charged with copyright offences.

4 Joint Committee on Human Rights, *Fifteenth Report: The Human Rights Implications of UK Extradition Policy*, UK Parliament Publications, 2011, para. 196.

5 We Are Babar Ahmad campaign, http://wearebabarahmad.org./ about-us/

6 Paul Gilroy, *There Ain't No Black in the Union Jack*, London: Hutchinson, 1987.

7 Nicholas De Genova, 'The Deportation Regime: Sovereignty, Space and the Freedom of Movement' in Nicholas De Genova and Nathalie Peutz (eds), *The Deportation Regime: Sovereignty, Space, and the Freedom of Movement*, Durham, NC: Duke University Press, 2010, 33–65.

8 Ibid.; Peter Nyers, 'Abject Cosmopolitanism: The Politics of Protection in the Anti-Deportation Movement' in Nicholas De

Genova and Nathalie Peutz (eds), *The Deportation Regime: Sovereignty, Space, and the Freedom of Movement*, Durham, NC: Duke University Press, 2010, 413–42.

9   Étienne Balibar, *Citizenship*, Cambridge: Polity Press, 2015; Gurminder K. Bhambra, 'Citizens and Others: The Constitution of Citizenship Through Exclusion', *Alternatives: Global, Local, Political*, 40(2), 2015, 102–14.

10 Nicholas De Genova, *Working the Boundaries: Race, Space and 'Illegality' in Mexican Chicago*, Durham, NC: Duke University Press, 2005; Étienne Balibar, 'Es Gibt Keinen Staat in Europa: Racism and Politics in Europe Today', *New Left Review*, 186, 1991, 5–19.

11 Geoffrey Robertson 'Cameron and Clegg Must Now Do Their Moral Duty and Save Gary McKinnon', *Daily Mail*, 27 May 2010.

12 Joint Press Conference by Prime Minister David Cameron and President Barack Obama at the White House, 20 July 2010, Prime Minister's Office.

13 Press Association, 'Abu Hamza Extradition Ruling Praised by David Cameron', *Guardian*, 10 April 2012.

14 James Slack, Michael Seaman and Christian Gysin, 'A Great Day for Gary and British Justice', *Daily Mail*, 17 October 2012; Paul Harris and Christian Gysin, 'Incredible! We've Done It, We've Won for Gary', *Daily Mail*, 17 October 2012.

15 Paul Gilroy, *There Ain't No Black in the Union Jack*.

16 Workers Against Racism, *The Roots of Racism*, London: Junius Publications, 1985; A. Sivanandan, *A Different Hunger: Writings on Black Resistance*, London: Pluto, 1982; Paul Gilroy, *There Ain't No Black in the Union Jack*.

17 Anandi Ramamurthy, *Black Star: Britain's Asian Youth Movements*, London: Pluto Press, 2013.

18 CAGE, 'About Us'. https://cage.ngo.

19 Asim Qureshi, 'Fight the Power: How CAGE Resists from Within a "Suspect Community"', *Palgrave Communications*, 3(17090), 2017, doi:10.1057/palcomms.2017.90.

20 Department for Communities and Local Government, *Preventing Violent Extremism: Winning Hearts and Minds*, DCLG, 2007.

21 CAGE, *The 'Science' Of Pre-Crime: The Secret Radicalisation Study Underpinning Prevent*, London: CAGE, 2016.

22 CAGE, *The Prevent Strategy: A Cradle to Grave Police-State*, London: CAGE, 2013.

23 CAGE, *Failing Our Communities: A Case Study Approach to Understanding Prevent*, London: CAGE, 2015. It is of note that the child who cited morning prayers as an excuse for his lateness to school was hiding that he was being bullied; the bullying was not picked up on by teachers.

24 Asim Qureshi, *Fight the Power*. For example, they released the

correspondence they had with Mohammed Emwazi who had been complaining about harassment from the security services.

25 Randeep Ramesh, 'Charities Can Fund Cage Campaign Group, Commission Agrees', *Guardian*, 21 October 2015; David Cameron, 'Speech on Extremism', Birmingham, 20 July 2015.

26 Robert. Verkaik and Ian Gallagher, '"I'm a Dead Man Walking": Jihadi John Tells of Paranoia at Being Shadowed by MI5 Before He Went to Syria in Bombshell Email to *Mail on Sunday*', *Mail on Sunday*, 28 February 2015.

27 David Cameron, 'Speech on Extremism'.

28 Patrick Wintour, Frances Perraudin and Nicholas Watt, 'David Cameron Believes "There Is a Case to Do More" in Syria', *Guardian*, 2 July 2015.

29 Camilla Turner and Steven Swinford, 'David Cameron "Knew British Pilots Were Bombing Syria" – As It Happened', *Telegraph*, 17 July 2015. The House of Commons had voted against military action in Syria in 2013.

30 Malia Bouattia, 'David Cameron Should Be Ashamed of His Speech on Extremism', *Vice*, 22 July 2015.

31 Andrew Gilligan, 'CAGE: The Extremists Peddling Lies to British Muslims to Turn Them into Supporters of Terror', *Telegraph*, 28 February 2015.

32 Nick Cohen, 'Feminism or Islamism: Which Side Are You On?', *Standpoint*, April 2013.

33 Chetan Bhatt, 'Human Rights and the Transformations of War', *Sociology*, 46(5), 2012, 813–28; Max Farrar, 'Why on Earth Would Leftists Go Out of Their Way to Support CAGE?' *Open Democracy*, 12 August 2015.

34 Richard Kerbaj, 'Amnesty Boss Blasts Its Link with Taliban', *Sunday Times*, 7 February 2010, 13. See also Gita Sahgal's full statement: http://stroppyblog.blogspot.com/2010/02/amnesty-reinstate-gita-sahgal.html.

35 Max Farrar, 'Why on Earth Would Leftists Go Out of Their Way to Support CAGE?'.

36 Rahila Gupta, 'Double Standards on Human Rights', *Guardian*, 9 February 2010.

37 It is of note that Sahgal's critique that the partnership with CAGE would do 'fundamental damage' to the human rights organisation, which was taken up by other liberal advocates that supported her stance, rested largely on one particular organisation and mostly one particular individual, so that the framework for addressing this critical question became centred around the character of Moazzam Begg.

38 Antonie Anghie, *Imperialism, Sovereignty, and the Making of International Law*, Cambridge: Cambridge University Press, 2005.

39 Tom Mills, Narzanin Massoumi and David Miller, 'Apologists for

Terror or Defenders of Human Rights?: The CAGE Controversy in Context', *Open Democracy*, 31 July 2015.

40 Amnesty International, 'Amnesty International Responds to the Global Petition and a Response from the Petitioners' press release, *Europe Solidaire Sans Frontières*, 1 April 2010.

41 Max Farrar, 'Why on Earth Would Leftists Go Out of Their Way to Support CAGE?'.

42 Nick Cohen, 'We Abhor Torture but That Requires Paying a Price', *Guardian*, 14 February 2010.

43 Regarding 'rights talk' versus 'culture talk', Mahmood Mamdani insightfully proposes that 'the language of protest ... bears a relationship to the language of power'. In this regard, the language of 'rights' and usually 'human rights' is typically associated with the Western liberal tradition. Mahmood Mamdani (ed.) *Beyond Rights Talk and Culture Talk: Comparative Essays on the Politics of Rights and Culture*, Basingstoke: Palgrave Macmillan, 2000, 2.

44 Suhaiymah Manzoor-Khan, 'Intersectional, Radical, Unpalatable and Abrasive; That Is the Feminism I'm About', *Brown Hijabi*, 31 August 2015.

45 Rafia Zakaria, 'Women and Islamic Militancy', *Dissent*, 62(1), Winter 2015, 11825.

46 Alan Travis, 'UK Terror Arrest at Record Level After Increase in Female Suspects', *Guardian*, 10 December 2015. This trend of women losing custody of their children is indicated in research we have been gathering as part of the wider Deport Deprive Extradite project.

47 Richard Kerbaj, 'Children put in care after Met's extremist hunt', *Sunday Times*, 30 October 2016.

48 Andy Worthington, 'Defending Moazzam Begg and Amnesty International', Andy Worthington, 10 February 2010, andyworthington.co.uk.

49 Gargi Bhattacharyya, *Dangerous Brown Men: Exploiting Sex, Violence and Feminism in the War on Terror*, London: Zed, 2008.

50 Richard Kerbaj 'Amnesty Boss Blasts Its Link with Taliban'.

51 Andy Worthington, 'Defending Moazzam Begg and Amnesty International'. Working for a range of newspapers mostly under Murdoch, Kerbaj has been consistent in his defamatory reporting of all things Muslim including, for example, his coverage of the Trojan Horse affair.

52 Richard Kerbaj, 'Amnesty Boss Blasts Its Link with Taliban'. In a separate post, Begg responded to the article countering the misrepresentation of his views to offer another reading of the question at hand. Noting that the reporting journalist had chosen to exclude the responses Begg had offered to questions posed, Begg explained that neither he nor CAGE 'support[ed] the ideology of killing innocent civilians, whether by suicide bombers or B52s, whether

that's authorised by Awlaki or by Obama'. Moazzam Begg, 'Letter to the *Sunday Times*', *Sunday Times*, 7 February 2010. He went on to state that the organisation believed a person's guilt should be decided through the law. Begg's personal response was that he had witnessed a series of human rights abuses by both the Taliban and the US administration and that just as he advocated for engagement and dialogue with the latter, he did so with the former. Moazzam Begg, 'Hatred and Another Agenda', *CAGE*, 26 February 2010.

53 Angela Woollacott, *Gender and Empire*, Basingstoke: Palgrave Macmillan, 2006; Naeem Inayatullah and Robin Riley (eds) *Interrogating Imperialism: Conversations on Gender, Race and War*, Basingstoke: Palgrave Macmillan, 2006; Gargi Bhattacharyya, *Dangerous Brown Men*.

54 Chandra T. Mohanty, 'Under Western Eyes: Feminist Scholarship and Colonial Discourses', *Boundary* 2,vol. 12/13 (3–1), 1984, 333–58; Nira Yuval-Davis, 'Intersectionality and Feminist Politics', *European Journal of Women's Studies*, 13(3), 2006, 193–209; Sriram Ananth, 'Conceptualizing Solidarity and Realizing Struggle: Testing Against the Palestinian Call for the Boycott of Israel', *Interface*, 6(2), 2014, 143–63.

55 Nira Yuval-Davis, 'Intersectionality and Feminist Politics'.

56 Ibid.

57 Pragna Patel, 'Back to the Future: Avoiding Déjà Vu in Resisting Racism' in Floya Anthias and Cathie Lloyd (eds), *Rethinking Anti-Racisms: From Theory to Practice*, London: Routledge, 2002, 128–48. In her infamous book *Is Multiculturalism Bad for Women?* (Princeton, NJ: Princeton University Press, 1999) Susan Moller Okin poses a similar question.

58 Nira Yuval-Davis 'Fundamentalism, Multiculturalism and Women in Britain' in J. Donald and Ali Rattansi (eds) *'Race', Culture, Difference*, London: Sage, 1992, 284.

59 Ibid.

60 Ibid., 286.

61 Saiqa Chaudhari, 'Bolton Muslim Girls School among Best Schools in Country', *Bolton News*, 2 July 2013; Rebecca Ratcliffe, 'Bolton Muslim Girls' School Breaks London's Grip on Excellence', *Guardian*, 21 January 2016.

62 Priyamvada Gopal, 'Speaking with Difficulty: Feminism and Antiracism in Britain after 9/11', *Feminist Studies*, 39(1), 2013, 98–118; Saba Mahmood, 'Feminism, Democracy, and Empire: Islam and the War on Terror' in Hanna Herzog and Ann Braude (eds), *Gendering Religion and Politics: Untangling Modernities*, Basingstoke: Palgrave, 2009, 193–215; Suhaiymah Manzoor-Khan, 'Intersectional, Radical, Unpalatable and Abrasive'.

63 Gargi Bhattacharyya, *Dangerous Brown Men*, 56–7.

64 See, for example, Centre for Contemporary Cultural Studies, *The Empire Strikes Back. Race and Racism in '70s Britain*, Oxon: Hutchinson & Co., 1982; Department for Communities and Local Government, *Preventing Violent Extremism*; Inspire, *Making a Stand Campaign*, Inspire website, 2014. The latter campaign which encouraged Muslim women in the UK to make a stand against terrorism, it later transpired, was funded and supported by the Home Office's Research, Information and Communications Unit, a unit responsible for disseminating counterterrorism narratives. See Simon Hooper, 'UK grassroots anti-extremism campaign produced by Home Office', *Middle East Eye*, 13 June 2016.

65 Gargi Bhattacharyya, *Dangerous Brown Men*.

66 Suhaiymah Manzoor-Khan, 'Intersectional, Radical, Unpalatable and Abrasive'.

67 Negative media representations were most notoriously made by the *Sun* whose front cover the next day read 'The Truth'. The newspaper claimed Liverpool fans had urinated on police offers, pick-pocketed victims and obstructed the police and the paper's editor was closely aligned with Margaret Thatcher. Harry Arnold and John Askill, 'The Truth', *Sun*, 19 April 1989.

68 For the campaign see stopisolation.org.

Conclusion

1 Suhaiymah Manzoor-Khan, 'This Is Not a Humanising Poem', Last Word Festival 2017, London, 8 June 2017.

2 Rafeef Ziadah, 'We Teach Life, Sir', Nuyorican Poets Café, New York, 30 September 2016.

3 John Stevens, 'EXC: Jeremy Corbyn Claimed Cyber Jihadis Had Not "Done Anything Wrong" Despite Them Fundraising for Terrorists', *Daily Mail*, 2 June 2017.

4 Jennifer Williams, 'The Deadliest Attack Peacetime Manchester Has Ever Seen', *Manchester Evening News*, 23 May 2017.

5 Charlotte Cox, 'All Those Arrested Since Manchester Arena Attack Released Without Charge as Police Issue New Images of Bomber', *Manchester Evening News*, 11 June 2017.

6 All those initially arrested in relation to the attack on London Bridge were also released without charge.

7 Theresa May, 'PM Statement Following London Terror Attack: 4 June 2017', Prime Minister's Office, 4 June 2017.

8 Ibid.

9 Stuart Hall, Chas Critcher, Tony Jefferson, John Clarke and Brian Roberts, *Policing the Crisis: Mugging the State and Law and Order*, London: Macmillan, 1978.

10 Ibid., 285; Stuart Hall, 'The March of the Neoliberals', *Guardian*, 12 September 2011.

11 Paul Gilroy, *Between Camps: Nations, Cultures and the Allure of Race*, London: Penguin, 2000.

12 Hannah Arendt, *The Origins of Totalitarianism*, London: Harcourt, 1968; Aimé Césaire, *Discourse on Colonialism*, London: Monthly Review Press, 1972.

13 Aime Césaire, *Discourse on Colonialism*, 36.

14 Barnor Hesse and S. Sayyid, 'The Postcolonial Political and the Immigrant Imaginary' in N. Ali, V. S. Kalra and S. Sayyid (eds) *A Postcolonial People: South Asians in Britain*, London: Hurst, 2006, 28.

15 Angela Y. Davis, *Abolition Democracy: Beyond Empire, Prisons and Torture*, New York, NY: Seven Stories Press, 116.

16 Hannah Arendt, *Origins of Totalitarianism*.

17 Paul Gilroy, *Postcolonial Melancholia*, New York, NY: Columbia University Press, 2005; David Theo Goldberg, *The Threat of Race*, Oxford: Wiley Blackwell, 2009.

18 Arun Kundnani and Deepa Kumar, 'Race, Surveillance and Empire', *International Socialist Review*, 96, Spring 2015.

19 Stuart Hall et al., *Policing the Crisis*.

20 Audrey Macklin, 'The Return of Banishment: Do the New Denationalisation Policies Weaken Citizenship?', EUDO Observatory on Citizenship, 2014.

21 Nisha Kapoor and Kasia Narkowicz, 'The Character of Citizenship: Denying the Rights of Asylum Seekers and Criminalising Dissent', *Open Democracy*, 20 May 2017.

22 J. M. Moore, 'Is the Empire Coming Home?: Liberalism, Exclusion and the Punitiveness of the British State', *Papers from the British Criminology Conference*, 14, 2014, 31–48; Arun Kundnani and Deepa Kumar, 'Race, Surveillance and Empire'; John Stuart Mill, 'On Liberty' in J. M. Robson (ed), *The Collected Works of John Stuart Mill, Vol. XVIII —Essays on Politics and Society, Part I*, Toronto: University of Toronto Press, 1977 [1859], 224.

23 Barnor Hesse and S. Sayyid, 'The Postcolonial Political and the Immigrant Imaginary'; David Theo Goldberg *The Racial State*.

24 Talha Ahsan, 'This Be the Answer,' in *This Be the Answer: Poems from Prison*, Edinburgh: Radio Ramadan Edinburgh, 2011.

25 Rafeef Ziadah, 'We Teach Life, Sir'.

26 Suhaiymah Manzoor-Khan, 'This Is Not a Humanising Poem'.

27 Arundhati Roy, *The Ministry of Utmost Unhappiness*, London: Hamish Hamilton, 2017.

28 Sally Weale, 'NUS President Malia Bouattia: "It Was the Most Difficult Year of My Life"', *Guardian*, 8 May 2017.

29 A. Sivanandan, 'Editorial', *Race and Class*, 15(4), 1974, 399–400.

Index